EXECUTIVE STYLE

EXECUTIVE STYLE

Looking It . . . Living It

Created by

MARY B. FIEDOREK

Written by

DIANA LEWIS JEWELL

New Century Publishers, Inc.

To David, Colin and Carver

Printing Code
11   12   13   14   15   16

Library of Congress Cataloging in Publication Data

Jewell, Diana Lewis.
  Executive style.
    1. Clothing and dress.   2. Beauty, Personal.
  3. Women executives.   I. Fiedorek, Mary B.   II. Title.
TT507.J48   1983   646'.34   82-25976
ISBN 0-8329-0254-3

CONTENTS

PREFACE

"I wish you a lotta luck, honey."

The doors of prestigious Seventh Avenue showrooms had always been wide open and welcoming to me when I was the "Better Dress" buyer for Bergdorf Goodman in New York. Once inside these hallowed halls of fashion, racks of rarified couture creations would be whisked in front of me, and I would quickly commit thousands of company dollars, ordering expensive, elegant little dresses in the $350–$700 retail range. At the time, it didn't matter at all to me that only a select market of women would ever buy these clothes.

An occasional comment would reach me about not having clothes for the "real world" (mostly from successfully employed friends who could afford to shop my department, but didn't). However, I didn't let that worry me. Dressed in the latest haute fashion look, as I had to be in my position, I simply wondered why these women weren't secure enough to wear whatever they pleased to the office. After all, they had reached the executive level in their firms. Surely they had enough confidence in themselves to wear anything they wanted do.

My mistake.

What I didn't understand then was the very specific dress code that does exist for the professional woman in conservative, male-dominated fields. Doctors, lawyers, accountants, architects, financial managers and corporate administrators *do* dress differently from art directors, magazine editors, advertising copywriters, soap opera stars—and even Bergdorf buyers. And it has less to do with a lack of fashion individuality than it does with the intelligent determination of what is appropriate and what is not in each particular professional environment.

As cavalier as my earlier "let-them-wear-fashion" attitude sounds to me today, it was typical of the retail community's response to the clothing needs of the fastest-growing segment of the female population. Flying in the face of Department of Labor statistics, retail management either dismissed this market as "not important enough," or created hodge-podge departments, ostensibly targeted to the "working woman," but without clear definition of who this woman was. Specialized career apparel boutiques began springing up in major stores all across the country, yet these departments were mostly amalgams of merchandise culled from other store areas. No one buyer was responsible for pulling together appropriate apparel for a specific, salary-targeted executive customer.

Perhaps because I was in the fashion industry, friends in conservative fields—both men and women—began expressing their clothing concerns to me. Time after time, acquaintances would take me aside and confide, "Mary, I work with this terrific lady. She's bright, has great ability, works wonderfully, but she looks like hell, and it's going to hurt her."

I began to realize that there were many professionally successful women who simply needed the kind of realistic wardrobe direction that fashion magazines and department stores weren't providing. In order to obtain solid information about the clothing preferences of these executives, I enlisted the aid of a market research firm. Together we selected focus groups of women earning at least $25,000 per year in conservative, male-dominated fields to participate in a series of round table conversations. Sitting in an observation room behind a two-way mirror, I watched and listened as each woman executive expressed her own clothing considerations. Hours of focus group discussions revealed a great deal of agreement when it came to what they wanted—and didn't want. Many of their comments helped to form the basis of the wardrobe management philosophy of this book, and quotes from these sessions will lead off every chapter.

After two years of research, I discovered that this select executive customer had very specific, and different, clothing priorities from the majority of working women. First of all, fashion for its own sake was not considered to be a significant reason for buying anything. In fact, it was more important to avoid something that was definitely "out" than to worry about wearing what was "in." Their common objective was unobtrusive dressing. "You don't want to be 'the one in the pink'," advised an in-house council. These women were not talking about innocuous dressing—they definitely wanted a personality to show through—but a daily fashion parade was deemed totally inappropriate. Developing a correct professional image had more to do with judgment than it did with stylishness.

Timelessness was perceived as a virtue; timeliness was not. Classic looks, quality fabrics and long-wearing adaptability were the three points brought up time and time again in defining ideal, efficient office looks.

There was also a sense of wanting to uncomplicate clothing decisions. Monday to Friday mornings were definitely not for playing mix and match. "I don't have time to make those decisions," one executive complained. What was wanted: comfortable, competent-looking clothes that didn't require much time to put together.

While not one woman was willing to forego flexibility in favor of a uniform, all agreed that the expression of individual style was the most difficult thing to accomplish within the strict parameters of professional dressing. Suiting up to look like clones of their male counterparts was offensive to them all, yet none of them wished to appear too provocative, too feminine, too fashionable, too *anything*.

The women in the focus groups were not indecisive about the kind of clothes they wanted for their professional lives. They shared the same instant recognition of what was right when they saw it. The trouble was, they weren't seeing enough of it. Most dreaded shopping, hated department stores, and didn't have the time to run from one store to the next coordinating their various purchases. What was lacking in the whole process was efficiency. Sizes were hard to find; a well-defined selection of merchandise was impossible to find; and service was virtually non-existent. Most of these women avoided the issue of shopping by relegating it to one frantic expedition every six months.

When the focus groups were asked what they needed to make their shopping lives easier, they agreed that services particularly suited to the working woman were clearly lacking in larger stores. What these busy professionals demanded were later hours corresponding to their leaving-the-office-late schedules. They preferred shopping nearer their offices to nearer their homes. And, wherever they shopped, delivery or messenger services were a must. In-store professionals such as wardrobe consultants and tailors were important to these women for more efficient utilization of their limited shopping hours. When it came to clothes, there had to be a carefully edited collection of appropriate professional attire and accessories, but with enough variety to allow for individuality.

I was convinced that such a store did not exist—but should. And in March of 1980, I opened Streets & Co. in New York. It was the first free-standing store designed to fit all of the qualifications set forth by executive women themselves.

With the advice and support of my financial partner, we decided to keep the name of the store and the definition of the merchandise as flexible as possible. Names like "Business Image," or "Office Politics" and a suits-only policy would have locked us in to one look ten years from now—and who knows where our remarkable woman customer is heading? As more and more women executives begin to set their own tone, they may take their professional dressing into entirely new directions. And we want to be ready with the right kind of merchandise and a name that alludes only to the action centers of business in America—"the street"—whether it's Wall Street, Broad Street, LaSalle Street, or even Main Street, U.S.A.

Selecting the name and a location was a lot easier than finding the best possible mix of merchandise to fill the shelves. While I did have entrée to many Seventh Avenue vendors from my previous incarnation at Bergdorf's, most of them just didn't understand what I was looking for when I began to buy for Streets & Co. Telling some of them that I was opening a store specifically for the professionally elite executive woman was enough to close some of the doors that had been open to me before. Some wouldn't take my calls, others wouldn't let me in, still others had no idea whatsoever of what I was talking about. I had expected a bit of cynicism. What I was finding instead was open hostility. When I couldn't convince a well-known designer that his black leather jacket, spiked down the sleeves with dinosaur-like points was *not* what "Park Avenue lawyers" were wearing this season, I practically had to fight my way out of his showroom. "I wish you a lotta luck, honey," was the least insulting thing he said to me.

The menswear manufacturers seemed far more receptive to my ideas of appropriate business apparel for women than the fashion firms on Seventh Avenue. In fact, they were like sponges, soaking up information about this potentially lucrative new market. Unfortunately, many of them simply could not incorporate drastic changes into their production lines. They were used to turning out straight lapels, soft shoulders, nipped-in waists, boxy jackets and back vents. Styles guaranteed to add ten pounds of hips to any woman wearing them. And the rather limited fabric choices reflected the fact that few women (other than the manufac-turers' wives) had ever contributed aesthetic direction to the menswear industry.

Some of these manufacturers worked long and hard to accommodate us, how-ever, allowing me to select more feminine fabrics from the fabric market for them; restructuring mannishly tailored shapes; shortening jackets. After the first season, when shorter jackets practically walked right out of the store, we had established enough credibility with these firms that more and more began to listen and, gradually, to change. Even the closed doors on Seventh Avenue swung open again, as the influence of this tremendously important customer was being felt.

There is still somewhat of a dearth of the right merchandise available in the market. And it takes a lot of hopping around to pull a piece here, a piece there, into a well-edited, cohesive collection.

Until that time when such a store appears in your city, you're going to have to do it yourself. And you'll be able to easily, if you follow the guidelines outlined in this book. Here's how to make the book work for you:

• Section I: Starting Out. If you're just beginning your job search, whether you're right out of school, or re-entering after twenty years, you'll need the infor-mation in this section. *Starting Out.* You'll find everything from how to help your wardrobe make the transition, to how to organize an effective interview look, to what professionals are looking for when they look at you. Read the *entire* section if you are unsure of any of this.

• Section II: Making It. This section will help you develop your professional image as you're on your way to the top. You'll find an efficient wardrobe manage-ment plan, as well as helpful information on all aspects of executive style, from how to spot quality, to how to have a successful business trip, to the best ways to take care of yourself.

Knowing what it takes to pull together the most effective professional look in the least amount of time is half the battle. Learning how to personalize it and adapt it to changing career needs is what will make executive dressing work for you. Whether you're well on your way up the ladder, re-entering the workforce, or just getting out of graduate school, there are certain codes for communicating competence. We hope this book will help you decipher them easily and efficient-ly so you can get on with the business at hand.

Mary Fiedorek
New York

ACKNOWLEDGMENT

Our special thanks to everyone listed below. They gave unstintingly of their time and energy and this book is a result of our working with them and their ideas:

Ann Abercrombie
Jane Ahrens
Martha Adger
Barry Allardice
Robin Baron
Pat Begley Beane
Jon Christoph
Marita Cluett
Susan Tichenor Congalton
JoAnn Daly
Penn DeYoung
Wendy Ehrenkranz
Kathy Ellis
Rena Ettlinger
Gerie Feldman
Bruce Fiedorek
William Friedrich
Elizabeth Grody
Dennis Hersch
Alexandra Hendrickson
Yerger Johnstone

John Kalish
Martha Neff Kessler
Kathryn Knudson
Donna Leahy
Denise Mack
John Mack
Marilyn Miglin
Dale Naylor
Janice Popalos
Gail Reiser
Sue Reville
Amanda Robinson
Elizabeth Savage
Bruce Schnitzer
Jan Sharry
LuRaye Tate
Paula Venuto
Sharon Wick
Walter Wick
Lindsay Zullo

INTRODUCTION
The New Work Force—You

"We're talking about not reinforcing men's preconceptions of women in business. There are so many battles to be fought, clothes should not be the battle you want to fight first."

Rich man, poor man, beggar man, thief. Doctor, lawyer, Indian chief. As you recite the lines from the familiar childhood chant, each character probably conjures up an unmistakable mental image. And what immediately distinguishes one from the other is what you imagine them to be wearing. Whether in top hat, tatters or feathers, each sends forth a kind of sartorial signal that determines your perception of just what he does—or does not do—for a living.

The acceptable professional apparel in any field has always communicated position as effectively as a business card. It's always been easy to tell a doctor in whites from a pinstriped, attachéed lawyer. Or, for that matter, a thief from an Indian chief. And we've had no trouble at all determining relative degrees of wealth. Until the working woman entered the picture.

Suddenly, there seems to be an occupational identity crisis, and men aren't any happier about it than the women who must select a correct professional image.

This kind of tailor-made typecasting has been going on almost as long as the human race has been covering itself. The more highly decorated a member of any society was, the more leadership he assumed. And it was always a he. Men began learning the importance of dress distinction probably somewhere near the year fire was discovered. Although times changed, and the idea of "less is more" has taken hold with men in positions of authority, their clothing continues to be based on class distinctions. Considering that the basic business suit hasn't really changed all that much since Victorian times, you begin to get a sense of consolidation almost to the point of conspiracy. They've purposely made it easy on themselves. With "more important things to worry about," men have managed to convey the same professional image for over one hundred years.

If slightly unimaginative, the message their clothing gives off is designed to be perfectly clear. It either says blue or white collar. There's never any doubt about who does what. It's a simple code. But it works.

Contrast this with the endless variety of fashion "looks" offered season in and season out to women. We can be anything we want to be with just a quick change of clothes: gypsy one minute, peasant the next, Victorian heroine the next, and queen of the jungle after the sun goes down. During some fashion seasons, it's been stylish to be everything from a rich man to a beggar man to an Indian chief, depending upon what party you were going to. Confusing at best, but we've brought it on ourselves. Just as men have been resistant to change, we've welcomed it, heralding it with collections, proclaiming it through designers. We've always understood, and accepted, the quick-change artistry required of us. Until we became doctors, lawyers, architects, accountants, financial managers and corporate administrators. And now we haven't got a thing to wear. We have not yet established our own dress code as instantly identifiable as that of our male business associates.

The first immediate impulse is to simply copy theirs. It's a phase most professional women go through as soon as they earn their MBA's, JD's or MD's. Severe, mannish imitations abound among entry-level executives—right down to the button-down shirt. Sturdy, loafer-like pumps and a strictly tailored, hip-covering jacket matched to a fairly straight, below-the-knee skirt complete the rather inconspicuous picture. It's safe, all right. But it's boring. And it's guaranteed not to get you noticed. While that may be a novice's goal as long as she's on shakey ground, imitation dressing is not going to get her off the ground. Blending in is not necessarily the best way to demonstrate clear superiority. There's such a thing as being too safe, too dreary. In response to the drab professional image of two female second-year associates, one partner in a law firm nicknamed them "the Sorrow and the Pity." This kind of apparel intimidation is as obvious, and as inappropriate, as flashiness. The trick is to demonstrate a bit of initiative and imagination within the confines of a conservative dress code.

"The men at our firm are always saying, 'Why do you women work so hard to look so severe?'," one financial account executive reported during a focus group conversation. "But yet, if we didn't . . . ," her voice trailed off, acknowledging the double-edged wardrobe dilemma facing most executive women in male-dominated fields. You must appear to be effective, decisive and authoritative while "fitting in" with the company's executive image. You must distinguish yourself as a leader, without being overly distinctive. And, in the midst of this apparent dichotomy, you must always, always be consistent. Conflicting clothing messages are interpreted as ambiguous at best, weak at worst. Without a clear visual identity, women executives have to work just that much harder to prove who they are—and what they can do. While clothes helped make the man, they certainly can un-make the woman on her way to the top. There is a direct relationship between appearance and the perception of effectiveness, and an inappropriate image can undermine even the most competent. Unfair as this sounds, the quicker you learn to capitalize on projecting the proper image, the easier it will be to direct associates' attention where it belongs—on your work.

WHO SAYS YOU HAVE TO WEAR A SUIT?

If "suiting-up" is one more reflection of executive role-playing, women are readily casting themselves in the part. While the formality of a man's business suit may set the tone in most corporate offices, it's the executive women of each firm who set the standards. Ask any male business leader to define proper dress for female executives, and he'll describe exactly the way their top women dress. Men, whether co-workers or clients, as a rule don't distinguish enough between different degrees of feminine dressing to know what the exact equivalent of a business suit might be. So they look around. What their women executives are wearing seems proper enough. And, right now, they're wearing suits. Most high-ranking women in conservative organizations are leading others, either by example or implicit policy, to dress to suit the stereotype of their profession.

If anybody is putting women into a predictable "power look," it's women themselves. We've found a common ground of agreement—you wear a suit, and I'll wear a suit—and the temptation is to stick with it. It's understandable, acceptable and automatic. The fact that a lot of professional women are already looking for alternatives, however, gives some grounds to the theory that executive dressing isn't where it's going yet. As more and more women assume managerial positions, clothing options are going to become as varied as they are in other industries where women executives are more prevalent. That's not to say the standards will relax. In certain professions a degree of formality will always be preferred. But without women executives automatically equating this with a suit, who else will?

THE TEN-YEAR TAKEOVER PLAN

The professional woman whose career is a principal focus of her life is the most important sociological phenomenon of the past decade. Whether attributed to the economic need for two-paycheck families, or the goal-oriented objectives of a maturing baby boom generation, women in the work force now exceed women who stay at home. In 1970, 43% of adult American women worked outside the home. By 1981, their number increased to 51%, and the Bureau of Labor Statistics expects it to reach 65% by 1990.

You've heard the statistics before—even though information by job classification is still sketchy, at best. But the woman-in-the-work force facts trumpeted in everything from business journals to sociological treatises sound phenomenal enough. Tracking future professionals by the percentage of women graduating with advanced degrees, we find an amazing 750% escalation in the number of women earning master's degrees between 1950 and the present; a 1200% jump in those earning doctorates. Although most of these were for traditionally "female fields" such as education, English, journalism, fine and applied arts, foreign languages and literature, nursing and library sciences, the Census Bureau does report a 1200% increase in the number of law degrees, and a 335% increase in the women receiving medical degrees between 1966 and now.

Compared to the total number of graduates of professional schools, 3% were women in 1968; 33% in 1982; and a projected 43% will graduate in 1990. Women specifically receiving advanced business and law degrees went up from 3% of all MBA recipients in 1966 to 35% in 1980, and from 5% to 35% of law degrees.

That's quite an impressive spawning ground for future professionals. But how are these women actually faring in the work force? Not as well as they're going to, projects the Bureau of Labor Statistics. Although there has been a 65% increase in women in professional or managerial positions between 1968 and the present, even greater strides will be made in the next decade. Today, 38.5% of all accountants are women. By 1990, almost 57% will be. The 32% of all financial officers who are women will increase to more than 51%. And over 32% of all lawyers and doctors will be women in 1990, compared to the current 14% figure.

You're part of the fastest-growing segment of the working population, with an income that is growing faster than the economy as a whole (8–10%, as opposed to 2–3%). And, although the executive woman currently accounts for only about 1% of all people earning $30,000 or more annually in the United States, the real income of this professionally elite group is increasing faster than any other subset of the economy. No wonder marketers are finally starting to sit up and take notice!

YOU'VE GOT CLOTHING CLOUT

Preparing for life in the executive lane takes more than a solid academic foundation. Like it or not, you've got to look the part—from the day of your very first interview until the day they wish you a long and happy retirement. Which means part of the costs of competing at the higher levels of the job market include spending about 8% of your income on appropriate apparel. Work-related clothing expenditures pull approximately $23.3 billion dollars from women each year, and this figure does not include all other incidental clothing purchases for leisure-time activities. Everything from casual sportswear to dressier "dinner" apparel to all-out evening wear must be bought to supplement a basic working wardrobe. And, dollar for dollar, there lies one of the most common discrepancies between the way men spend money to acquire a professional image, and the way women must. "How many corporate events have I gone to," lamented one marketing manager, "where the women all wear nice, non-office dresses, and the men wear the same old suits we see them in day in and day out." When there used to be a major cost differential between what a man would spend on a suit, and what a woman could, having to have special wardrobes for weekends and entertaining wasn't so exasperating. But as the costs between men's and women's professional apparel began to close, and in some cases reverse positions, the resentment widened. If a suit works in almost every situation for a man, some women are determined to make it work for them as well. More and more are going directly from the office to dinner parties or other social situations without so much as the change of accessories advocated by women's magazines to switch from a "day" to an "evening" look. After all, how many men change their ties at 5:00 P.M.?

Simplification seems to be the key in all wardrobe areas other than those clothes a woman can wear to the office. No matter how high her income, an executive will think twice before adding another silk dinner dress to her closet, but will consider an additional suit a necessity.

Apparel manufacturers may have been slow to spot this switch in the way women were buying their clothes, but some were at the right place with the right merchandise. At least seven of the top ten menswear firms had added women's lines by the early 1980's. And even Brooks Brothers, the last bastion of the male conservative dresser, now attributes 15% of their business to women's clothing sales.

According to *Forbes* magazine, Evan–Picone, one of the most popular suit-suppliers, went from a $4.75 million division of Palm Beach, Inc., to a $110 million moneymaker in just eight expansive years. The quietly tailored look that is Evan–Picone's trademark instantly appealed to the growing female executive market, and the price of a typical suit was targeted directly toward their increasing salary scale.

They know you're out there. And the more you make, the more they'll offer you quality clothes with quality price tags. The economics of this burgeoning market have already established that career women spend twice as much on clothing as their non-working counterparts. They know you have the money and they know you're going to spend it. Maintaining a professional image is a priority consideration among today's successful working women. *But*, what they also know—and what many otherwise aggressive, confident and secure women executives have yet to acknowledge—is that *you* determine what that professional image will be. You put yourselves in suits, and accounted for a 70% jump in suit consumption in one year alone. The apparel industry is not arguing with such phenomenal success. More and more manufacturers are turning out conservative, well-constructed jacket and skirt coordinates. But some are beginning to wonder what you're going to want next. Will the dress come into its own? Is the dress/jacket combination an acceptable alternative? Will you one day reject suits entirely? Will sweaters ever have the same authority as jackets? Will the worry over being in a "uniform" finally relax? You have their attention. And you've already demonstrated your economic influence. In the coming decade, your definition of what is acceptable business apparel will determine the direction these manufacturers will go in.

But what happens now? Before the percentages of women reach a comfortable level in male-dominated professions, you're going to have to cope with preconceived ideas of what your professional image should be. It's hard enough getting where you want to be, and clothes may indeed not be "the battle you want to fight first." While you are part of a gradual clothing evolution, you still must exist—equally—in a professional environment that has been prescribed by members who know only one way to dress for success. This book will help you live in that world while asserting your individualism with a clothing style that is both appropriate and adaptable to your career needs.

It's going to take a little time and thought, after all, it took your male colleagues a century of subtle evolution to come up with their appearance code. But work with us on the following pages. Don't just read them. Experiment with them. After reading each chapter, try at least two new things you never would have thought were "you." Then try them out at work. Monitor the responses. You'll be able to gauge what is acceptable, and what is not, in your particular professional environment. It takes a bit of judgement to develop your own personal clothing code, but you'll never be able to exercise it if you stick to imitation dressing. Now is the time to set your own standards. The apparel manufacturers are ready—and waiting—for your direction. And so are 43 million other women.

EXECUTIVE
STYLE

SECTION
I
STARTING OUT

☑ TO READ

- If you've just graduated
- If you're re-entering the workforce
- If you've got an interview lined up
- If your clothes are too (college-y) (housewife-y)

☑ TO SKIP

- If you've got the job
- If you need to sharpen your executive image, not define it

CHAPTER

1

Your New Image: From College to Interview

"Coming out of business school, my wardrobe sort of ran down, and I didn't feel good in anything."

After four, six or even eight years of preparing for a professional career, it can come as a bit of a shock to find you may still not be ready to enter the "real" world of corporate positioning. No matter how impeccable your credentials, how unassailable your academic references, if something is missing from your personal presentation, you're just not ready to play the game.

Coming out of the cocoon of academia means it's also time to shed your student image, no matter how comfortable it's been. Those safe old wardrobe standbys that saw you through years of hard labor aren't going to do you a bit of good when you join the labor force. Even if your clothing choices did take a more serious turn once you got to grad school, chances are wardrobe-building was not a priority consideration. With the escalating costs of a professional school education, and the academic emphasis on performance, it's perfectly understandable if appearance took a back seat. But now you are faced with the inescapable paradox of professional employment: clothes *do* count. So much so that, all things being equal (which they frequently are among entry-level job applicants), appearance becomes the single most important factor determining who gets hired—and who doesn't.

You acknowledge that fact, fair or not, from the moment you begin to wonder what to wear to your first interview. At that point, it's best to simply pitch your well-loved, well-worn turtlenecks, corduroys, crewnecks and textured tights and create a professional image for yourself. There are virtually few clothing items that can make the switch with you, so take a deep breath (and a charitable tax deduction) and begin.

What goes? Anything that you don't want to run the risk of wearing in a weak moment. Unless you have a totally isolated area of your closet for "weekends-only" clothes, discard most of what even smacks of casual. You will *not* wear a cotton knit turtleneck under a suit, no matter how many times you consider it. Saving it will only clutter up your closet and confuse your options. For less decision-making in the morning, it's best to have only what's going to work hanging there. That corduroy blazer-and-skirt that was as close as you ever got to a suit? Out. It's too country–suburban to make much of a professional, on-top-of-everything impression. That cabled crewneck? Wrong. Even with a strand of pearls. You simply can't get away with dressed-up preppy for long. While some may think it's a great going-in look, it typecasts you as the new kid on the block, and could keep you in a junior position.

What about those wonderful crunchy, cowl-neck sweaters? Nope. Too bulky even if you *could* get them under a blazer. About the only adaptable sweaters that will work for you now are thin cashmere cardigans or sleeveless sweater vests. Wear them for warmth (for *function*) under a suit. Use the sweater vest alone to finish a blouse and skirt. If it's thin enough and subtle enough, it can be belted at the waist to pull together a suitable professional look. If it's bulky, brightly argyled or obviously patterned—out it goes.

Speaking of skirts, what about all those separates that were the mainstay of your college closet? If they're classic shapes and colors, you could consider them. The ones dated by hem length, fabric pattern or obvious silhouette (too full, too tight, too tricky) have got to go. The classic skirts should then be divided into two piles: "soft" and "strict." Any skirt with a little bit of waist or hip interest (dirndles, inverted pleats, all-around pleats, soft gathers, wraps) goes into the "soft" stack. A-lines, straight skirts, skirts with thigh-high splits go into the "strict" group—and out. A competent professional should never be confused with a commanding officer. The closer something is to strict, the quicker it's going to feel like a uniform. And the sooner you're going to be bored with it.

The next step is to match every remaining classic skirt with a corresponding top. A jacket would be fine; a softly tailored blouse-and-skirt combo would be worth saving for future reference. In some of the less conservative firms, unmatched jackets and skirts will be acceptable and you will be able to get some use out of these separates. If a skirt hasn't got a partner at this point, however, don't think you're going to be able to get it one. Especially if it's a holdover from your first years at school. Better to take the tax write-off and start out with a skirt that's as new in the marketplace as you are.

Pantsuits should be pitched; good, tailored gabardine slacks should be put far back in your closet with your weekend wear; and jeans should never be seen, except perhaps on company "outings." Pants, in any form, have not yet succeeded in achieving executive status.

With any luck, you should have very little left in your post-college closet. That's the way it should be. Not much will translate well to your new way of dressing, and there's nothing more time-consuming than trying to make leftovers work. At the moment your motto should be, "When in doubt, throw it out." Necessary? Definitely. You've got to make a clean break, and your closet is the best place to start.

IT'S TIME TO DEVELOP A NEW CLOTHING PHILOSOPHY

A successful "pitch session" is one of the best ways to clear out old clothing attitudes as well. You're going through an important transition between the end of educating yourself and the beginning of marketing yourself. While creating an image was inconsequential in school, it is essential now. Where proletarian student garb made you look as inconspicuous as possible, clothes must now be a distinctive presence. And, although you once may have considered spending money on clothing incongruous, you've now got to believe it's entirely appropriate. Even the very function of clothing must be perceived in a new light. You can no longer see it as a simple covering for the body. Clothes now have to become communicators, conveying a very specific message.

It will not be easy for everybody to adjust to these necessary attitude changes. Those who can't will take a stand for ability over appearance, and they'll lose out to someone with equal ability every time. Those who have a little trouble rethinking wardrobe priorities will be reluctant to part with many old favorites from their college wardrobes. If you find yourself identifying with either set of symptoms, fight it. Changing undergraduate clothing concepts is absolutely intrinsic to accepting your new image. You can't do one without the other. Although putting on a professional look may help you play the part for a while, nobody's going to believe in you if you're uncomfortable with your own appearance. And, believe me, it will show. Something will always be not quite polished about the way you put yourself together. The time to establish your new sense of self is right now, while you're discarding the clothing chrysalis of your student life. Before you buy one new thing, take advantage of the time you spend sorting out your closet. Really examine your motivations for wanting to keep certain things. "It might come in handy" isn't enough of a rationale for clinging to items that aren't instantly recognizable as appropriate. Since the key to successful decision-making is often to follow your instincts, listen to yourself. If you're questioning something, chances are others will, too. Eliminate it, and indecisiveness vanishes with it. The more uncluttered your closet becomes, the clearer your new self-perception will be. And the sooner you'll be ready to replenish your wardrobe with appropriate professional looks.

FROM SELF-PERCEPTION TO IMAGE PROJECTION

Part of your new way of looking at clothes requires recognizing them as instant communicators, signaling competence, judgement and confidence in one quick visual code. The message your appearance conveys is interpreted instantly—and irrevocably—during the first few moments of any encounter. And, for better or for worse, that impression is set in stone until you contradict it through words and deeds. But sometimes you never get the chance. In casual associations, or in an interview situation, what a person sees is what he or she expects to get. Or reject.

It's human nature to form instant impressions based on appearance. Differentiating between species or threatening/non-threatening situations is built right into our genetic heritage. But we've honed this instinctual response to a higher degree. Immediate, at-a-glance determinations of a person's net social or occupational value save the critical time and energy involved in any weeding-out process. Those we choose to associate with, or employ, must conform to our own personal standards of acceptability. If they set off the wrong kind of reaction at first sight, our initial response is like a warning bell. Once it goes off, all other efforts are likely to be overlooked.

Because it is absolutely critical to set the right signals in motion when you begin to market your professional skills, you must be able to determine—in advance—what your clothing says about you. Look for clues in fabric, cut, color. Do all three send out the same message? A well-tailored suit in a bright blanket plaid contradicts itself. The intent to be appropriately dressed is there, but the sense of seriousness is missing. The same thing holds true for conservatively cut apparel made from obviously inexpensive materials. Nice try, but it still doesn't work. The overall impression will only be one of inappropriateness. Few people will take the time to interpret conflicting messages, especially when there are more important determinations to be made than what went wrong with your look. If your clothing code is undecipherable, your interviewer will avoid the confusion altogether by registering only a simple visual "tilt" signal. He or she may not even be aware of anything that is specifically wrong, but the feeling that something about you is not "quite right" will remain.

Image consistency must be a head-to-toe proposition. Even minor details could be dead giveaways that you are unaccustomed to your attire. Check hair, accessories, makeup. Ankle-strapped, open-toed shoes send a decidedly different message than the businesslike blazer on top. Obvious, clanking bangles say you're not ready to get down to work. A plastic belt belies the quality of the skirt you wear it with. A too-casual hairstyle says you might not be as serious as your suit. And blatant makeup calls taste into question. Clue by clue, it all adds up in about ten seconds.

Dressing to communicate a singular, professional image is the best way to project your understanding of the environment you'll be entering. It is by no means a frivolous or unnecessary preoccupation. There's a lot riding on your presentation—not the least of which is a reflection of your judgment and attitude. You must demonstrate that you are aware of the varied situations you will be expected to perform in, and that you are capable of representing the firm in each. Showing a clear understanding of the company's image and having the good sense to adopt it is a strong indicator of management potential. In effect you are saying, "I know the rules of the game and I'm prepared to play."

Reflecting the very image of a company's executive employee at an interview is a bit like an actor auditioning in full costume. Imagine the advantage he would have convincing the director to cast him! In a sense, the outdated fashion use of the term "costume" hits closer to the mark today than it ever has. With the proper wardrobe, you don't have to rely totally on your powers of persuasion during an "audition." If you know what role you want to perform within a corporation, you can use clothing to help you get the part.

The best news is, role-playing works both ways. The more you look the part, the more you'll act the part. In many cases, what we wear determines what our behavior will be. Wear pants, and it will be hard to resist propping your legs up on something. Wear a silky blouse and skirt, and your movements will become more graceful.

The influence clothes have on the way we act was first acknowledged in the formation of corporate dress codes. Their original intention was to prescribe proper conduct as well as dress. Attire that was too casual was not deemed conducive to work. It was thought that a relaxed way of dressing would soon lead to a reduction in efficiency. And there is something to that. Characteristic mannerisms do alter with a change in clothing, and that sets in motion a whole perception–response chain reaction. Those around us are affected by the changes in our behavior. When they respond to us in a new way, we adjust our actions accordingly. And on and on it goes. From an employer's point of view, it's far more comfortable—and less disconcerting—to surround yourself with people who live up to certain set expectations in appearance and performance. The two are not mutually exclusive.

Just as the wrong attire can adversely affect the way others react to you, wearing what is perceived as the most effective professional look can do wonders for your credibility and your confidence. When you like the way you look, you show it. You automatically behave more assertively, caring less what others are thinking when they look at you. All the insecurities about the image you're presenting get out of the way, and you get on with your work with more assurance, more authority. It doesn't take much to prove this to yourself. Keep track of your activities on the days you feel great about your appearance, and on the days you don't. On which ones do you tackle the important tasks, challenge a client, solve a problem? If energy isn't directly related to appearance, courage certainly is. It isn't just by coincidence that hurdles are handled on days you feel you look capable enough to conquer them. As one junior account officer put it, "When I look good and competent, I feel I'm doing a better job."

THE ESSENTIAL INTERVIEW SUIT—A NECESSARY INVESTMENT

The investment you've been making in yourself over the past few years doesn't end the day you get your degree. You've got to be prepared to spend a little more on "packaging." Second only to the cost of your education, a well-constructed interview suit is the best outlay you can make. You've got to go in looking like you know what you're doing, and a conservative, classic business suit is the quickest signal of executive potential. Although it is not the *only* answer. A well-tailored jacket and dress duo is formal enough for some firms, but if you're not totally confident when it comes to pulling together a polished professional image, or you want one look that will be appropriate everywhere you interview, stick with a suit. It will simply be more convenient at this stage of the game.

The trick is to know how to invest your money wisely. An "all-purpose" suit will only have longevity if you'll continue to wear it after you've got the job. While you'll want the suit to fit the corporate image of as many firms as you'll be interviewing with, you'll also want it to fit your personal image. Otherwise, it will become a uniform, to be shed the day you're hired.

How do you make the merger between personal style and corporate style? The trick is to go for quality first. Make that your priority requisite, and a lot of second-rate looks are going to get weeded out. That doesn't mean you must run to the designer rack. Most interviewers (and statistics show most interviewers *will* be men), wouldn't know, and couldn't care, who's label you're wearing. But they can spot quality across a conference room. Tip-offs are usually the smallest details: an uneven hemline, a too-short jacket cuff, a too-shiny fabric. Look for well-finished tailoring and avoid synthetic materials. Anything polyester is simply out of place. Stick to thin, lightweight wools, and you've got yourself a ten-month-a-year option. Go for the finest quality you can afford, and it will amortize itself over and over again during the first few years of your professional career.

The second characteristic you should look for as you make your selection is subtlety. Does anything stand out about the suit? The color? The cut? Are there any obvious fashion details? If so, save it for a different situation. You don't want your interviewer to remember your double-breasted brass buttons. You want him to concentrate on you. Although you don't have to give up all forms of personal expression, there is a fine line between making an impression and attracting unnecessary attention.

It is possible to look formal and feminine, as long as the details you choose to add can't be interpreted as frivolous. Concentrate on presenting a clean, no-frills, business image. Let the way you put yourself together establish your personality, without exploiting it.

The third guideline for finding the perfect all-purpose suit is to gauge its degree of formality. Your potential employer will be formal—you should be, too. A mismatched jacket and skirt—even if carefully coordinated—just doesn't have the same seriousness. Although you may get mileage out of blazer and separate skirt team-ups later on, only a suit is formal enough for an interview.

A fourth important qualification is comfort. While the comfort level of what you wear does have something to do with fit, it also has more to do with how you perceive yourself in your interview look. If there is anything about it that makes you feel insecure, pass it up. The last thing you'll want to be worrying about is if camel is too casual a color! Things to avoid: revealing splits, pencil-thin skirts, extreme shoulder pads, too-tight jackets. Don't think you can get through an interview if you're the least little bit uncomfortable. You'll show it. And it's almost impossible to resist fidgeting with the thing that bothers you most.

Now that you've narrowed down your choices by scouting for quality, subtlety, formality and comfort, the perfect interview suit should stand out from the other almost-appropriate alternatives. If you need further criteria, think in terms of color. Navy and grey are generally safe bets, although they do not have to be

The floppy bow is one of the best neckline finishers. Try it in various widths, various prints.

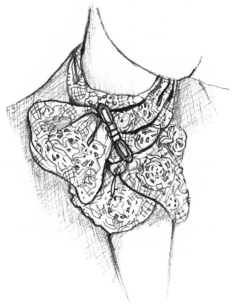

For a softer stock-tie effect, wrap around a feminine fabric—like lace. Bow the ends, and secure with an interesting bar pin.

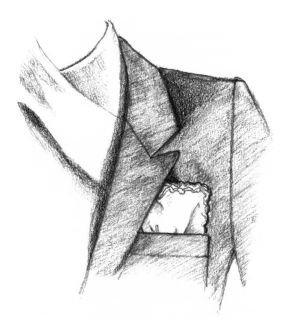

A pocket square doesn't have to mean a menswear foulard. Look for lace, silk, anything with scalloped edging!

A classic reptile belt never goes out of style. In a basic shade (black, wine, taupe), it will go on forever.

solid. A muted glen plaid or the subtlest fleck would convey the same appropriate message. (Leave obvious tweeds for the country, however.) If navy or grey isn't your color, don't feel you have no choice. A deep burgundy, soft tan or even white in the summer would be equally appropriate—if you're confident in them. If you're considering other colors, apply the subtlety/formality specifications to them. You simply can't compromise with those conditions. Any color that's not subtle enough or formal enough just won't allow you to feel comfortable enough.

Don't worry about locking yourself into a look-alike look. It's the alternatives you choose that will individualize your interview image. Soften (but don't *clutter*) your neckline with a small fabric bow or a soft, floppy tie. Since your suit will be somewhat precise, select collar treatments with a slight feminine twist to them. Don't opt for the classic stock-tie-and-pin approach. It's far too regimented to show any imagination. Look instead for silk, moiré or even lace treatments. Be experimental with fabrics—they're what will make your added touch a bit different. Choose a color that will pick up your predominant accessory shade. Match it to your belt, shoes, or bag. And, speaking of those items, you'll get the most mileage out of them if you select neutral shades such as taupe or burgundy. Don't worry about matching blue shoes to a blue suit and brown shoes to a brown suit; the same threesome you select for your interview suit should be able to work with a whole careerfull of clothes. That's if you buy with an eye toward quality. Accessories set the tone of your whole appearance. So go ahead and spend $25 on a belt, insist on really good shoes, don't consider a handbag or a briefcase unless it's real leather. You don't want to take away from the impression of quality you've created. Incidentally, it is *not* necessary to carry a briefcase with you before you land the job—unless you're tempted to pull your resumé out of a brown paper envelope!

WHO IS THAT STRANGER IN THE MIRROR?

Now that you know exactly what you're looking for, it might come as a surprise to you when you find it. Especially if you've spent the last four years or so in down parkas and turtlenecks. You need to ease into your new professional appearance, or you'll never accept it as the "real" you. Some graduate schools are now considering it a part of your formal education to introduce you to the appropriate attire of your chosen profession. One young lawyer acknowledged the kind of advice she got in school by telling us, "The seeds of the way I dress now were sown in law school. They told us what *not* to wear there." Even in the reverse, such guidance is extremely helpful. It's a step up to know the expected, accepted dress code of your colleagues.

If you can't observe proper professional dressing firsthand, and they forgot to include it in your curricula, the best strategy to know what's going to be expected of you is to attend as many executive apparel seminars as you can. Streets & Co., for instance, has been invited to hold both professional school and corporate seminars for such institutions as the Wharton School, Harvard Business School, New York University Law School, and several New York law firms. We've found that many companies taking the initiative to instruct women in the art of executive image-making do so at the request of their employees—both women and men! They feel what's needed is simple knowledge of what is appropriate and what is not—not fashion expertise. You'll be one beat ahead if you look like you have that knowledge. Watch the newspaper for store announcements of professional dressing seminars, or attend with a friend whose firm is giving one.

Try On Your New Image

When your idea of the way you're going to look begins to take definite shape, it's time to try your image on. Pick one store that can deliver personalized attention to you, and go during a non-peak shopping time. You'll have to give your new appearance some serious thought. This is not going to be one of those grab-it-and-run sessions, but it needn't be an ordeal either. Try to make it as pleasant as possible for yourself by choosing a store that has a knowledgeable consultant who can work with you and leave everybody else at home. If you don't know exactly what you want to look like yet, your mother/father/working sister/brother/boyfriend/husband's opinions will only cloud the issue. It's your identity you're after—not their idea of it. The natural assumption that a man who's been out in the corporate world for a few years can offer concrete advice is not necessarily a valid one. Resist the urge to bring a token male executive with you. If he's coming from a button-down, pinstriped world, he'll see no harm in your looking exactly the same. And the first mistake you can make is to think you are entering a man's world so you should dress like one.

Equally handicapping is the idea that you don't need an interview suit at all. Some women will insist that their credentials will carry the day, while others resent any hint of conforming to pre-set standards. Their attitudes register from slightly defensive to openly defiant on the Richter scale. One such customer at Streets & Co. was firmly convinced that men do not judge women on the basis of their appearance. A male stockbroker, shopping for a present for his wife, overheard the conversation, and pointed out to the woman that men judge other men on their appearance, so why wouldn't they apply the same discriminatory eye to women? In his office, he went on to explain, the ones who look like clerical workers—male or female—are generally treated as such. At the root of this woman's feelings was her reluctance to accept the idea that a suit was the only answer. And it isn't, after you've passed "go." When we pointed out that it is necessary to be accepted on equal terms during a first encounter with a company, however, she eventually agreed that a suit did give her a polished professional image.

Insecurity about one's evolving image can take many forms. Another woman came into the store ostensibly looking for an interview suit. After an hour of browsing without finding anything to try on, she finally admitted that she did not want to wear anything that even vaguely reminded her of a "uniform." Convinced that her MBA was really all she needed, she didn't want to risk seeing herself in any sort of "success" look. By not even trying a suit on, she didn't have to acknowledge the difference that clothes could make in communicating her competence. When we convinced her to try just one classic flannel suit, complete with accessories, we guessed the response would be immediate—and it was! Calling it "capitalist chic," she ordered a second suit in navy.

Whatever the rules are, we at Streets & Co. didn't invent them. They exist. There simply is a right way to dress effectively in male-dominated, conservative professions. The days of wearing whatever you want are now called Saturday and Sunday. If you can't see the need to adopt a formal set of clothing standards equal to your male peers, keep in mind that, even today, only a little over 6% of all working women are in managerial positions. You will, somewhere along the interview path, be appraised by a man. And while you aren't necessarily dressing to please him, you are dressing to be taken as seriously as the three-piece-suiter behind you. It's not "selling out" or "suiting up." Looking appropriate for the situation simply demonstrates that you know how to act on the information you've been given.

The only thing you have to guard against is a preconceived idea of what the best suit for you will look like. One customer in her early thirties thought she knew what a "female version" of a man's business suit should be. Read: substitute skirt for pants. When the suit of her choice had a slight slit in the back of the skirt, she instructed the tailor to pin it closed. It was only after she couldn't walk comfortably in the skirt that she realized kick pleats do serve a purpose. When she accepted it as functional, rather than fashionable, the suit was sold. The moral of the story is; don't automatically shy away from every bit of detailing. If it's got a reason for being, it's not unnecessary.

Recognizing the "New" You

Seeing the "new" you in the mirror is often a shock you'll want to postpone any way you can. And after you finally get yourself into a whole new image, the temptation is to get it off as quickly as possible. Don't. If you feel uncomfortable with the person in the mirror staring back at you, spend some time getting to know her. Move around, sit down, stay in that suit even if your first inclination is to feel "silly" in it. You've got to get used to your own reflection, so hold a dress rehearsal. Try on all the accessories you'll want to wear with it. When the look starts coming together, the suit will look less out of place on your body.

It will also help to have some makeup on and the proper hairstyle. Dashing into a store with a casual "Saturday face" won't convince you that you look professional in anything you put on. There's no sense in studying neckline and collar variations when you plan to have four inches of hair trimmed tomorrow. It's a good idea to consult a hair stylist before you begin your wardrobe makeover. Know what you're going to look like from the neck up while you're considering your dress from the neck down. Image integration is the key. A tousled, sexy hairstyle can throw off even the most serious professional look. One focus group executive noted, "The way women wear their hair to the office is often more revealing than how they dress." Although the days of the severe chignon have mercifully passed (unless you look wonderful with your hair skinned back), it is always advisable to avoid any style that calls attention to itself. Your hair look should meet many of the same qualifications your clothes must. The most successful styles will be subtle, formal (as opposed to fly-in-the-face casual) and comfortable. Any look that has you twisting ends around your finger needs revising.

Work with a good local stylist to come up with the most flattering way for you to wear your hair given those prerequisites. Length is not really at issue. If you refuse to lose one little inch to your profession, simply learn how to demonstrate effective management.

To get you thinking about ways to give your hair professional status, here are some suggestions.

Short. A layered cut will be the easiest to care for, and a *good* layered cut is absolutely essential. Judge it by trying to shake your hair into place without combing. If you can see the right line as it falls, you've got a good cut. If you can't, find another salon. Wash and wear hair is great for your busy life, but it takes body to hold the look together. If your hair hasn't got it, you might end up looking mousy. Don't be afraid to try a body wave. It won't give you permanent frizz, but it will put enough "oomph" into your locks to let them be practically maintenance-free. The only thing you'll have to worry about is keeping the shape of your style by having it trimmed every four weeks.

A short, no-set style doesn't have to trap you into just one look. Here are three variations on the same layered cut.

Add easy-to-care for curls with a perm or curling wand. Shape is the key thing here to keep from looking like a fuzz-head. Brush sides back and away from face. Secure with combs, if you have to.

The same look, sans curls. A quick blow-dry sweeps hair back at the sides. Keep brow uncluttered with either very short or side-swept bangs.

Slick this more sophisticated look into place with styling gel first, then use a diffuser on your dryer to prevent blow-away. Hair is brushed *up* and back at both sides, allowed to curl softly forward in the center.

Medium. You've got to know what you're getting into if you opt for medium-length hair. It's probably the hardest of any length to maintain. You'll have to blow it or set it into shape at least every time you wash it, and often between washings. With this comes the risk of overworking or overdrying your hair. It will help to never blow your hair completely dry. If you stop just short of bone dry, your style will hold together without doing as much damage to your hair. Frequent conditioning will also guard against your hair just giving up.

On the plus side, however, is flexibility. A good chin-length blunt cut trimmed every six to eight weeks will give you maximum adaptability. Here are just three ideas to try:

The simplest no-fuss look is often the most direct. Ends are turned under all around (use three large rollers if blow-drying leaves ends too straight). Bangs can be side-swept or straight across, depending on what's best for the shape of your face.

Change a basic blunt cut by twisting side and top hair back and securing with combs. Don't be symmetrical. If you take both sides back, you'll look too much like the ingé-nue.

If the shape of your face doesn't work with straight hair all around, you can still wear it medium length. Layers will give it more fullness, more "oomph." Keep sides brushed back and keep curl going strong with a body wave.

Long. Shoulder-length or longer hair is easy to care for if you select a simple, no-fuss style. Keep it away from your face and off your neck. Nothing looks messier than the shoulder line of a suit cluttered with fly-away hairs. Somehow, the three hundred or so that are supposed to fall out every day seem to do so on the back of your navy blue suit! The name of the game is control. Pull it back, pull it up, or both. Braided chignons are newer than "buns," and the image they create is far less librarian. And hair accessories such as combs, bands and clips can work wonders. They can be pretty, but keep them non-commital. Avoid anything in the "cute" category.

Long hair, more than any other length, needs to look shining clean, even if it means getting up an hour earlier every morning! And even if you never took your long locks to a salon your entire college career, plan on having them trimmed every six to eight weeks. In this case, there *can* be too much of a good thing!

Although your style options are virtually endless, don't ever fall back on the pony tail because it's easy. You'll look fine—for summer camp. Develop a knack for creating a finished look. Learn to do rolls and braids effortlessly, or they'll take all the time you have in the morning. Start by experimenting with these styles, then ask your hairdresser to show you a few quick tricks of the trade.

Hair accessories are important for keeping long hair off the face. Stick to a simple, one-length style. Add levels by pulling hair back with combs, clips, wraps.

Up-do's are elegant, as long as they don't get too Gibson Girl. Save the curls and stray wisps for evening. For a more serious, non-nonsense look, keep sides and top flat. Twist ends, roll and tuck at sides and top. In the back, French braiding, a twist, or a neat braided chignon.

Keep everything under control with a simple non-intricate cut. Blunt is best for long hair. Layers mean you'll have to curl—and too much curl with too much length can look too frivolous for the office. Keep top flat, ends turned under.

SAVING FACE—THE MAKEUP THAT LOOKS RIGHT

Where signs of sexuality are consistently frowned upon in male-dominated environments, somehow makeup has remained unscathed. The proper amount of emphasis is always acceptable and, in most cases, preferable to no artifice at all. Most women simply look better with a bit of color added here and there. If you prefer to leave well enough alone, nobody is going to fault you for it. But it's absolutely the wrong move to stop wearing makeup entirely because you think you might look too feminine for the job. As long as the application isn't obvious, you don't have to go through the "give-ups." Many first-year professionals automatically abolish eye shadow, nail enamel—even cheek color—from their beauty routines. But that's really not necessary. Most employers appreciate any extra effort you make to look as attractive as possible.

Color seems to be the determining factor. As long as it doesn't distract, you're okay. The best way to avoid making blatant mistakes is to stick with a slightly browned palette. Choose taupe, faun, grey or beige over blue, green, gold or violet for eyeshadow shades. The same subtly browned tones can also work for cheek, lip and nail colors. Pick a pink or coral with a warm brown undertone, and it will look far more natural than anything fuschia, berry, wine or red. Save fashion colors for time-off.

Use color only in areas of natural shade (along eye crease, under cheekbones). Never extend, rim, or create a contour that simply isn't there. Unless you're very adept at it, and you can afford to allow lots of time for proper blending, makeup "techniques" are going to show in office lighting.

Another item on the endangered species list is perfume. Many junior-level executives have wondered if it's ever appropriate in an office environment. To them we say, "Have you ever considered a man's after-shave scent inappropriate?" As long as it's subtle, it's neither offensive nor excessively feminine.

The same common-sense rules apply whether you're selecting your first interview suit or your final splash of fragrance: keep it in good taste, and don't let anything be overpowering. All of the elements that go into an executive look—accessories, makeup, hair—must work together to project one singularly successful image. *Your* new image.

CHAPTER

2

Executive Material: What They're Looking For

"Men wear clothes that are serviceable, comfortable, not provocative, and meet all of the qualifications. We should be looking for the same thing—but not necessarily the same clothes."

The last thing an interviewer wants to see is a woman who is trying hard not to look like one. And that's the first thing that gets noticed. Denying your own femininity is as obvious as it is irritating to those who are assessing your employment potential. "There's no sense in pretending you're not what you are," a senior partner in an investment firm insisted, "That shows a certain lack of self-esteem." "We're waiting for women to begin showing a little flair," a vice president of an ultra-conservative corporation noted, "and when they do, it will loosen things up for them."

There seems to be a consensus among most executives in hiring/promoting positions that women play it too safe for their own good. "The biggest misconception," said a corporate lawyer, "is there is something wrong with being attractive." Attractiveness has always been an asset for men in the business world, but women instinctively shy away from it. Understandable enough, given the incriminating associations attractiveness has had for women in business. Traditionally, its connotation has been entirely different for women than it has been for men. While it may be associated with effectiveness for male executives, it has had little to do with perceived professionalism as far as women were concerned. But all of that is in the past, executives tell us today. It may have been true ten years ago, but it's no longer an issue, they insist. Suddenly, it's okay to be attractive—whether you're a woman or a man. "You women have overreacted," is a frequently heard male complaint. A little smug, perhaps, but the generalization is too often true.

In an attempt to project seriousness, many women executives go through a period where they only succeed in projecting dowdiness. And while there is no lack of thought that goes into the way they present themselves, male colleagues perceive it as such. Time after time we've heard the same plaintive plea: "Women should put more thought into their appearance." "Women don't bother to put the

19

whole thing together right." These observations couldn't be further from the truth. If anything, the way women dress for their careers has to do with too much thought . . . and not enough courage.

Clearly, the executives we interviewed—both male and female—expressed a desire to see more personality in a woman's professional appearance. But as encouraging as this attitude sounds, just how close is it to reality? What happens when a woman—or a man, for that matter—wears anything slightly unexpected? "If you walk in on Monday wearing something noticeable, you know it before 10:30. And tomorrow it doesn't happen," the head bond trader at an investment bank told us. When interviewing candidates for a job, a fourth-year associate admitted, "If a woman stands out because of something she is wearing, it could be for the better, but it's risky. It all depends on the mindset of the interviewer." Women are treading a very thin line here; small wonder most opt for the security of unobtrusiveness. Success—even employment—is at stake.

Still, things are easing up a bit. When we asked a representative sampling of executives from conservative industries about specific items of apparel that were considered out of the question as recently as two years ago, they were almost unanimous in their acceptance of them. Such "feminine" things as nail polish, open-toed shoes, sheer colored stockings, diamond ear studs, silk dresses and makeup were all perfectly acceptable to everyone interviewed. As long as they suited the personality of the woman wearing them.

On the other side of the coin, two items of apparel were rarely deemed appropriate: pants of any sort and mink coats. "There's too much of a showgirl, mistress, golddigger association to fur," one investment banker commented, "Mink is conspicious consumption, and that's just the wrong image to present." While raccoon or other more casual furs were acceptable to some, most agreed that, unless you were going out for the evening directly from the office, there was simply no reason to bring the mink to work.

And here all agreement ended. Our sampling of executives representing conservative legal, fiduciary and corporate institutions showed a dramatic difference in viewpoint between men and women. It wasn't surprising to find the men all in favor of more experimentation in clothing styles—"as long as it remains within the boundaries of appropriateness and good taste"—and the women more strict in their definition of what is acceptable and what is not. Yet all acknowledged that innovation has to come from the younger employees up. Once new-hires go through a period of conservativism even more pronounced than the senior members of their firm, they begin to develop their own sense of style as they move up within the organization. Until women feel comfortable enough, and confident enough, to walk into an interview situation wearing whatever they want, real change is going to have to come from within. Underneath all the progressive-sounding sentiments for change runs the implicit caveat: Get in the door first. Show some initiative, but don't overdo it. Wait until your performance speaks louder than your clothes.

We've condensed all interviews from each professional field below. While the opinions expressed are fairly translatable to any conservative profession, you'll notice a slight tightening of the reins when it comes to prescribing proper attire for lawyers. If you're in doubt about the degree of flexibility in a field not represented here, and you want the most conservative definition of professional dressing—look under the section titled "Legal Advice."

INVESTMENT STRATEGIES

Whether you're a banker, broker, portfolio manager, securities analyst, institutional trader or corporate money manager—no matter what side of the "street" you're on—there is a solid strategy to compounding your perceived assets. The correct conservative image, say the following professionals, is determined by the industry; standards are not set by individuals, be they men or women.

Senior Partner, Investment Banking

"In our business, you're trying to influence people, trying to earn credibility in a very quick way. You've got to earn a client's respect by demonstrating self-confidence. Appearance is a very big part of this. You've got to look successful. In any business situation, presentation is 50% of the ballgame. It's just as important as content. And the same amount of professional thought should go into it.

"If everything else is equal, I would clearly go for the person who presents a more attractive appearance. We're looking for folks who are ahead of the pack. Attractiveness in both women and men is an underutilized asset. People ought to play to their strengths. A woman should play up her attractive features in an appropriate way, just as I would expect a man to play up his attractive features. I wouldn't want to hire a woman or a man who was afraid to look attractive.

"Right now, the women at our firm present a solid, reliable image. But they're much too dowdy for their own good. It's a kind of compensation, but the net effect is they look like they don't put much thought into the way they dress. They ought to pay more attention to themselves. This strict uniform that they've adopted is kind of laughable in a way. I think they ought to loosen up a little bit. I'm not looking for a woman who's trying to look like a man.

"On the other hand, they have to show good taste; good judgement. I don't mind a bit of flair, but anything that's too informal, too sexy, too extreme or too dramatic is an instant red flag. There are some very elegant ways to look attractive, however.

"I don't remember what a woman was wearing for her interview specifically, but it sort of fits into a general overall impression. I don't make mental notes, but if I see someone with sloppy grooming, or totally unimaginative dressing or inexpensive or poorly fitting clothes, that reflects something about that person's attention to detail and organization. You can tell a lot by just looking at people.

"Most of our senior people have a very straightforward, Ivy league, unimaginative style of dressing. But it's a generational thing. You don't have to dress that way to be at the top. There are some imitators among the younger leaders, but we're beginning to see a bit of expressiveness and flair. I think it has more to do with your peer group, not your power group.

"Is there an interview uniform necessary for a woman? It's safest. That's what I'd do. You can bet I was in my best grey flannel!"

Vice President, Risk Arbitrage

"During a preliminary screening situation, you have to decide if you're willing to risk more time with a person, if you're willing to go on to the next step. Initially, you'll only spend about 20 minutes deciding if someone warrants a second, longer interview, and appearance is about 40–50% of this decision. I've found you really can tell a book by its cover. At the actual decision to hire, however, appearance drops to about 25% of the total consideration of a candidate. Still, it's always a factor.

"What registers with me is the absence of anything extreme. I'd rather not notice what someone is wearing. Dress should not be a distraction, but if you do happen to focus on it, it should be appropriate and well thought-out. There are two interview types that I do notice—in a negative way—the minute they walk in the door. The first is what I call the "ultra-executive." She's the woman who looks too much like a man, too much like a clone. I have to wonder if maybe she's stretching beyond what she can do. The second stand-out is the high-fashion approach. Everything is too perfect, too stylish. There are only so many hours in a day, and I automatically think this woman spends too many of them concentrating on coordinating her clothes! Someone who looks too dolled-up is just as off the map as someone who's sloppy. If a man is too well-dressed, I have to sort out the possibility of a silver spoon—and that is a factor to consider. With a woman, I really can't tell if she's being chic or conspicuously wealthy or what. I can't recognize women's clothing styles that easily. It just registers in a wrong way.

"I feel more comfortable with someone who looks comfortable—like they're not stepping out into some other groove, whether that's too masculine, too power conscious or too fashionable. Proper attire doesn't always have to be a suit—especially if the suit looks like it's wearing the woman! My advice is to wear something that simply looks right on you.

"I clearly remember what a woman was wearing at her interview when we review resumés. More so than I remember what a man was wearing. Maybe that's human nature, but most men pay more attention to the way women dress. I know this is going to come off as sexist, but being attractive isn't a liability. I'd rather work with attractive women. I'd rather work with attractive men, too.

"Most of our women executives are very conservative in their dress. They don't have any fun. Men do. We might wear a stupid tie or a pair of bright suspenders. But right now women don't seem willing to risk anything. It works for them at first. Being conservative is not to their disadvantage at the beginning of their careers here, but there is room to have some sport. It's always a challenge to stay non-average, to stay off the norm just a little."

Third-Year Associate, Investment Banking

"I notice if a person takes pride in their appearance before I notice if they're fashionable or not. Such things as grooming, neatness, the way clothes fit, the fabrics they're made of are more important to me than the latest success look. If a person takes care to present a clean, business image, it says a lot about their self-esteem, and that carries over into their work.

"My first impression of a prospective employee is based on roughly 25% appearance, 75% ability. Of course, such intangibles as poise, grace and charisma enter into it. But if a candidate were borderline, I think appearance would finally determine whether I hired them or not.

"Perhaps because I am a woman and I am interested in clothes, I remember every detail of what an interviewee was wearing—from their shoes on up to their accessories. This is true for both male and female applicants. I'm also conscious if someone is better dressed than I am, but I don't hold it against them. I admire them for it. If someone came in here absolutely perfect from their hair to their nails to a very finished, professional look, I'd certainly be impressed.

"There is such a thing as looking too severe, however. A woman who's trying to dress to fit her idea of what an investment banker should look like is trying too hard. I'd rather see a little creativity. It's much more important to be feminine. But on the whole, most women dress to deny their femininity. They're the ones putting too much of a role model on themselves, and they end up looking frumpy. Sometimes it's better to go with a safe, conservative cut than to risk being dowdy.

"Around here, people tend to wear things according to the time they entered the organization. And, of course, income enters into it. Those in the upper echelons do tend to dress better, but there's no pre-determined style that says, I made it. They still wear the same type of looks they wore when they first started, only the quality may be better. Right now, separate skirts with blazers are gaining acceptance, but they still have to look finished in some way. For instance, a cotton shirt with the collar opened is just too casual. Even open-toed sandals are too casual here. We're just beginning to understand sling-backs!"

Fourth-Year Associate, Investment Banking

"The first thing I notice when a woman walks into my office is her face—specifically, her hair and makeup. If nothing is too outré there, I go on to look at her clothing. It's interesting to see which women don't wear any makeup and don't allow themselves to be feminine. Usually the look is carried through to a very mannish suit. Not that there is anything wrong with that, necessarily. People don't lose points with me unless they're wearing something bizarre. In the investment banking world, people expect a certain kind of conservative dress, and it always has to be in good taste. It has a range, but it's a much narrower range than, say, dressing for a career in advertising.

"I don't think I pay any more attention to a woman's appearance than a man's in an interview situation. There's no reason to judge women any differently. I apply the same criteria to both. The way they choose to present themselves is all a part of who they are; you can't help but be influenced by their appearance. If a man or a woman is so unobservant as to be oblivious to the impression they're making by the way they look, that kind of person probably wouldn't work well here.

"It is possible to look too perfect, too studied. You wouldn't expect to see a very lacquered kind of look in this environment. I don't mean that I object to an interviewee who is obviously better dressed than the interviewer. Sometime's it's obvious they're sitting there in a brand new suit that looks like it's never been worn, and we're sitting there in suits we wear every day to work in. But that's to be expected. They don't work—yet.

"It's rare that you see a woman inappropriately dressed for an interview here. I've seen sport jackets and slacks—which is definitely wrong—worn by some men, but, by and large, most women seem to dress the same way for an interview. It might be better if they were to stand out a little more. I don't think a suit is all that mandatory. As long as the clothes were in good taste and flattering, it wouldn't adversely affect the way I viewed a woman. I don't think they have to pretend to be non-feminine to be good investment bankers.

"Women, particularly in Wall Street professions, tend to imitate the male too much. They tend to be too conservative, and it doesn't really fit their image. It's really a shame. Women are different, and they should use it to their advantage. In addition to the stereotyped suit look, things like chunky, fat heels just look too mannish, too masculine. When you wear something extraneous to your personality, it sticks out immediately. Of course, a woman has to be confident enough to bring off something other than a uniform look. But, I think as she becomes more powerful and more secure in her position, she should dress whatever way is most comfortable to her. If that turns out to be in a conservative style, than that's fine. If not, then as long as what she's wearing is in good taste, it should be equally acceptable. Here, however, you don't notice a difference in the dress worn by women at the top. I have to say you don't see that much change in what men at the top wear, either—maybe a few more monogrammed shirts, a few more custom-tailored suits, but that's about it. Quality seems to be the differentiating factor."

Vice President, Investment Banking

"I have a bias for people who look professional, for people who look like they would fit in in a business environment. And most people do who interview here. I don't see many people who look less than professional. Of course, if an undergraduate comes in for an interview, they just might not have the kind of clothes they need for the working world, and I can't hold that against them that much. You can have a terrific candidate in spite of the way he or she is dressed, but I'll tell that person to know how to dress before they show up for work! Believe me, if they don't show up in an interview uniform, we will suggest the proper way to look to them once they get here.

"The appearance factor may be overrated as to its importance in evaluating someone. We're looking at an overall profile. Psychologically, it may be there, however. If someone looks too well-groomed, for instance, you might think, do they ever roll up their sleeves and go to work?

"I think it's natural to pay more attention to the way a woman dresses for an interview, only because there's more variety there. With a man, you know he's either going to have a dark or light suit, depending on the season, and a tie. With a woman's clothes, there's more to notice. But I don't necessarily remember what anybody was wearing—man or woman—as I review their resumé. Unless something was definitely unusual about their appearance.

"Clothes simply aren't that big a deal at this institution. We don't spend a lot of time thinking about it, and there's not that much of a distinction in the way junior level and senior level executives dress. Of course, there aren't that many women at the top, either. In my own development here, I noticed that I did begin to wear brighter colors, and, sure, they elicited comments, but I didn't care at that point. Although when I first started out, my initial response was to look as conservative as possible. Actually, I looked downright dowdy; my skirts were probably too long, my colors were probably too dark. As I saw myself grow within the organization and my confidence began to grow, I began to deviate from the norm a little. I think when most people first enter an organization, it's very important to establish credibility, so they tend to start off on a very conservative tack. It's a stage we all go through, but I don't think we necessarily have to.

"There still must be a certain degree of formality to the way women dress. A blazer with a skirt is acceptable, but it's clearly associated with the day-before-vacation mindset. You wouldn't wear it on a day you're seeing clients. And with a suit, there are certain accessories that are just too informal: tinted hose or open-toed shoes, for instance. Sling-backs are less inappropriate, but I'm still not wild about them. And if you wear pants—ever—you're likely to be taken for a secretary. We just can't be that casual."

LEGAL ADVICE

Corporate, international or litigational law careers require the most conservative of all professional wardrobes. There is little fashion latitude, whether you're representing a client or representing your firm. Confidence-inspiring looks are considered essential; "power" looks are not. The effect to create is one of outward calm and inner security.

Senior Partner, Litigational Law Firm

"I think women have to indicate a characteristic confidence in themselves by the way they dress. It's very important in our business. A client has to look at you like a counselor—which is what a lawyer is—and, frankly, clients aren't used to looking at women that way. That's simply because there always have been more men than women in this business.

"We start off with a given here: anyone who walks into this office probably has the brainpower to be a lawyer. In fact, during an interview, I very rarely talk to anybody about legal things. I assume if they got to this point, they're good enough technically to be in the running. That makes personality and appearance the two most important things I'm looking at. I'd say the decision to hire is at least 50% based on appearance, and I probably pay just slightly more attention to the way a woman dresses for the interview than a man. If a candidate's overall personal habits indicate a lack of concern about themselves, my guard goes up. I figure if they don't take care in their dressing, they might show the same lack of concern about their work.

"It doesn't matter to me if a woman wears a standard interview suit, but I think most of my male colleagues would react differently. A traditional suit allows the majority of men to feel comfortable interviewing a woman. There are no surprises they have to contend with. I'm certain this attitude will change, but right now, I'd say a suit is definitely necessary.

"The most important thing a female candidate can project is a certain ease with herself. If she's too turned-out, she's not going to look natural or relaxed. I'm likely to interpret this as probably a lack of confidence. Another mistake they make is not to show they're women. That's an advantage, and they should use it. I'll tell you, I have an easier time hiring an attractive woman than an unattractive one.

"Men at the top dress the same way they did 25 years ago when they started. Personally, I think women at the top should wear silk dresses. Even if attitudes change and more women start dressing more fashionably, it's unlikely that men will change their style of dressing that drastically. The most important consideration is how will your clothing style affect your client's impression of you. This holds true no matter where you go. You've got to know how to dress to suit the people you're dealing with in various parts of the country. New York is the most conservative; I'd wear my senior-partner-pinstripe here, but if I've got a meeting in Los Angeles, I'd take along a sportcoat. I'm looking for someone who demonstrates that same kind of ability to judge what is appropriate for the situation by the way they dress at their interview."

Ninth-Year Associate, Corporate Law

"There is an acceptable range of clothing for a law firm, and most people operate within that range. Although some people restrict themselves more than they have to. Most of the women at this firm don't go to extremes as far as projecting an austere appearance goes. The women who are partners here tend to wear dresses probably more often than suits. Whatever they wear, it seems much more feminine. That may be because they feel more expansive about the range they can wear.

"At first, it's important to demonstrate that you have enough judgment to dress appropriately for the occasion. That's why you'll never get into trouble in an interview suit. In the summer, maybe you could show up in something else, like a dress, but it has to have the same clean lines. A fresh appearance is always preferential. Something frilly or blatantly sexy, or clothes with what I call a lot of "street appeal" would be absolutely the wrong thing to wear here. When sizing up a person's potential is limited by time, the first impression is pretty crucial and clothing plays a substantial part of it. It's certainly connected to other qualities. The fact that a person didn't have enough judgment to wear the right thing for the occasion might also reflect their lack of judgment in other areas.

"What's definitely out of place in this firm is something terribly trendy. Someone who looked too up-to-the-second in clothes would bother me because I'd feel that they were spending too much time in that endeavor and probably weren't interested in a lot of other things. Also, I find it disconcerting if a woman has every hair in place, the nails polished, the toenails polished, everything just perfect. It makes me uncomfortable. I begin to wonder if I have anything out of place!

"However, an outfit that didn't show any thought whatsoever would make me suspicious. We're a client-based corporation. We have to have people who can represent the firm without feeling that we have to give some kind of explanation for their appearance. We also try not to be more conspicuously well-dressed than our clients. The whole firm's style is a conscious effort to look tasteful and understated. That's why a woman wearing a fur coat would be wrong. You don't want to look like you're making tons of money off your client and others like him.

"I think a lot of people really don't know what they look like in certain things, and that's where they can go wrong. For instance, diaphanous, see-through blouses may look pretty in the stores, but in the office they're just totally inappropriate. I don't think seeing a woman's bra through her blouse is any more attractive than seeing a man's undershirt. It's certainly not sexy or appealing in this environment. Too much gold jewelry is another example. It just looks out of place to see gold bracelets, gold necklaces, and gold earrings on a younger woman. It's just not the time or the place for it. Other details that tend to ruin a woman's appearance are severe hair styles and clunky shoes. For me, open-toed shoes and even open-heeled shoes are preferable on a woman to the heavy-looking clunkers many of them feel they should wear. Those white shirts with bow ties are cute once a week. They look good up to a point, but there's no doubt that it's a look copied from the men. If a woman wore it every day, I'd think it was a little too dyke-ish.

"Women do have the edge when it comes to being able to wear a sport jacket and a skirt. That looks fine, although men can't get away with anything less formal than a suit. And when they move up in the firm, the only change they make in the way they dress is to go to the higher range of Brooks Brothers suits. Women at least have the opportunity to be a little experimental, and they should use it."

Fourth-Year Associate, International Law Firm

"We once had a woman who came in here for an interview wearing a tight red sweaterdress, and she had about ten associates wanting to interview her. But she did not get a job offer. I think she made the two worst mistakes you can make in your selection of what to wear: color and fit. Something bright is just as bad as something that doesn't fit well, although men tend to notice fit more than women do.

"Neatness is the first thing I notice about someone. If a person cares enough to dress well, then it's an indication of their attitude toward work and their employer. You tend to give more emphasis to appearance in an interview situation than you do in evaluating someone's performance on a day-to-day basis. When you first meet someone, however, their clothing is a significant factor in your overall impression of them.

"The ideal effect to create is that you really look wonderful, but it didn't take a great deal of effort to achieve. If anything looks fake, it's instantly recognizable. Sometimes the grey or the blue or the black interview uniform looks like the woman put it on in the morning and can't wait to get it off. This turns me right off. I like a person who looks well in their clothes, but also looks comfortable. Otherwise, it seems that they just haven't put enough thought into the way they want to present themselves.

"We have a range of acceptable clothing styles for women at this firm. Some wear suits, but I rarely do. I prefer dresses. If I were interviewing at another law firm, however, I would wear a suit. Maybe in navy or beige. And definitely a silk shirt. I think cotton shirts are too mannish, although I do like them worn with the floppy bow ties. Occasionally, women here do wear skirts with non-matching jackets—but no more than once or twice a month. Suits or dresses are considered more appropriate office wear. Open-toed shoes always elicit a lot of negative comments around here. And pants can set the whole place buzzing! It has only happened twice that someone has shown up in pants, and the reaction was mainly one of unconcealed surprise.

"As women move into higher positions, there is no well-defined clothing code. You'd want a few more suits, and clothes of higher quality. I guess the key thing is to be more conscious of what you're wearing, but less self-conscious about it."

CORPORATE POLICY

Financial and legal careers aren't the only ones requiring a conservative way of dressing. At many supply-side corporations, a correct professional image is equally essential to success. Without one particular industry group regulating the standards, a general corporate clothing code is a bit more difficult to formulate, but it is apparent all the same. The professionals below, from as widely divergent fields as recruitment, insurance and city government all share a common recognition of an appropriate business look that works across the board.

Executive, Recruiting Firm (Financial and Legal Specialists)

"In any service business, you have to look impressive. You have to look like you have some credibility—like there's a reason someone is paying you. Part of that, a good part of that, is appearance. I'd say it's 75% of any decision to hire.

"My first impression of someone has more to do with grooming than it does with style. Sloppiness is inexcusable. I look to see if a person presents a neatly cared-for appearance. If there's a spot anywhere, I'll find it! I'll only remember the negative things that tend to stand out. When I'm favorably impressed by someone, I tend to attribute it to other qualities, rather than the clothes he or she was wearing.

"Women have more of an opportunity to make mistakes with their look than men do. With a man, not too much can go wrong. You might notice a tasteless tie, or an inexpensive suit, or socks that don't match, but that's about all a man can do to ruin his image. If he gets those three things right, he's passed with flying colors. But, since a woman has more diversity in the way she can pull herself together, she can miss the mark in many more places. You have to pay more attention to a woman's interview look for this reason. There's a lot that can go wrong.

"Maybe a suit is the safest answer, but it's certainly not mandatory. A jacket with a dress would be perfectly acceptable to me. But most women don't risk it. Suits are fine, too, but I do look for some personality in what they wear—a little bit of pizzazz.

"The worst mistake a woman can make is not to update her looks. You can stay too collegiate or too conservative for too long. The style level of women at the top is improving, but it's coming up from the younger female executives. It would be wise for the older executives to take notice. People tend to follow leaders—at whatever level on the executive scale they are. When I was first starting out, I wanted to be totally inconspicuous. I wanted them to think only one thing when they looked in my direction, and that was that I was doing a good job. Now I'm more comfortable wearing clothes—and colors—that might be noticed. You owe it to yourself to look a little interesting. Being too fashion conscious is something else again. Whatever's in style can usually be spotted on secretaries—for $12.99.

"You can't be too casual, however. I don't think sportswear separates are ever acceptable for work. Men don't wear them—why should women? If a woman came in here with a camel blazer and a plaid skirt, I'd think she didn't get dressed up enough for the interview."

Vice President, Chief Financial Officer, Insurance Brokerage

"I'm looking for some sense of self, a personal style, in the way a prospective employee dresses. There is a certain level of expectation; a professional woman tends to dress within a certain range. And any deviation from that range is likely to be viewed more positively after you can evaluate the person's performance. You can be more tolerant about appearance at the promoting stage than you can at the hiring stage. At that point, you're simply looking for signs as to whether or not a person is going to fit in and be comfortable.

"The higher the position you're hiring for, the more important appearance becomes. Somebody in a senior capacity usually has their sense of style pretty well set. They aren't going to change at that point, so they have to look like the right image for your company to begin with.

"Performance is profoundly related to appearance. When you get dressed in the morning, you deliberately choose to present a certain façade. And that façade, like it or not, is a reflection of your personal priorities. There's a definite relationship between what one looks like and what they act like.

"If someone shows up for an interview in something too sexy, too showy, too cheap—which doesn't mean inexpensive, by the way—you've got to think there's something wrong there. Either the person doesn't understand the job, or they're badly off base in terms of interpreting what is culturally appropriate, or they're trying to get the job for the wrong reason. Whatever the problem, there's obviously something the matter with that candidate.

"I personally have an aversion to the boy banker look in men and its counterpart for women, although I wouldn't *not* hire someone because they conformed to that mold. If you're going to play it incredibly conservative, however, you better have suits of extremely high quality. Otherwise, the whole look misses by a mile. As far as suits go, softer ones are safest for women. Something in a tweed or a soft color. It should still be tailored and have clean lines, but it shouldn't be strict. The grey or blue "man's suit" is just too severe. Done very well, it's terrific, but most people don't do it well enough. Personally, I think professional women look best in dresses.

"If someone is particularly attractive physically, that can be a problem. First, because an awful lot of people out there are going to start off with the impression that they must be stupid. Secondly, people are naturally defensive about anybody that presents too good an appearance. People want to believe that anybody that's so perfect has to have some faults, and they instantly assume one of them is that the person must spend too much time on himself or herself. They think something—like their work—has to suffer. It's a partially defensive reaction.

"A sport coat and skirt are perfectly acceptable for women here, but a cotton shirt with an open collar seems just a little too sporty. Colored hose is not for beginners; you've got to know what you're doing with them. It's not too far from there to looking cheap."

Budget Director, City Government

"A general level of attractiveness is what I look for in a woman. That doesn't imply sexiness. There are qualities that all have to fit together: hair, makeup and complexion, the way she carries herself and the clothes she wears. This isn't a sexist thing; appearance is just as important for a man. Ideally, it should be 30–40% of your total evaluation of someone, but in reality, it probably hits closer to 50%. The nicer you can look at an interview, the better.

"I think we're seeing a standardization of the way professional women dress developing. There's a tendency to a more tailored look—a lot of suits and jackets. Although women at lower-end jobs tend to be more casual. What's too casual on anybody in this business setting is pants. They indicate a lack of professionalism and are not appropriate in the corporate or financial spheres we deal in.

"One thing I place considerable value on is femininity. I don't like a mannish appearance. But that doesn't necessarily mean a tailored look. Some women can wear very tailored clothes and still be feminine. It all depends on how you carry yourself.

"The main thing I see going wrong with the way some professional women dress is the lack of self-confidence their clothes reveal. The uniform look is not necessary and, besides that, it's boring. Sometimes this shows a certain narrowness, a tendency not to be able to cope with change or stress. I would like to see a sense of style in a woman. Jackets with different skirts, for instance, are acceptable and can show a range of imagination. I'm disappointed when a woman walks in wearing the Brooks Brothers suit and tie look. It's too stereotyped, too easy. You don't want to show a lack of attention to yourself. The way you feel about yourself does affect the way you work; it's all interrelated."

WHAT YOU'RE WEARING NOW

There isn't a great deal of difference between what prospective employers want and what employed women executives are wearing. If anything, they err on the side of safety. In spite of the indication that the working world is ready for a few less suits, they are still the number-one attire most favored by women in managerial positions.

Recently an Executive Dressing Questionnaire was distributed to the women customers of Streets & Co. who hold senior level positions. You'll find an abbreviated version of it at the end of this chapter. Answer the questions yourself to see how your analysis of what is, and what is not, acceptable in your field match up against the women we surveyed.

The responses we received from women representing over seventeen different industry groups* confirmed that conservative is still the key word when it comes to selecting professional apparel. Most maintained that there is an appropriate way to dress in their field, and specified a well-groomed, tailored look as the most acceptable image to have. What was interesting was that the majority of responses

---

*Investment banking, commercial banking, corporate finance, securities analysis, management consulting, corporate public relations, brokerage research, real estate investing, law, advertising, publishing, data processing, tourism, mental health/health care administration, architecture, office products, scientific instrument systems coordination.

denied that women consciously copy male dress patterns, yet over 86% acknowledged that the male perception is involved in some way in the way they dress. Fifty-one percent agreed that it is the men who set the standards of dress, although in the case where there are few women in senior positions, many respondents indicated that it is difficult to determine whether these women set their own standards or merely reflect those already established by senior male associates. All were conscious of the affect their dress would have on the men they would have to deal with. Virtually 100% of these women executives insisted that avoiding overtly sexy clothing was their top consideration. Second to that was their avoidance of anything that made them look like a man. The third look they could do without was anything trendy. Following these considerations, in order of importance, was the desire to look as authoritative and as conservative as a man. While 47% of the respondents said they compared the seriousness of their image to that of their male counterparts, only 15% opted to copy the same colors worn by men.

Role Models or Fashion Models?

Other sources of image inspiration are few for these highly visible executives. Only 60% felt that women intentionally copy other women's style of dressing, and none of them felt they could turn to fashion magazines for realistic wardrobe information. Thirty percent said they never read them. Of those who did, exactly half of them felt the looks presented to the readers were *never* applicable to the conservative demands of their professions. "Who wears these clothes? They're crazy!" one respondent wrote in the margin of her questionnaire. About the only help considered somewhat worthwhile by the women we surveyed was the services of a qualified fashion consultant. Although most of them had never used one, almost 60% of them said they preferred to be advised while shopping.

The Perception of Performance

Not one woman felt the subject of developing a correct professional image too frivolous to be taken as seriously as they took their jobs. Over 80% felt that a woman's appearance is directly related to the perception of her performance. Less (67%) felt the same holds true for men. Although the majority agreed that appearance was more important in the perception of competence for women, they also acknowledged that the dress code was somewhat stricter for men. In the absence of an established, formalized dress formula, it seems that appearance takes on much more importance. Where it is noticed and critically evaluated for women, it is more strictly defined and more easily dismissed for men. No wonder the female professionals' initial reaction was to develop an equally noncommital style of dressing! But it didn't work. Today, only 26% of the executives we surveyed said they purposely select clothes that won't be noticeable.

What Works Now

By far the suit is the single apparel item executive women feel most comfortable wearing. Nearly 80% of the Streets & Co. respondents indicated they feel most appropriately dressed in a suit, seconded by 47% who will wear a skirt and a jacket. While a dress felt right to only 20%, a dress with a jacket was acceptable to nearly one-third. We weren't surprised when the collegiate connotations of a sweater and skirt combination kept its acceptance level to just above 10%. Nor were we surprised (given the variety of industries represented in the survey) that pantsuits and pants with a jacket got the go-ahead from exactly one executive!

The Need to Personalize

The women we surveyed expressed confidence in their own personal determination of what was appropriate for their profession, yet most revealed a need for individuality within the framework of their clothing code. When we asked what questions they would ask a fashion authority, most of the replies were variations on this same theme: "How can I jazz up my total appearance without losing my professional look?" "How can I look professional and feminine and distinguish myself as an individual?" "How can I dress in an appropriate, 'take-me-seriously' style and still be feminine, stylish and show some personality?" "How can I look tailored, but not as boring as everybody else?" "What are some ways to make each outfit, especially suits, distinctive, unique and interesting?"

Expressing individuality is a significant enough cause of concern among professional women that this book is dedicated to exploring all the options we can. Imagine—and many of you can—the frustration of looking into your closet and feeling the same limitations imposed upon you as this young lawyer described: "Since I've been working, I just can't wear what's going to express my personality. I have an entirely different attitude to clothes now." We say that is exactly the wrong attitude to have. Given the expectations expressed by professionals in hiring/promoting positions for some degree of flair, and the desire of most female executives to show a bit of personal pizzazz, change does seem imminent. But it's not going to happen as long as we choose to cling to stereotyped, unimaginative images. Over 52% of the executives we surveyed indicated that they did not expect their clothing style to change as they moved up within their organizations (although most admitted that standards for women's office attire have changed within the past 2 years). Obviously, a conservative professional look works in the business world. What's needed are more ways to make it work for women.

THE STREETS & CO. EXECUTIVE DRESSING QUESTIONNAIRE

The following is an abbreviated version of the questions we asked our executive customers. Try answering them yourself. It's a good way to begin analyzing your own wardrobe considerations. You may be surprised at the real reasons behind why you dress the way you do!

1. Is there an appropriate way to dress in your field? _____ yes _____ no

2. If yes, describe briefly what is considered appropriate attire. _____

3. Who sets the standards?
   _____ management—women
   _____ management—men
   _____ immediate superior
   _____ other (please explain) _____

4. Do you feel women at your office consciously copy male dress patterns?
   _____ yes _____ no

5. Do you feel women at your office consciously copy the dress of successful women in the organization? _____ yes _____ no

6. Is the male perception involved at all in the way you dress for the office?
   _____ yes _____ no

7. Please check off any of the following statements that apply to your considerations when selecting office attire:
   _____ I avoid overtly sexy clothing
   _____ I don't want to look like a man
   _____ I follow the conservative look of the men at the office
   _____ I don't want my dress to be particularly noticed
   _____ I don't want to appear trendy
   _____ I try to look authoritative
   _____ I choose the same colors preferred by male counterparts
   _____ I compare the seriousness of my image to male counterparts
   _____ Other (please explain) _____

8. Do you take the time to read fashion magazines?
   _____ yes _____ no _____ sometimes

9. Do fashion magazines present realistic office looks?
   _____ yes _____ no _____ sometimes

10. Do you feel a woman's appearance is directly related to the perception of her performance? _____ yes _____ no

11. Do you feel a man's appearance is directly related to the perception of his performance? _____ yes _____ no

12. Do you feel perception of performance is based more on appearance for women than for men? ____ yes ____ no

13. Is the accepted dress standard for men stricter than for women at your office? ____ yes ____ no

14. If there is one dress or accessory symbol of authority for women where you work, what is it? _____

15. Have standards of dressing for women in your office changed at all during the past two years? ____ yes ____ no

16. If yes, in what way? _____

17. Which look do you feel most appropriately dressed in?
    ____ a suit
    ____ a skirt/jacket
    ____ a skirt/sweater
    ____ a dress
    ____ a dress/jacket
    ____ a pants/jacket
    ____ a pantsuit

18. What is definitely considered inappropriate attire at your office? _____

19. Have you ever used the services of a personal fashion consultant? ____ yes ____ no

20. Do you like to be ____ advised or ____ left alone while shopping?

21. If you could ask a fashion authority just one question concerning your professional wardrobe, what would it be?

    _____
    _____
    _____

22. Do you feel your dressing style will change as you move up in your organization? ____ yes ____ no

23. If yes, in what way? _____
    _____

CHAPTER

3

Starting Over: Re-Entry Strategies That Work

"I didn't have any clothes in my wardrobe that were right when I decided to go back to work. I had hoped that I could use some of the things in my closet, but I really couldn't."

Returning to the work force can be just as mystifying as approaching an interview at 22. You're still starting out—you're just starting later. Some women find, however, that every year "out" adds ten times the insecurities to the whole process. "I wouldn't be this nervous if I had my youth, my skills and my knowledge at the same level as the competition," a 39-year-old mother of three insisted.

Still, it is possible. In fact, the re-entering worker is the phenomenon of the decade. Women are leaving the serenity of the suburbs, the hum-drudgery of housework, and seeking gainful employment in unprecedented numbers. Some are searching for self-actualization, some are supplementing family incomes, and some are suddenly on their own and have to work to survive. For whatever reason, more than 1,185,000 women between 35 and 54 will re-enter the work force this year.

Re-entry women are swelling the ranks of the 11–14 million women expected to join the employment market during this decade. Estimates indicate that two out of every three women will be employed by 1990, and the average woman will work more than 34 years of her life. If you've taken a few of those years off to get married and raise a family, you have a bit of catching up to do! If you've never worked at all, the chances are good that you will. Predictors say 90% of all women will be employed outside the home at some point in their lives. According to a survey conducted by Laurie Ashcraft and Elizabeth Nickles for *The Coming Matriarchy*, 30% of non-working women have definite plans to enter the work force in the near future, and an additional 50% are considering it. So you're not alone. The Bureau of Labor Statistics expects the participation of women aged 25–54 in the labor force to increase nearly 70% during this decade.

Going back to work is not something that only married women do when the kids are old enough. Statistics show 77% of single women aged 35–44 are bringing home the bacon, too. Including both divorced and displaced homemakers, this group returns more out of necessity than any need to establish an identity. Considering the grim prediction that one out of every three currently married women will eventually divorce, and only 14% of divorced women are ever granted alimony, it's easy to understand the economics behind the fact that 74% of all divorced women were in the labor force as far back as 1979. And that number continues to grow. At least 4 million displaced homemakers—those women finding themselves suddenly alone after being completely supported by their spouse—find they must venture into the workforce for the first time in their lives. The woman who assumes head-of-household responsibilities (and 14% of all families are now headed by women) also must become the chief breadwinner.

Married women are getting into the act with as much determination, but perhaps different motivation. The U.S. Bureau of Labor Statistics reports that only 37% of all women today are full-time homemakers. Many of those opting to join the labor force do so to maintain the family's standard of living in the present economy. Others are financing their children's education funds. Still others are seeking to improve self-esteem, and gain a sense of their worth as individuals separate from the family structure.

With the increasing visibility of aggressively successful women in the workplace, many full-time homemakers simply feel left out of the mainstream when the topic of conversation turns to the inevitable, "What do you do?" "I wasn't bored into going back to work," a returning portfolio manager explained, "certainly I had more than enough to do. But I was tired of being defensive about it. No matter how valuable a contribution I thought I was making, underneath it all, I didn't feel very stimulating." In fact, it has been demonstrated in study after study that employed women do feel more self-confident, more attractive and are more extroverted than their non-working counterparts. And the more they engage in activities outside the home, the greater their need for self-fulfillment becomes. For the re-entry employee, nothing succeeds like the first taste of success.

Individual motivations aside, the positive feedback—either emotional or economical—from being a part of the working world is enough to attract the 56% of all women in the labor force who are married and living with their husbands. And it's enough to generate government speculations that, by 1990, three out of every four wives will be working outside the home.

KNOCK, KNOCK. WHO'S THERE? NOBODY.

But what about mothers? Surely someone's staying at home. Wrong. Today, women are waiting an average of only 3–4 years after childbirth to re-enter the work force. The number of working wives has tripled during the last few decades, and it's the mothers who are leading the parade. In 1940, it was almost unthinkable to abandon children for a career; only 9% of all mothers with children under 18 did it. But then the numbers began to escalate: to 28% by 1950; to 58% in 1980. Within one year alone, from 1980 to 1981, the participation of mothers in the work force with children under six jumped from 30% to 48%. Currently, the Labor Department reports, more than half of the country's children have mothers who work away from home. And the absenteeism is expected to increase. By 1990, it is estimated that two-thirds of all mothers with children under six will be working and both parents will be employed in three-fourths of all two-parent families.

Clearly, many women are starting over. But the difference between the re-entry generations is the number of years they've been away. Those closer to the younger end of the scale tend to take less time out. That's a key factor in evaluating your chances of a smooth re-entry. The more years you've been away, the more you'll have to work at it.

WHAT'S STOPPING YOU?

If you've put off doing something about re-entering at a professional level, you must have your reasons. But will you recognize when they turn into rationalizations? Too many women postpone taking any job action because of misconceptions about what's "out there," and what they can contribute. If your excuses fall into any one of the categories below, it may be time to re-examine your reasoning.

Guilt: The "they-can't-manage-without-me" syndrome is responsible for stopping many women before they start. When, in fact, most who return to work find the family *can* manage. Very nicely. When there is the proper spirit of cooperation, family members can even develop new skills. More and more teenagers, for instance, are becoming expert meal planners and food shoppers, spending 40% of family food dollars. Guilt can also be the motivating factor behind the "super-woman" routine. Women who expect to both excel in their careers and single-handedly keep things running as smoothly as ever at home are often operating out of a deep sense of desertion. The unfairness of it all is that it puts undue stress on both fronts, sometimes hindering the woman's chance of success at either. If you've made the decision to return to work, you've got to nip guilt in the bud—or it will nip you. Concentrate instead on enlisting family aid for *specific* duties. Organize and delegate. Think of it as good training for your new position.

Fear: More than ignorance, fear of failure is the main deterrent preventing many women from re-entering the marketplace. The feeling that you can't hold a candle to the competition is a powerful procrastination tactic. It's all too easy to underestimate your own ability to perform. That's why many returnees automatically set their sights too low. Limited expectations restrict many to seek low-status, low-paying positions. Jobs that utilize more familiar public-oriented skills are the ones re-entry women are most likely to go after: retail sales positions, nursing, teaching, secretarial and clerical duties. These traditional "pink collar" fields attract 80% of all working women. Currently, four out of five American women who work outside the home hold less-than-executive positions. This contributes to the fact that, on the whole, women's salaries are still only 60% of men's. It is also often pointed out that only 6% of working women are in management. That's not as hopelessly low as it sounds, however, since the opposite side of the coin reveals that only 14% of men are. The fact of the matter is, however, only 7% of the 1,185,000 women between the ages of 35 and 54 who will re-enter the work force this year will do so in professional positions. And fear is one of the principal reasons why.

Values: It's going to take some serious value re-evaluating to turn you into a competitive, aggressive career woman. After years of cultivating relationships, many women are unable or unwilling to place less importance on keeping the peace. The success-at-all-costs survival instinct simply isn't there. If you feel your personal responses would run counter to corporate interests, you'll need to do all you can to redefine the way you deal with people. Being popular isn't always possible. Being well-liked is far less important than being respected. Protecting a friend is never preferable to being effective. The inability to delegate responsibility, the proclivity for forming friendships rather than working relationships, and the tendency for women not to be selective in forming office associations can all be traced to conflicting social/professional roles. Women who have been out of the work force for a long time find they have to "toughen up" interpersonal attitudes.

It is difficult enough to develop a competitive edge, but almost impossible to get ahead without one. Internal power plays *can* effect your career, whether you approve or not. If you don't want to play the game, you at least must develop an awareness of what's going on. The mistake many women make is to think they can rise above all internal intrigue. They can't. It's important to recognize the impact corporate politics can have. Read books. Talk to people who have successfully negotiated their way through the professional power maze. Attend women's association workshops. Acquaint yourself with the games people play before going in. Naïveté is no excuse for failure.

While you're re-examining the way you interact with people, be prepared for long-standing friendships to change. Many re-entry women find that, as their schedules and interests change, and as free time becomes more limited, friends feel either left behind or left out. Don't be surprised if jealousies develop. Loneliness is a common complaint of women who, at first, feel caught between two worlds. Not entirely committed to a career initially, they feel out of their "element" at work and disassociated from their friends at home. As the personal and professional feedback becomes more positive from the job, this early conflict is resolved. Studies have shown that, as a woman's self-concept improves, she feels less torn between traditional values and her new role outside the home. The early need to closely examine personal priorities, re-evaluate values, and reformulate interpersonal attitudes is enough, however, to stall the progress of many prospective re-entry women.

Lack of support. Lack of confidence: The two often go hand-in-hand. Changing your entire manner of living is not an easy thing to contemplate, and, without encouragement from friends and family, it's almost impossible to overcome a natural insecurity. In interview after interview, women who had successfully made the switch from homemaker/mother to employed executive credit family support and cooperation as major factors in the ease of transition. Unfortunately, the opposite holds just as true. A woman's initial ambivalence about the merits of trading in one full-time career for another is greatly exaggerated by lack of understanding and encouragement. The best advice is to resolve any resistance on the homefront before you even start your search. Get to the real root of all objections. At the base of many "my-wife-doesn't-have-to-work" arguments lies a more practical fear of loss of services. If you have to hire a part-time housekeeper to make sure the laundry gets done on schedule, do it. Proving that things will get done goes a long way toward easing tensions.

The loss of affection is an even greater threat, and women who were expected to give up their careers when they got married are more susceptible to it. Training and generational mores have made male approval so paramount to this group of women that many are afraid to risk losing it. Establishing one's own place in a competitive marketplace may be too challenging to a mate, and many women simply don't want to upset the status quo. Insecurity over loss of affection is compounded when the spouse fears alienation as his wife enters a much more stimulating world. Making an effort to improve the quality of the time you do have to spend with each other is both reassuring to the relationship . . . and stimulating in its own right. It takes some organization, but the busier many executive women become, the more they make time to do.

Lack of knowing where to start: Many women never leave home looking for a job because they just don't know where to begin. It's easier to put something off if it's a great unknown. Without a concrete course of action, you can wile away endless hours with the want ads, without ever having to take any action at all. Actually, the want ads aren't a bad place to start. They give you an idea of who's hiring, what they're paying, and what experience is expected today in your field. Unless you can sit right down and write a resumé with all the required qualifications, you'll need to continue your exploration beyond one attack on the classifieds. Find out what new knowledge there is for your occupational area. Contact local professional women's organizations, get a schedule of their upcoming seminars and workshops and plan to attend the ones related to your field. Many "brush-up" programs will give you a good overview of what's required when you re-enter the work force. Attending a few of these won't be a waste of your time. You can get specific about locating courses of study that apply to your particular category or personal development skills once you've done your first general research. Whatever you do, don't sign up for an expensive, three-year course of study without investigating all the alternative routes for getting where you want to be. Most women who have been out of the job market for a long time *do* find that they lack up-to-date skills, current education in their field, or even the advanced degree required today. Studies have shown that the more education a woman has, the more likely she is to go to work. But determining that you need more education to go back to work can put a crimp into even the most ambitious plans.

GOING BACK-TO-SCHOOL. AT YOUR AGE?

Many of the same reasons that stop re-entry women from seeking a job at an executive level also stop them from furthering their education to ensure their worth in the marketplace. And the longer a woman has been out of school, the greater her fears are likely to be. Apprehension about dulled intellectual abilities and outdated information leads older students to believe their opinions are not as valid as those held by younger classmates. Self-doubt at a new time of self-identification often results in initial anxiety. The schools that offer re-entry women special attention in personal, career *and* academic counseling are the places to apply. You'll be able to judge them by the amount of information they give you about the often confusing re-entry process. Lack of familiarity with the multitude of academic procedures, coupled with institutional inflexibility, can discourage the most determined student. If a school provides special personnel to help you through the maze, you can be somewhat confident that their programs will be sensitive to the very particular needs of re-entry women.

Insecurity about dusty skills necessary for academic success—such as taking notes, recalling material, writing papers, taking exams and using the library services may be a powerful deterrent. Most women need to refresh, upgrade and update basic academic skills before they tackle their first course. The Project on the Status and Education of Women lists the following skills as vital re-learning targets:

1. Studying
2. Improving reading ability
3. Taking exams
4. Writing college papers
5. Brushing up on math and science
6. Communicating and giving presentations
7. Managing time and juggling schedules
8. Using new information resources in the library, language lab and classroom

In addition, students must also be able to critically analyze information, assert themselves in the classroom and make decisions. These skills are as essential in determining your academic performance as the ability to take concise notes.

Even if you were straight Dean's List in your last academic experience, a lot has changed in new information systems. You won't be able to find the facts you need if you don't know how to do a computer search in the library, access videotape, or find the right microfiche.

If it all sounds too overwhelming, fear not. The re-entry woman is a valuable new source of student revenue to declining application figures, and the savvier schools are doing what they can to make your transition to student as painless and as successful as possible. Check for pre-entry workshops and refresher courses.

Writing labs, reading clinics, exam skills workshops, math anxiety workshops, career retraining projects, assertiveness training programs, communication and speaking technique workshops, time management training and college technology resource reviews can all help prepare you to compete academically—or professionally! Take a brush-up course or two at a local college before you sign up for Advanced Economics 301.

In addition to personal concerns, two very practical obstacles to re-entry involve both institutional and situational barriers. Application and admissions policies, unrealistic scheduling for off-campus students, and unacceptable transfers of credit all keep re-entry women away, as do family and financial responsibilities. Almost 70% of all women 35 and over who were enrolled in school in 1978 were also in the labor force. Colleges that can accommodate women juggling time, transportation, children and careers offer the following options:

Part-time study: In addition to evening and summer programs, some schools have now instituted weekend colleges. Courses are offered from Friday afternoon through Sunday evening several times a month. The student is encouraged to stay on campus during that time to allow for intensive scheduling and full use of the college's informational facilities. Undergraduate degrees in business, management, communications and human services are among those most often available in this format.

Experiential learning: Over half the colleges and universities in the U.S. accept some type of credit for what has been learned outside the classroom. The kind of experience re-entry women most often draw upon includes community and volunteer activities (fund-raising, editing a newsletter, organizing and running a committee, publicizing an event, etc.); homemaking (teaching children, managing finances, interior decorating, etc.); and job-related experience. An institution will examine proper documentation (often required in portfolio form with actual work samples), and designate the number of credits acceptable. Although it is next to impossible to earn or transfer such credit at the graduate level, experiential learning can put you several steps ahead in an undergraduate degree program. After all, you haven't stopped learning just because you've been out of school. And colleges are finally beginning to recognize that fact.

Just testing: You can demonstrate your accumen in areas where you already possess a body of knowledge by "testing out" for credit. The College Level Examination Program (CLEP), devised by the College Entrance Examination Board, provides general and subject examinations for specific courses. CLEP exams are held during the third week of each month at more than 1,000 centers in the United States. There is also a Proficiency Examination Program (PEP) provided by American College Testing, offering standardized tests correlated to both upper and lower division courses. Although most institutions limit the number of credits it is possible to earn through testing, a year's worth of credit is not unusual. It is even possible to earn complete undergraduate degrees through testing at some schools.

Credit-through-contract: Students can devise their own curriculum without benefit of classroom-type instruction. External degrees may be earned for off-campus learning. The usual procedure is for both student and school to draw up a "learning contract," specifying what will be learned and required in order to receive credit. The number of credits required for graduation is the same as the number required in a traditional undergraduate degree program. Since the student works at her own pace, however, it can often take longer. External degrees are every bit as valid as those earned in the classroom. Of those surveyed with such a degree who applied to graduate school, 89% were admitted.

Graduate schools are attracting a high percentage of women returning to upgrade their value in the marketplace. In fact, there has been a significant upswing in the number of re-entry women. The good news is, almost all women who complete graduate school go on to do productive work in their field. The bad news is, evidence suggests that returning women students at the graduate level often experience more conflict with their husbands, parents and friends than returning undergraduates. And the discrimination doesn't stop there. It is more difficult for re-entry women to be admitted to graduate than undergraduate programs. Although reasons vary with each school, generally the criteria precludes part-time participation and credit acceptance from interrupted education. Re-entry women are often viewed as non-serious candidates who will have too much difficulty picking up where they left off. Over 86% of re-entry applicants admitted to encountering a negative reaction during the required personal interview. And, if all of this weren't discouraging enough, the Graduate Record Exam (GRE) usually required for admission is valid for only 5 years. For women who don't apply within that time frame, having to take the GRE over again is an additional source of anxiety.

Still, no matter what a woman has to go through to get herself into prime employable condition, re-entering an educational program must be working. The number of women 35 and older enrolled in college has doubled since 1972. And more than one-third of all college students are at least 25 years old. The largest segment of this adult student population is composed of women, who now account for more than two-thirds of all adult students. And they're good students. As a whole, they earn higher grade point averages than younger students. Educators believe that re-entry women tend to have clearer career goals, more experience and/or transferable skills than their younger counterparts. Motivation is the key that accounts for the tremendous growth in the numbers of women returning to school (up 187% according to the latest Census Bureau figures). This percentage is almost four times higher than the number of men who returned to school during this same period. For the first time since World War II, women now outnumber men in the non-traditional age bracket. And projections for the future forecast that this phenomenon will continue. A study recently completed by the Carnegie Council predicts that, by the year 2000, 50% of all undergraduates will be over the age of 22.

Economic factors are often the single most important cause for returning to school. Re-entry women students are serious about parlaying their educational experience into a self-fulfilling, financially rewarding job. Education and training offer the greatest opportunity for entry into other positions. But there's no guarantee. The grim employment prospects of many June graduates attest to that fact. Women have to realize that returning to college is not a magic carpet ride that will automatically end in the career of their dreams. Especially when job-related undergraduate opportunities are most often awarded to men. Male students are traditionally chosen for activities that give them a marked advantage in the job market later on. And the informal network that exists among students, faculty, administrators and the business community accounts for many more placements than the school's Placement Office. A returning woman student has to develop her own strategy for making sure her learning experience leads to an earning one!

SEVEN STEPS TO TURN EDUCATIONAL EXPERIENCES INTO A JOB

1. Attend a variety of seminars on career planning and vocational information. Know what's out there and where the courses you have selected fit in. Take only those courses that will specifically equip you for the field you wish to enter. To do this, you must know the exact job demands of your chosen profession.

2. Contact local professional women's organizations in your field. They may have scholarship or internship programs available. Besides gaining valuable information, you will be making your first industry contacts.

3. Investigate internship-for-credit courses. Work/study scheduling helps you to adjust classroom theories to on-the-job application. This gives you a wonderful opportunity to explore your career direction (and change it if you don't find the actual job interesting!), and it often leads to future job possibilities. When it comes to hiring, corporations give the edge to applicants who have successfully interned with them. The feeling that you know the company and can "hit the ground running" makes you a more valuable applicant in the eyes of the employer.

4. Establish a rapport with professors. Don't wait for professorial plums to be handed out to the male students. Volunteer to share authorships, participate in research projects, attend professional conferences. Do not confuse this with offering to type manuscripts, schedule appointments, or do other secretarial duties.

5. As your degree gets closer, attend workshops on resumé writing, job application and interview procedures. Prepare a professional-looking resumé, with proper job objective/skills emphasis for the businesses you plan to interview with. You may have several versions of your resumé. Print up quantities of each.

6. Establish contacts with successful graduates in your field. Attend university receptions that introduce re-entry students to local business and professional women who have graduated from your school. If such events don't exist, initiate

and organize the first one. You'll make even more contacts if you have to person-ally invite all professional guests.

7. Contact head hunters and career counselors. Ask for directional advice. Learn what you need to do to market yourself. Establish a list of possible employ-ers, and send out your first letters of inquiry. Don't forget to enclose your resumé. Follow every letter up with a phone call to schedule an interview.

While you're waiting for a positive response, take encouragement from this thought: many employers actually prefer mature re-entry women. They don't leave to get married or to raise a family. And they're often more appreciative of employment—and advancement—opportunities within the company. As one senior investment officer put it, "A woman who takes the trouble to re-enter the work force at an executive level is not a job-hopper. And she generally takes her professional responsibilities as seriously as she's taken her family ones. She's defi-nitely a good hire."

YOU GOT THE JOB! NOW WHAT ARE YOU GOING TO WEAR?

That, literally, is the last of your problems. We've heard of women waiting until two weeks before their starting date to begin getting their wardrobe into working order. Most find that very few things translate from their past to their professional lives. In interviewing women who had been out of the work force for 9 to 29 years, we found not one of them was satisfied with her pre-professional wardrobe. Even women who had periodically held non-executive or part-time positions felt the clothes that had been suitable for those jobs were not appropriate for their new status. Skirt/blouse/jacket put-togethers did not equal the polish of a suit. Sweat-ers and sportswear pieces did not have the right businesslike connotation. Dresses worked the best, if you need to save some of your wardrobe for a quick-switch transition. Either one- or two-piece dresses can be updated with the right add-ons. At the end of this chapter you'll see how the addition of only five easy pieces (shoes, bag, belt, jacket and scarf) make all the difference between a suburban shopping look and a slick professional appearance. It can be done, if you've got the right basic components in your wardrobe. Most prospective executives who have been out of the work force for a while do not.

To a woman, all believed that having the proper clothes became increasingly important. "I never paid that much attention to the impact clothes could make," said a returning PhD, "until I found myself employed at a corporation whose image is very conservative. Deciding to place greater emphasis on my own image was a turning point in my career." "I used to only buy sale clothes," confessed a 40-year-old MBA recipient, "then I realized the value of my time. Now it's well worth it to me to buy the best clothes I can. Quality always lasts longer, in terms of style and wear. Who has time to replace items every year?"

Although shopping for an appropriate business image was sometimes post-

Turn a suburban look into a professional one in five
easy steps:

1. Add neckline finishing.
2. Add a belt.
3. Add a blazer (with pocket square).
4. Change to a tailored bag.
5. Switch to businesslike pumps.

poned until the last moment, no lack of thought went into it. Most of the women we interviewed, faced with the prospect of presenting themselves in an entirely new light, carefully planned their purchases. "I gave up on everything red and purple—my two favorite colors—and made myself buy basics like navy, khaki, grey," reported a woman who had just passed her law boards. Many took two to three years to conscientiously build their professional wardrobes, discarding at least a third of their "former life" fashions every year. "It takes discipline to turn your wardrobe around, but you've got to strive for a singular image," noted a financial analyst. "Showing up like Harriet Homemaker one day and Veronica V.P. the next will only confuse your co-workers. You're either coming from one camp or the other—and you should look it."

There is a danger in looking too matronly, and many executive women advised against falling into that trap. Because you may be older than many of your peers, there is a tendency to cast you into the "office mother" role. Do everything you can to avoid it. The experience that's respected in this situation may have nothing to do with your expertise on the job. If you find co-workers asking for your advice on everything from raising children to handling delicate personnel problems, you'll know to instantly switch your image. You're doing something wrong. Check for too many prints, too much polyester, too little tailoring. Although it's never necessary to assume an overly severe "power look," your clothes should say business and not coffee klatch. The best collective advice of all re-entry executives is to stick to well-defined staples. "Until you know what's expected of you and where your freedoms lie, it's best to play it on the conservative side," advised a returning statistician.

The wait-and-see policy was endorsed by the majority of starting-over executives. "You've got to guard against buying too much, too soon," suggested one computer analyst. "What you think is right may be far too inflexible." Returning executives all agreed that, the older a woman is, the more she can deviate from the dress code. What looks right on 24-year-old management trainees often looks out-of-character on 45-year-old entry-level executives. When you reach a certain age, you're expected to have your own sense of style. If you don't have it, don't expect to develop it by following the fashions of younger employees. It's far better if they emulate you. Once re-entry executives get the lay of the land, however, most feel confident enough to personalize their dressing style through softer silhouettes or slightly brighter colors. "I went in wearing my all-purpose suit," said a new office manager, "and I'm glad I did, because that established my attitude toward the job. But 3 months later I felt secure enough to switch to more feminine looks. And the younger people started copying me!"

SECTION
II
MAKING IT

☑ TO READ

- If you need effective wardrobe management
- If you've got to get organized
- If you want to upgrade your look
- If you have to travel on business
- If you're looking for a few personal perks
- If you've just gotten a big promotion

☑ TO SKIP

- If you were offered the senior-vice-president-in-charge-of-corporate-planning position after your very first interview

CHAPTER

4

Your Wardrobe Game Plan: Appearance Management

"You have to think in terms of three to four year spans when buying clothes, not just one season. Our attention span is longer than the fashion industry thinks."

Buying with an eye toward wardrobe accruement requires the same kind of thought process as developing any investment strategy. It takes research, logic and discipline. You start with the premise that there's going to be an initial outlay of funds and go on from there, carefully assessing, adding and resisting impulse!

Expenditures for the kind of quality clothing you need to project a successful professional image are going to be on the high side, so it's best not to be haphazard about your buying decisions. Know what you want—and why you want it—going in. If you train yourself to give prospective purchases the careful consideration they merit, you'll develop your own apparel investment style, and it will keep risk to a minimum throughout your professional career.

LONG TERM OR SHORT TERM? THAT ISN'T THE QUESTION

Since trendiness is somewhere next to joblessness in conservative corridors, you don't have to worry about buying anything while it's "hot." In fact, the minute you begin to spot the same look over and over again in every store in town is the time you should consider finding a personal tailor. You don't want to wear anything that can be summed up in an instant fashion phrase. If you can define any garment with the latest copy catch-word, forget it. In-again, out-again looks are short-term investments. Even if they weren't highly inappropriate for your professional image, the financial outlay is seldom worth the return.

What works best are classic, well-tailored items. If you have to ask yourself if something is classic, it probably isn't. Truly timeless pieces—in all apparel categories—are instantly recognizable. You know them when you see them. How? It has to do with color and cut. Basic shades such as navy, greys, beiges, browns, burgundy and some shades of olive are always considered classic, as are the simplest silhouettes, for example, calf-length, clean-line skirts (as opposed to those with flounces, flairs, tiers or wraps). Classic dressing is not an attempt at "adult preppy," as one of our survey respondents defined it. That connotation is far too casual, and it implies a regimentation that simply isn't there. Classic apparel in no way obviates imagination. Rather, it is a way to be close enough to the fashion mark, without actually sacrificing wardrobe longevity. When you think in terms of long-term apparel investments, classics will give you the highest return on your fashion dollar, and should form the basis of your professional wardrobe.

STARTING

If you've decided to start from scratch and want to build up the most workable professional wardrobe in the least amount of time, plan your first acquisition list to include the following. You'll need:

> 2 suits
> 1 skirt
> 1 blazer
> 5 blouses
> Accessories in a basic coordinating color: a few soft bows/ties; one belt; one good pair of shoes; one attache, tote or portfolio

Pick a three-way color strategy, such as grey/camel/blue; black/grey/red; or beige/ burgundy/navy and select everything within that range. With the right kind of coordination, this combination could get you through 45 working days, assuming all jackets work with all skirts and blouses. Since this is rarely the case (suit jackets, especially, are tricky to switch around), you can realistically expect to get something closer to three weeks' worth of switchability out of your initial invest- ment. Still, it's a start. And if it's well thought-out, you'll have enough variety in your appearance to satisfy your personal need for change, without interfering with your professional need for consistency. Remember, you don't want to wow 'em with a quick-change act. If your strategy is too obvious, it will be self-defeating.

This core wardrobe could cost between $1500 and $2000 for starters. And while that may sound like a lot for one outlay, you've probably been spending more than that if you're from the hit-and-miss shopping school. One-at-a-time purchases can add up faster than you think. And, if they don't fit in with the total scheme of things, they really cost you more in the long run. It's best to bite the bullet and buy your basic start-up wardrobe in one fell swoop.

BUILDING

What you add next depends primarily on how well what you have has worked for you. You'll begin to get a definite feel for the most successful looks you own. They're the ones you save for a particularly important client meeting or a day when the impression you make is absolutely critical. Before you consider any new acquisitions, it's helpful to analyze exactly why these certain looks make you feel more confident than the other clothes in your closet. Take them out and line them up. Look for a common thread that runs through all of them. Are they similar in color? Cut? Fabric? Whatever clues you pick up will help you make better buying decisions when you're surrounded by unfamiliar clothes in a store. If you know that you feel more successful in a certain skirt silhouette, for instance, you should quickly eliminate anything else from the dressing room.

The next trick is to know what you want to add in order to *develop* your wardrobe capabilities. Don't simply repeat items, or you'll bore yourself to death. And don't rely solely on the replacement technique. If you buy only to restock favorites that have seen better times, you won't be building a wardrobe. You'll only be replenishing it.

In order to take your wardrobe in the direction it needs to go to give you the most appropriate selections, ask yourself three questions:

1. Do I have any mistakes in my wardrobe?
2. What do I need most?
3. What do I need least?

It isn't enough to think you know the kinds of things you'd like to add. You have to be able to pinpoint the places where you could go wrong. Knowing exactly what doesn't work for you saves you from both expensive impulse buying and brink-of-buying decision dilemmas. The "should I take it or not" quandry can be resolved much more quickly if you can determine whether an item falls into the "need most," "need least" or "big mistake" category.

Remember when we brought up discipline as a necessary adjunct to any investment strategy? Well, now is the time to exercise it. Whether you think you know what your next purchase is going to be or not, take out a sheet of paper right now and write down your answers to the three questions. To get your thinking started, here's what some of our survey executives had to say.

"DO I HAVE ANY MISTAKES IN MY WARDROBE?"

It's a rare woman who doesn't. Nearly 80% of the executives we asked admitted to owning clothes they wished they didn't. An attorney regretted having any dresses without matching jackets. An advertising vice president took it one step further when she recognized that she had "too many things that don't go with anything else." Fabric and cut were often the chief causes of complaint. Mistakes along those lines? "Anything ultrasuede," lamented a commercial banking associate vice president. "Jackets that are too long for the rest of my body," a real estate investment associate acknowledged. When it came to color, brights were rarely signaled out as mistakes (probably because they were avoided in the first place). Surprisingly, brown and brown-based tweeds were voted least likely to succeed in the most formal situations. Both attorneys and bankers alike said they considered owning anything in the brown family a basic mistake.

"WHAT DO I NEED MOST IN MY WARDROBE?"

Seasonal considerations were strong here. Many female executives saw a real need for suitable summer-weight clothing with the same sense of seriousness as heavier suits and blazer/skirt combinations. A financial analyst wanted to find "fall/winter shades instead of typical summer pastels." A lawyer asked for "less frivolous summer dresses and comfortable suits for really hot days." And an office products analyst needed something more professional-looking to replace thin cotton dresses. Clothes that were "travel-worthy" and "versatile" also hit the most-needed list. Over 60% of these women said they often went out directly from the office, and many wanted dresses that would go from 9:00 A.M. through dinner.

Selectivity was the key to being satisfied with wardrobe choices. Less than 40% of the executives felt they needed more clothes in their wardrobes. Most felt they just didn't have enough of the right clothes, and only 16% said they didn't need to buy another thing!

"WHAT DO I NEED LEAST IN MY WARDROBE?"

Pants won the who-needs-'em vote by a landslide. Nobody said they didn't wear them for leisure, but not one respondent put them on the priority buy list. Although almost 95% insisted their social wardrobes were different from their professional ones, they didn't want to buy "cocktail dresses" or evening clothes, either. One administrator, after surveying a closet full of professional looks, said the item she needed least of all was "another suit!" Moral: There is such a thing as overkill. When you're beginning to build a wardrobe, a bit of variety should be a prime consideration.

Once you've sorted out the personal pitfalls you want to avoid, you're ready to extend your basic nuclear group. For more flexibility, don't go for another suit right away. Add another skirt, another blouse, another blazer instead. When your finances permit, think dresses next. A two-piece one will give you even more mileage if the blouse works with your other skirts and the skirt works with the jackets already in your wardrobe. Now's the time to pick up a few more accessory items as well.

Your three buying phases, then, should look like this:

	2 suits
	1 skirt
Phase I	1 blazer
Core	5 blouses
Wardrobe	Accessories in a basic coordinating color: soft bows, one belt, one pair of shoes, one attaché/tote/portfolio

	1 blazer
Phase II	1 skirt
	1 blouse

| | 1 two-piece dress |
| Phase III | Accessories in a second coordinating color: one pair of shoes, one belt, one bag |

The object is not to have a lot of clothes. At the end of these three building phases, you'll still only have four jackets, four skirts, six blouses and one two-piece dress. You won't have a clothes-horse closet by any standards. But the point is, you will have the *right* clothes.

A well-edited wardrobe should save you from time- and budget-consuming mistakes. You can waste an awful lot of money on them if you don't follow some sort of predetermined plan. It's too easy to be lured by "bargains" or unrelated pieces if you don't have a sound strategy. When you feel a threatening urge to buy something you hadn't anticipated, at least make sure it doesn't violate these cardinal rules:

1. *Never buy anything unless you absolutely love it.* Liking it a little bit is not enough. Something you feel terrific in always does come along.

2. *Never buy anything without trying it on.* Grabbing it and running is the quickest way to guaranteeing returns. And some stores won't let you.

3. *Never buy a jacket or skirt without buying something to go with it.* Right then. You won't find it later.

4. *Never buy anything that has nothing to do with the rest of your wardrobe.* It probably isn't your style, if what you have goes off in a different direction entirely.

INVENTORYING

Knowing what you have, and what you need next, is nothing more than taking inventory. It's the way men have been managing their wardrobe acquisitions for years. Do you know many who go out and buy one shirt at a time? Most take stock of what's running down, then go out and purchase in multiples. Mainly because it saves time. Taking inventory is just a more efficient system of wardrobe maintenance.

Once you have your wardrobe in optimum working condition, you shouldn't need to totally revise it with every new fashion season. But you will have to update it with a few key pieces on a regular basis. To make it easy to overview your wardrobe at a glance, copy and use the Wardrobe Management Inventory Chart included at the end of this chapter. Fill in all your business clothes that you plan to use for a particular season. Complete separate inventory charts for fall/winter and spring/summer periods. Note the colors/patterns of each item, and the year it was purchased. You can expect the lifespan of a quality suit, jacket or skirt to last about four years. Dresses and blouses will require more frequent replacing.

Keeping a running inventory of your wardrobe may look like a case of over-organization, but once you buy according to a schedule, you'll find that your closet will fall together much more easily. Tack completed charts to the inside of your closet door for instant updating. You'll be able to see easily when something is about to "expire," and just how its replacement will have to fit in with everything else you own. After you've carefully coordinated your professional wardrobe to be able to use as many pieces as possible in as many ways as possible, you wouldn't want to throw the whole scheme off balance by buying the wrong thing at the wrong time. If you use an inventory chart consistently, it really shouldn't happen.

KEY PIECES

Suits

The suit seems to be the culprit in any claim of "defensive dressing" leveled at professional women. If there were a clear delineation between what women wore and what the rest of the work force wore, no one would accuse anybody of wardrobe me-tooism. Yet, with suits all around, it's easy to place the blame. What was once the only acceptable apparel option for women first entering the management fraternity is now considered the least imaginative alternative. It's still the most popular, however, because it works.

Today, investing in a few good suits comes more from economics than insecurities. There's just more mileage in them. If they were defensive in the past, they're certainly considered sensible now.

Ideally, each suit could function as well as separates, with the jacket and skirt leading independent lives. But don't expect this. Because of fabric and cut, some jackets simply won't translate well as blazers. Ditto for some skirts. Don't be disappointed if a light-weight, thin wool herringbone suit jacket looks too mild-mannered over a bulkier flannel sportswear skirt. Even if the color is a perfect match, some things were never meant to be worn together.

Where you can ensure flexibility, however, is in the shape of your suit components. If you select different collar and skirt treatments, you won't feel that you're stuck in a uniform "rut." Jacket styles will change slightly with the fashion influence of the times, but the modifications should be subtle enough to give you several years' worth of wear. Wider or narrower, there will always be notched and peaked lapels. Collarless styles come in cardigan, band-collared, or jewel neck

Peaked lapel

Traditional notch lapel

Collarless band neckline

Collarless cardigan neckline

Double-breasted jacket

Bouclé weave

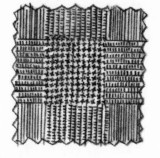
Glen plaid

Herringbone stripe

treatments. And special effects include double-breasted and shawl-collar shap-ings. The illustrations following should give you an idea of the kind of differences a collar can make.

Jackets can be varied in their body lines as well. Continental styles seem to go longer and straighter. Waist-length jackets can be boxier, sometimes with puffing at the shoulder. Fitted jackets are sewn in tighter toward the waist for a very feminine, nipped-in silhouette.

There are a lot of jacket options to consider before you even get to color and fabric. And that's where the obvious differences come to the fore. Subtle textures and patterns, like the bouclé, glen plaid and herringbone stripe illustrated here add even more interest—enough to get any suit out of the strict, imitative classifi-cation altogether. There's a whole world of feminine, conservative suiting beyond navy pinstripe. Your best bet is to seek out subtle slubs, flecks, muted plaids, shadow stripings, heathered tweeds—any effect that softens the overall appear-ance of the fabric. If you're set on a solid, at least look for a slightly brushed texture. You won't tire of a suit as quickly if it's one step removed from strict.

Blazers

It's easier to coordinate a blazer with a suit skirt than to find a skirt that will work with a suit jacket. That's why additional blazers are absolutely indispensable to extend the options of your professional wardrobe. It's good to have at least two per season in good, basic, go-with-everything shades. I'd pick one solid and one subtly patterned fabric for variety. Depending on where you live, go for black, navy, beige or white for the solid shade, then look for an interesting, sophisticated tweed, stripe or novelty fabric. The only thing to make sure of is that the overall tone coordinates with your basic wardrobe color scheme. Look for combinations of two of your predominant shades: beige/black, grey/blue, or burgundy/navy, for instance. You might want to vary the weight of each blazer, too, to create a different feeling with the same skirts. A raw silk would add a dressier touch than a flannel or a tweed. In all instances, however, a blazer with a skirt will have a less formal connotation than a suit. Keep your business day in mind before you plan to wear any jacket and skirt match-up. But do remember, when you're wearing a jacket with a skirt, it should be shorter, as a general rule, than the jacket you wear with pants.

Skirts

Use the bottom line of your look as another element to add variety. Don't limit yourself to only one style of skirt; dirndls and A-lines aren't the only conservative cuts in the market. You can be somewhat adventuresome in shape, if you stay with conservative colors. The four styles sketched here are each equally appropriate under businesslike jackets. The trick is to find the silhouette that works with *yours*. If a pot belly is a problem, pleats—either stitched down or released—aren't the answer. Look instead for *soft* gathers just at the waist band or trouser tucks. A slight fullness in the skirt takes attention away from the slight fullness in you. If you wear pleats, you owe it to yourself to have at least two of that kind of skirt in your wardrobe. They make a world of difference in the mood of any jacket you put with them. There's more movement, more femininity, to a skirt with some pleat detailing—either stitched at one side; hip-stitched and released in a centered, inverted V; or pleated all around. Try it teamed with a shorter jacket, and see how you feel. In the right colors, the net effect will be every bit as conservative without appearing so dead-ahead serious.

Proportion plays a part in the ability some skirts have to pair up with certain jackets. A longer jacket, for instance, needs a skirt with some slimming through the hips. A cropped-to-the-waist jacket can take on soft gathers or dirndled waist-bands. If you're not sure about which jackets will work with which skirt shapes, work with a competant sales professional. Shop only in a store where you can find a knowledgeable, helpful advisor and bring several of your own jackets with you to try with prospective skirt purchases.

Styles do change from year to year, although less so for truly classic skirt shapes. Still, the eye gets used to new proportions quickly, and what looked great last year may suddenly seem dated in one short season. If simply lengthening or shortening a hem doesn't give you a more current proportion, the next step is to alter the length or shape of the jackets you wear with the skirt. If it's worth it to you and you like the garment enough, go to a good tailor and see what can be done. Take the skirt and the jacket(s) at the same time to make the new proportions work together. You've got to see the potential for at least another year's worth of wear, however. If you can't make it "right" enough, don't bother. You'll end up passing it by more often than not, and it will cease to be an integral, functioning part of your wardrobe. Better to give it to charity, take the tax deduction, and replace it.

Dresses

After struggling to coordinate suits, blouses, blazers and skirts five different ways, dresses seem like simplicity itself to some women. They certainly uncomplicate matters in the morning. If there's no belt, all you need to do is add one.

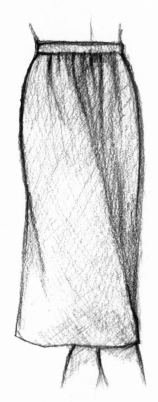

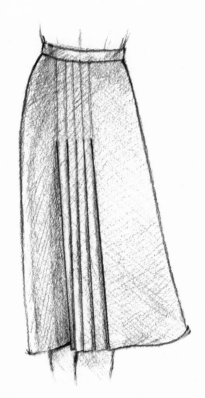

Softly gathered dirndle waist

Side-stitched pleats

Hip-stitched, all-around pleats

Straight trouser skirt

Why more executive women don't opt for dresses over suits may be due in part to the fact that there are not enough professional-looking dresses on the market. Somehow, dresses tend to go trendier, and fewer classic styles have evolved. There is the shirtwaist, of course, and the two-piece variation of it. But that's about it. Which means you have to make the judgment about whether a divine little silk number is too fashionable for its own good. And many women simply don't want to bother making that decision.

Add that to the fact that what you gain in simplicity you lose in versatility. Unless you have an endless supply of interesting jackets, a dress isn't going to go very far. What you see is about all you get. There's not the same switchability that separates can provide. Still, executives are clamoring for more dresses. When the fashion industry catches up with appropriate-looking ones, expect to see many more in corporate corridors.

When you do see a dress that looks professional enough, grab it. It will add a fresh spirit to your working wardrobe, and it's an awfully nice alternative when you've just got to get out of a suit. Play it by the same rules, however. Make sure the color is subtle enough and the lines are clean enough. Now is not the time to break out in little girl ruffles. Even the fabrics should meet the same standards of quality as those in the rest of your garments. Natural fibers like silk, linen, cotton and wool challis are preferable to slippery synthetics. They feel better on the body, although you can expect them to wrinkle.

Blouses

Ten blouses are plenty to see you through a season. And if you think that sounds like a lot, you probably have more hanging in your closet right now. Blouses are things women tend to collect; men buy them seven at a clip and they're done with them. There's a certain efficiency to that.

We're not recommending that you follow their lead and buy the same collars and bodies in a few different fabrics, however. That's where they lose all hope of variety. Fortunately, women haven't gone that far toward standardization! Pick as many collar treatments as you find appropriate (six suggestions are illustrated here), but stick to only two fabrics. Cotton and silk choices will simplify your selection process, and they're far more executive-oriented than sheer polyester georgettes or slithery silk imitations.

A cotton blouse will take more finishing than a silk one. Left to its own devices, it runs the risk of being almost too casual. There's a slightly sporty feeling there, and you'll take it right over the edge if you keep the collar unbuttoned and un-adorned. You can't overdo it, either. Cotton is only going to get just so dressy, and all the jewelry in the world is never going to jazz it up. The only thing that will work for round, pointed or button-down collar styles are string ties finished in a bow or tied twice around with just the ends showing. A slightly wider crêpe de Chine or foulard tied in a soft, droopy bow is another variation, but you must watch that, whatever it is, it fits neatly under the collar in back. That's one reason

The classic cotton shirt

The wing-collar

The notch collar

The band collar

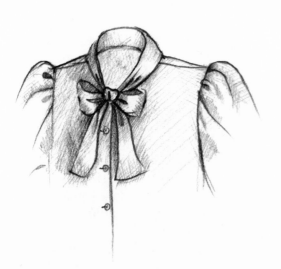

The bowed blouse

The tucked-front tuxedo

why scarves or ascots are generally too cumbersome. And there's no room at all for jewelry, since the top button should always be closed.

The wing collar will give you greater options. Especially if you're creative with unexpected pieces of jewelry. Try pushing a pretty stickpin through a top button. Or take a pair of pearl stud earrings and poke them through the wing tabs. Gold— even tiny diamonds—might be used for a dressier look. Earring posts will cause less damage than stickpins, and they're ideal to use in a variety of interesting places. Experiment!

The camisole   The Victorian ruffled blouse

The notch collar is really the only one that's right with simple neck jewelry. You can add pearls or a small gold chain, but it's not the place for anything exotic. Leave your clunky hammered metals and carved tribal beads out of it. Actually, a notch collar can be perfectly effective with no jewelry whatsoever. Take the focus to a new place by adding a contrasting pocket square to your jacket.

There are some blouse necklines that are better off left alone. Band collars, for instance, usually require nothing; the band itself is enough. High mandarin styles, embroidered collars, side-tied bow treatments and ruffled Victorian effects should also stand on their own. You don't need to add a thing. Blouses with body detailing, like tucked fronts, also require no additional finishing. This again is where pocket squares become handy little items, adding a lot of individual style whenever jewelry would be inappropriate or excessive.

WE RECOMMEND	I HAVE					
FOUR SUITS						
SUG. COLORS						
NAVY						
GREY						
CAMEL						
BLACK						
TWO BLAZERS						
SUG. COLORS						
NAVY						
CAMEL						
TWEED						
FOUR SKIRTS						
THAT CO-OR.						
W/BLAZER						
OR SUIT						
JACKETS						
TEN BLOUSES						
COTTON-SILK						
SOME OF						
THESE						
BLOUSES YOU						
WILL WEAR						
YEAR ROUND						
TWO DRESSES						
TWO PR. SHOES						
ACCESSORIES						
BRIEFCASE						
HANDBAG						
COAT						
MISC. ACCESS.						

* WARDROBES SHOULD BE PLANNED FOR A FOUR-YEAR LiFE EXPECTANCY. BLOUSES, OF COURSE, REQUIRE MORE FREQUENT UPDATING.

** NATURAL FIBERS LOOK BETTER THAN SYNTHETICS, BUT THEY MAY WRINKLE.

THE WARDROBE MANAGEMENT INVENTORY CHART

Use this form to keep track of what you've got—and exactly what you need to add or replace. Time your purchases by the lifespan of your clothes.

High collars need careful scrutinizing before you accessorize them. Sometimes they can take an interesting touch, sometimes not. It all depends on how high they go. The funnel neck, for example, drapes softly enough to hold a thin ribbon or a small bow or flower. Even the stud earring trick works well, if they're tucked in right along the folds. A stock tie, on the other hand, has enough going on without your adding another thing to it. If you wrap it around once and put it into a soft bow, it will look a lot less hunt club.

A word about color. You can go a bit brighter with silk blouses to freshen the look of a conservative suit. Don't shy away from a jade green, a deep violet, a clear red. And include at least two subtly patterned ones to break up solid skirt and jacket combinations. Avoid obvious motif designs, and look for small overall "no-pattern" patterns like tiny checks, foulards, geometrics. If you're only buying a few blouses, however, the most important thing to consider is how well the colors coordinate with the greatest number of items in your wardrobe.

Coats

You can get away with one good coat (in addition to a classic raincoat), if you do not invest in the latest fashion look or color. The simpler the line, the better. Reefers, wraps and Chesterfields in conservatively dark tones will take you any-where. Black is probably your best bet, since it can double easily as an evening coat. Spend your money on the quality of the fabric. If you can afford it, go for cashmere. And make sure the fit is easy enough to accommodate blazers and jackets underneath. Arm holes that are cut too high can cause you to carry your jacket to work! *Tip*: Have all belts tacked on at the back. That's usually the first thing that goes!

5

Accoutrements: Adding Up A Look

"Accessories are where you can express yourself, within the requirements of an acceptable professional look."

"**A**ccessorizing a look" sounds like a magazine editor's ploy for building multiple sales among the fashion savvy, and confusing all others who aren't. There seem to be so many ways to wrap waists, tone legs, tie scarves, perk up necklines, swathe on shawls, and balance with boots that it's amazing anybody gets to work on time! Even if adding the right item the right way weren't time consuming, the sheer variety of the latest accessory alternatives available each season is enough to boggle the mind and bite deeply into the budget. At some point, you're going to wonder if all this is necessary to keep your working wardrobe current. The answer is emphatically *no*. To the contrary, your objective should be a sleek, pared-down, professional look.

Nothing dates a look faster than the wrong accessory at the wrong time. By their very nature, the latest trend-setters exist in a specific period. They instantly update any look because their sole reason for being is to confer timeliness. But they age very quickly. Last year's sculptured buckle is this year's concha belt is next year's sashed waist, and on and on it goes. Sometimes, if you're lucky, an accessory comes in, goes out, and comes back so quickly that only a few years pass before it's "important" again. Witness the instant rebirth of the shawl every 2 years or so. The question is—which ones to save?

You can avoid the trendy trap altogether by adding only accoutrements to your professional wardrobe. The difference between accessories and accoutrements is the difference between timeliness and timelessness. Both can confer status, but one confers fashion status, one confers professional status. You want the latter.

FINISHING A LOOK

It's never important to "accessorize" a look for the sheer sake of accessorizing. It *is* always necessary to finish a look, however. And it needn't take a lot of thought.

Without professional finishing, your clothes have no clout. The look on the left does nothing to create a conscientious, executive image. There's no focal point, no initiative. The look on the right shows forethought, planning. The right accoutrements make all the difference.

Men have it down to a science. They know they have only so many focal points to their finished look, and there's never any question about what goes where. In less than five minutes flat a man can grab a tie, cufflinks, watch, pen and, in the winter, a cashmere scarf. He may switch among only two or three different pairs of shoes, with the wide variety of black or brown socks to choose from. That's all that's necessary to finish a formal suit look. It's not confusing. It's not time-consuming. And it's enough to convey a polished message.

Think of the message that's conveyed without these accoutrements. When the tie's loosened, or off completely, when the shirt sleeves are rolled up and the jacket's off, everyone gets the signal. Usually, it's "Go away. I'm not having meetings, I'm not presenting myself to the public. I'm knee-deep in work and I'm going to keep at it until I get it done." That's the nonverbal communication of an unfinished look. We're used to interpreting this as an emergency stance, not a daily professional appearance.

An unfinished look sends a harried signal—for both a man and a woman. It does not communicate composure. Once in a while, "rolling up your shirt sleeves" is acceptable—even commendable. But if this becomes your daily look, both your competence under pressure and your ability to get the job done may eventually be questioned.

That's the power of the items you select to finish a business look. Nothing determines the way your overall appearance is interpreted as quickly, or as critically, as the accoutrements you choose to compliment what you're wearing. And picking just the right ones can be a tricky proposition. Overdo it, and you can look too fashion conscious or cheap. Underaccessorize, and you'll look as unprepared for the public as the executive with the loosened tie.

HOW TO CHOOSE THE MOST EFFECTIVE ACCESSORIES

There are a few simple guidelines to follow every time you find yourself wanting the item of the moment. If it can fit the following stipulations, buy it!

1. Keep things uncomplicated. If we can learn anything from a man's five-minute finishing, this is it. And it's the most important consideration of all. You don't have time to experiment with clever accessory tricks in the morning, and you shouldn't have to worry about what goes with what, either. It's better to have fewer items that work with everything than multiples that you can only wear one way. Clean the accessory clutter out of your drawers, and simplify everything.

2. Choose items of obvious quality. The "less is more" philosophy will allow you to concentrate on quality as opposed to quantity. Instead of three belts in different shades, it's a wiser investment to buy one really good one in a reptile or neutral-toned leather. You won't need earrings in every color if you've got classic gold, silver, pearl or diamond studs. If you don't buy bangles in multiples, you can have one really fine gold link bracelet. And necklaces need be nothing more than a unique pendant hung from a cord, a thin gold chain, or a string of pearls.

In any category—jewelry, bags, belts, shoes—buy the best you can afford.

Look for the finest leathers, the real McCoy metals and stones. Even if it means waiting a bit, avoid obvious imitations. It's always worth the investment in wear and what having fine things says about you.

3. Pick classic shapes, clean lines. Accessory styles come and go with the fashion mood of the moment. One year everything is bold and primitive, the next year, softly romantic. Unless you're an avid collector of a certain period style (like Art Deco stickpins), stay with traditional, timeless shapes in both jewelry and leather goods. Avoid ornately decorated belt buckles; covered ones never date themselves. Choose bags for function first, form second. If they can hold everything that's necessary without becoming too bulky to fit into an attaché or tote, that's what you're looking for. Shape should be the least impressive thing about a bag; look for the leather first, the lining second, and the quality of construction third. Pick watches with simple, unpretentious faces and bands. The clearer it says "functional," the better. It's never necessary to wear the latest "status" watch. Our research showed very few equated a certain watch style with a symbol of executive rank.

4. Have a core group of accessories that always goes with you, and keep them in an accessible place. A man uses a valet stand or a dresser tray to hold items he needs everyday: watch, keycase, billfold, cufflinks. And it's not a bad idea for women, either. A single, organized spot for all essential accessories saves precious time when you have to grab and go, and it helps you remember the basic items you want with you at all times. I'd keep a few go-with-everything gold earrings and pins there, as well as an appointment book, credit or business card case, gold pen, watch, basic leather belt, key ring and sun or eyeglasses. If there's room to hang two basic handbags at the sides, do it. You'll be ready to switch them with all the essentials you'll need right there. It's a far better way to get your look together quickly than searching through drawers or jewelry cases for your everyday essentials.

5. Show originality with a few unexpected items. It's possible to add interesting accoutrements to a limited collection without getting into accessory one-upmanship. Think only in terms of basic items, and create one way to vary them. A tailored wine-colored cummerbund might replace a leather belt for a variety of skirt shapes. A small triangle of lace would add a totally different touch than a foulard pocket square. A small, fresh flower (remember boutonnières?) might perk up a lapel more than a pin could. The best part about the changes *you* choose to create is that they will express your own personality far more than following the latest accessory fad would. It's totally up to *your* imagination. But you need to develop it. Try—right now—to think of at least one different way to replace the following three items.

1. Instead of a bow at the neck, I'll wear a
   _____ .

2. Instead of a stickpin on my lapel, I'll try a
   _____ .

3. Instead of pearls, I'll fill in the neckline with a
   _____ .

6. Select some items only with an eye to function. The only professional credentials some accoutrements need is whether they work or not. Fashion—or the lack of it—doesn't enter into the picture. It doesn't matter, for instance, if your umbrella is a brightly printed fabric or a somber, solid nylon; as long as it's seriously wind-proof and easy to open. Boots are other items that are perfectly acceptable in an office environment, as long as they look like they have a reason for being. Spikey-heeled, butter-soft, thigh-high leathers worn in the midst of a blizzard, however, would be interpreted as strictly frivolous. (No boots at all would be equally foolish. If you don't wish to wear them through the day, tuck a pair of alternate shoes into your tote or attaché case.) The appropriateness of attachés is also based on whether they serve a purpose or not. If you don't need to lug around a lot of paperwork, a thin leather portfolio would seem less a superficial symbol of authority, more a necessity. Gloves, mufflers and hats can be anything that does the job. Don't worry about imitating a mannish fedora when you're bundling up against the cold. Berets, knitted caps and hoods are all equally acceptable. You have more leeway with all items that appear to fill a need. Anything that is even slightly questionable for executive attire stands a better chance of being considered appropriate if its function is immediately apparent.

THE BEST ACCOUTREMENTS TO OWN

Certain styles, no matter who makes them, stay very close to classic. Although you may find slight variations in particular items, the following illustrations will help you spot the most universally recognized executive accoutrements.

The Best Shoes

You can get through with two pairs per season in basic, neutral colors. No less will do, since it's healthier for your feet (and your shoes!) to alternate wearings. You need to give moisture a chance to evaporate from the linings in order to prevent foot odor and inhibit the growth of fungus. Choose a heel height that is comfortable and doesn't restrict a free, natural stride (1½ inches or lower is usually the best bet, although the higher and narrower the heel, the better the leg looks). If you need to compromise, try a lower heel with a tapered shape. There's no excuse for wearing clunky, squat heels. Try always to choose shoes that are feminine, as well as comfortable. Look for slimming, elongating touches like sling backs or open toes. Taupe, wine, beige and black are neutrals that will work with any item in your wardrobe.

Styling is secondary to quality finishing. Always check seams, lining and soles for workmanship. Stitches should be small and smooth. Exposed seams or rough irregularities can lead to painful problems. Don't expect repeated wearings to smooth things out! Look for leather linings and leather soles. Your feet will breathe easier for it, although it's a luxury that affects the cost and lifespan of a shoe. Synthetic soles wear longer and provide better protection against the pavement. In either case, check to see that the sole is stitched or cemented securely to the upper portion of the shoe. Also examine all heel, shanks and backs for rigidity. The higher you go in heel height, the more stability you'll need.

The classic pump in neutral tones goes everywhere, with everything.

Open-toed shoes can be business partners as long as they're serious-looking. Perforations, stacked heels and deeper shades keep them out of the too-dressy category.

The Chanel-toe is one of the most elegant shoe looks around. Either the sling-back or the closed pump is perfectly proper for the office.

The Best Jewelry

Jewelry is used to feminize and soften a look. It's as essential as makeup, and you shouldn't go out without it. No matter what other ways you choose to emphasize a look, you should always, always add a pair of good, classic earrings and a no-nonsense, plain-faced watch.

Necklaces can be as simple as one gold chain (keep it in the shorter 16-inch choker range); one 24-inch strand of pearls; and one 30-inch cord that can take on your favorite pendant(s).

Bracelets should be as bulk-less as possible. Bangles are bad if you have to rest your arm against a desk. Try narrow gold links or flexible three-quarter cuffs. You won't need to gang up two or three at a time, or wear matching ones on each wrist. The object is *not* to look like Wonder Woman.

Rings that are not wedding rings should be as simple and close-to-the-finger as possible. Band-style rings are less conspicuous than stones in any setting. Anything that extends more than 1/4 inch above the finger is generally too fussy for the office.

The most versatile pins to own are stick pins and bar pins. (Also, take your pierced earring sticks and use them as stick pins.) They can go anywhere: shirt collars, lapels, pockets, without appearing too complicated or heavy. Look for unusual ones with interesting metal or semi-precious stone motifs. If you find one that you really like, try buying two. Paired-up bar pins create an imaginative effect on a lapel, as long as the shape is cleanly geometric.

The Best Bags

A good bag is going to be expensive—there's no getting around it. But it's worth it. A cheap bag is the easiest thing in the world to spot. The grain and the softness of quality leather are dead giveaways. If you scrimp here, you'll end up wishing you hadn't—especially when the strap lets go at the wrong time, or the closure keeps popping open. Although expensive bags aren't necessarily repair-free, bargain bags usually can't be fixed. Most leather repair places won't take the trouble, or if they do, they'll want to charge you more than the bag was worth to begin with!

Although the shape of the bag you select for your professional life is secondary to the quality of its leather and construction, it is an important consideration. Size and silhouette are directly related to function—and that should be what a bag is all about. If you prefer a structured shape, check for strong welt seams and a solid foundation. There's nothing sloppier looking than a tailored bag that has stretched out of shape. Since this style has more body rigidity, make sure it will hold everything you need without having to pack things in tightly. Before you buy it, transfer everything from the bag you are carrying, and see if it fits. If you decide a different style of wallet will make the difference, buy it right there on the spot.

A softly constructed, pouch-style bag will enable you to carry a lot more, but you run the risk of fishing for items that disappear in the depths. Disorganization gives this style a bad business reputation, but if you find one that's not too deep and not too sporty, grab it. From a practical standpoint, unconstructed bags hold a lot more. In some cases, even the contents of your briefcase.

You don't want a hold-everything-from-your-boots-to-your-exercise-leotard-to-your-budget-report-bag, however. Anything too oversized just does not present a neat, professional appearance (imagine lugging it to a business lunch!). You'll have to be able to locate a pen and extract a credit card as quickly as a man can

The classic, uncluttered watch means you're serious about your time.

Classic ear designs can be pierced or clip-on. Look for small circles, knots, geometric designs.

You don't want your bracelets to bang against the desk. Choose something flexible, or cuffs that don't go all the way around.

Pearls in the 24″ length and gold chains in the 16″ length are your best neckline fillers.

Classic geometric shapes add pin interest to lapels, necklines, scarves.

lest your manner of transporting essentials be deemed less efficient. Struggling with clutter is perceived to be disorganized at best, frivolously feminine at worst. A compact, mid-size bag is your best bet. Something too tiny presents just as much of an organization problem as something too deep. Have you ever had to remove your compact, checkbook, lipstick and card case before you could fit your wallet back in? *Not* impressive.

Men seem to have a secret dread of any sort of clutter in a woman's bag. And that applies to the outside as well. Keep trim to a minimum; avoid tricky closures or too much hardware. No matter how expensive the bag, "gold" detailing eventually does wear off. The less metal you have on your bag, the better.

How you choose to carry a bag is purely personal. Shoulder straps do free up your hands, and they're not automatically considered too sporty, as long as the bag hits you about waist-high. A longer strap should be shortened—it's too casual, and there's also more of a security risk if your bag hangs down to your hips. Unless you plan to tuck a clutch bag into your briefcase, or you have nothing else to carry (not even a newspaper), don't consider it. Anything cumbersome gets in the way of a slick, professional presentation. The bag you want must be neat, serviceable and accessable.

The Best Bag Accessories

What goes into your bag is just as important as what's on the outside. Don't let inexpensive, plastic accessories belie your regard for quality. Remember, wallets, checkbook covers, credit card and eyeglass cases often come out in the open, and they must be able to stand scrutiny. Make sure each item is leather, and constructed solidly enough to serve without losing shape. Parachute cloth or other flexible fabrics simply do not maintain a neat appearance. The most organized wallet you can own is one that holds everything: credit cards, business cards, checkbook and

The softly constructed camera bag shape and the more structured pouch bag are neithe. too deep, nor too tiny, to carry work-day essentials. Note that trim is kept to a minimum.

money (including change.) Don't waste time with ones that fold cleverly into smaller shapes—you'll be tempted not to close it properly when you're in a rush. If you prefer to carry your credit cards in a separate case for security reasons, choose one that stays flat when filled and zippered shut. A small leather notetaker says something about your preparedness to jot down important ideas on the spot, and it saves hunting for scraps of *anything* to write something on. In fact, the less little bits of paper (receipts, gum wrappers, tissues, parking lot tickets) you have floating around in your bag, the better. People *do* see in, often when you least expect it. It's a good idea to "edit" out non-essentials once a day, so they don't get ahead of you.

Every executive, man or woman, knows the importance of being able to produce a fine pen whenever necessary. And three ballpoints with your dry cleaner's logo on them are better left out of your bag—you'll always find them first. Pack only one gold retractable point pen, or a fountain pen, if you prefer. Although these can get a little messy, they have a certain professionalism to them that is always impressive. Do avoid matching pen and pencil sets, however. There's such a thing as looking too methodical!

The Best Totes/Portfolios/Briefcases

The first thing to do is analyze your size requirements. If you tend to carry bulky items—anything from thick books to winter boots—a tote with wide side gussets might suit your needs better than a structured, unexpandable briefcase. If papers are all you ever take home, a thin leather portfolio might be all that's necessary. Never carry anything larger than you need—you'll only end up filling it up!

While fine leather is a luxury in an item this size, it is a good investment. A quality case should last through many career years. If you're not ready for the expenditure, a cloth tote will start you out nicely—as long as it's not bright canvas (too picnic-y) or covered with designer's initials (too unprofessional). What you really must watch for are finishings and closings. Make sure any case has a sturdy, reinforced handle and secure strap attachment devices. Foil pickpockets by avoiding any open-at-the-top totes. And make sure all zippers, snaps and locks work smoothly. Open and shut a case several times before buying. If there's anything that can go wrong, it will need repair eventually. The best strategy for the longest wear is to pick the plainest style in the store. And the best one you can afford.

The Best Appointment Books

Nothing signals the importance of your agenda better than a no-nonsense appointment book. It doesn't have to be impressive—gold-edged leaves and leather bindings are nice, but unnecessary—but it does have to be totally functional for you. If you need to jot down daily expenses as you go, make sure there's adequate

The briefcase. The most structured take-home tote. The framework will keep it from expanding, so make sure it's deep enough to carry all you need before you buy.

The tote. There's more flexibility for bulkier items here. Look for expansion extras like zip-open, zip-close side gussets.

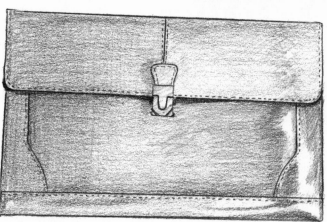

The portfolio. A thin leather envelope. Perfect for carrying papers—but not much else!

space for entries. If you need to schedule an entire department's activities, make sure you can see last month's and next month's calendars on every page. If you tend to book appointments half an hour apart, hourly time notations are not enough. Even if your company provides executive appointment schedulers, buy your own if the standard kind isn't serviceable enough for your business day. It will set you apart as someone who takes her time seriously. Carrying a pocket-sized version of your appointment book is a good idea only if you remember to transcribe the information you jotted down in it to your desk appointment book—and vice versa! If you must take your desk book with you wherever you go, make sure it's a manageable size. You don't need one with maps of the world and twelve pages of currency conversion charts. Whatever size you prefer, a simple leather or cloth-bound book with removable fillers will do the job nicely.

The Best Scarves

You don't need a wardrobe of scarves to add unlimited fashion mileage to your outfits. Unless you're terribly adept at tying them in a million intricate ways, they

A lightweight hanging garment bag and carry-on tote is all you need to take traveling. Look for them in sturdy nylon.

really won't give you that much variety. Your best bet is to let a beautiful scarf speak for itself. Drape it softly around a neckline and don't try anything tricky with it.

The most useful shapes are large squares and oblongs. Wear the square tied or untied with the point either in the front or back. Just make sure there's ample fabric for draping. A skimpy scarf at the neck looks just that—skimpy. Oblongs will give you a bit more versatility. You can loop them; bow them; slip them untied under a lapel; or wrap them at the waist for a non-office alternative. Don't overwhelm yourself with too many scarves, however. They usually end up accessorizing the inside of a drawer. Two that you really love in each shape will do it. If you want one other option, add a manageable shawl (nothing more than 52-inches square.) Every once in a while, it's a nice addition over a businesslike blazer or blouse. If you have to figure out which way to wrap it, however, don't be afraid to take a few lessons from a trained salesperson. In fact, someone who really knows her stock is the best person to help you coordinate a workable scarf wardrobe.

The Best Flight Bags

A matched set of hard, constructed luggage is the worst investment a traveling executive woman can make. Remember, you might have to actually move the steel-framed wonders without a redcap in sight. If you don't trust soft-sided bags out of your sight, take only those pieces that go on board with you. A hanging garment bag is absolutely indispensable. It's the most accommodating piece of luggage you will ever own. Clothes arrive wrinkle-free and ready to hang in the closet. Plus, you can stuff enormous amounts of extras into it. Look for one with a handle in the middle rather than at each end. You want your clothes to be able to hang down from either side. If you need to pack extra foldables, cosmetics, or other essentials, add a matching carry-on shoulder strap bag. The trick is to take everything with you. Waiting for bags wastes your time and that of your associates who may be meeting you or traveling with you.

Most travel-seasoned executives don't bother with the status or the high-ticket cost of luxury leather bags. A sturdy nylon bag with or without leather trim is impressive enough. You don't want to look like you're doing the Grand Tour when you arrive in Grand Rapids for a one-day conference!

6

Company Policy: Questions Professionals Ask

"You set standards of dress yourself by gauging the reaction people have to you, depending on what you're wearing. What you want to do is capitalize on what makes you the most effective."

The women executives who are setting their own clothing codes proceed with a basic understanding of what is, and what is not, acceptable at their firms. But we've planned enough professional wardrobes to realize that many women, no matter how high up on the corporate ladder they are, do not share an instinctual recognition of appropriate office attire. Since many of the same questions come up time and time again, we've kept track of what executive women want to know most about their wardrobe selections. Even if you think you already know the answers to many of the following questions, it will be helpful to see where the major uncertainties about appropriate professional dressing lie.

FIT AND PROPORTION

By far, the vast majority of questions have to do with the way jackets and skirts should fit. It's not as easy to determine as you would think. Anything that fits closer to the body is far easier to judge than jackets that seem to change their basic silhouette season in and season out. One year, they're better if they're big and boxy. Next year, the newer ones are nipped-in and cropped. To this extent, fashion influences do play a part in the way we perceive fit. What the eye gets used to is what looks right. The difficult part comes when you're trying on a new silhouette for the first time. When you're not used to wider shoulders or skinnier lapels, or any departure from a shape you're accustomed to, how do you determine if the fit is right for you?

The best way to gauge proper fit is by taking a long look at the overall proportion; the way the pieces balance each other. Even the slightest imbalance—a bow that's too big for your face; a skirt that's too long for your legs; a jacket that's too long for a skirt—can throw the whole look off. Often this is interpreted as poor fit, when, in reality, only an adjustment in proportion is needed.

Pulling things into proper proportion is one of the trickiest things to do. Some have an eye for it, most don't. And it's not a skill that can readily be developed. If easy judgment escapes you, you're by no means alone. But you should seek the services of a knowledgeable salesperson. Anyone that says, "That's the way they're wearing them this year" is *not* the one to ask! Here's the sort of advice you should expect.

"How can I tell if the fit is right for my body?"

With a jacket, the shoulders are the most important starting point. If it doesn't fit well and lie flat from shoulder to shoulder across the back, there is almost nothing you can do to make the jacket look as if it fits correctly. Check for ease by crossing your arms over each other in front, then swinging them around to the back. It's not necessary to button your jacket as you do this if you wear it open as a rule (most women do). Use the arm swing only to judge the degree of movement the shoulders will allow. When trying on a jacket, it is never necessary to button it if you normally don't wear it buttoned. If you like the way it fits everywhere else, don't take a larger size just in case you might button it. You never will, and the jacket will just end up looking baggier than it should. And never button the jacket during pinning for alterations.

Check the back of the jacket in a three-way mirror to make sure it tapers properly, without extra bulk at the side seams, or widening gaps at the vents. (We don't recommend vents on women's jackets, but if you're considering one with them, make sure they don't flap open!) While you're studying the rear-view, notice where the jacket ends. If it hits the hips, it's only going to accentuate them. The biggest myth in the world is that you can hide behind anything that covers your hips with excess fabric. Who needs excess *anything* back there. Everybody looks better in a jacket that ends just above the hips, short and tall alike. Not to mention large and small! It keeps the net effect lighter, and doesn't drag the eye down to the continuing length of the skirt. If you're terribly thin, you might like the option of one longer jacket with a longer pleated skirt. But with shorter, straighter skirts, you need a shorter jacket for balance. Sleeves should end just below the wrist bone, and no, your cuffs do not need to show beneath. Take the time to notice, and correct, if necessary, sleeve length. Even a half-inch too long here can make the entire jacket look too big.

Don't be afraid of alterations. You can always tell a "greenhorn" shopper by her aversion to having things fitted properly. Alterations are as important for women as they are for men. No man walks out of a store with a ready-to-wear suit, and you shouldn't expect to, either. Proper fit can make the difference between you wearing a suit, and a suit wearing you.

"What about hem length?"

It's wrong to say that only one length is ever appropriate. Styles change, and newer lengths eventually gain acceptance. While you don't want to be the first (and maybe the only) one in your office to wear the shortest or the longest length, you probably will wish to have about 4 inches of leeway: from just at the knee to slightly above mid-calf. Remember, the tendency for professionally conservative women is to wear skirts slightly longer than they should. Try to fight it. You run the risk of throwing the proportion off and the overall effect can be just plain dowdy. Aside from current fashion trends, the style and the fabric of a skirt can indicate its proper length. In general, lighter colors and softer fabrics can be a bit longer. Darker, heavier fabrics shouldn't drag down a look. They can go shorter. Movement also compensates for more length. A swingy, pleated skirt looks fine if it's longer; a straighter dirndl should stop somewhere around the knee. It's not a complicated formula. The mirror should tell you all you need to know. If your eye goes immediately to a solid, dark, immovable mass of skirt, you need to lighten up. Both top and bottom halves of your look must balance each other equally.

SHIRTS VS. BLOUSES

The second major concern is what goes best with a businesslike look on top. Most women don't want to copy the man's cotton-shirt-and-tie look, but they aren't entirely comfortable with more feminine alternatives. Here are some of the questions we answer over and over again.

"Are button-down collars appropriate for a woman?"

Oxford cloth, button-down shirts tend to look more casual on a woman than they do on a man. It's a man's tie treatment that dresses them up. Unless you plan to formalize them with a floppy bow, save them for sportier attire. Even manufacturers relegate these shirts to their sportswear lines.

"Can I leave a shirt collar open at the neck?"

Absolutely not. Although we covered this in Chapter 4, it bears repeating. Never leave a neckline unfinished. A basic shirt collar, especially in cotton, needs something soft at the neck. A collar with some detail, like a flat notched collar or a band collar, does not necessarily need accessorizing, although you may wish to add one classic gold chain or pendant necklace. The further away from the man's shirt look you go, the more freedom you have with finishing.

"Are ruffles acceptable?"

Of course, as long as they are not overly frilly. There's nothing wrong with looking pretty and professional. But watch the ones with romantic overtones.

"Can I wear a sleeveless blouse in the summer?"

If you wear a jacket over your shoulders most of the time, it's fine. You'll probably want to, anyway, with the chill factor of most office air conditioning systems. Warm-weather dressing is an area where women executives have more options than their male counterparts. Take advantage of them! Remember, looking cool is almost synonymous with looking competent. Avoid picnic-colored plaids or ruffly peasant toppings, however. A cool summer blouse must look every bit as efficient as a long-sleeved shirt. And don't count on a blazer to turn a sundress suddenly serious! Accept the fact that you're going to be warmer in a proper professional look than the women who can wear Indian gauze and stocking-less sandals to their offices. But do look for ways to take the heat off within the parameters of your executive requirements. Look for cotton or cotton blends. Save silks for chillier days. Keep colors lighter (try a beige/white/grey palette if you think pastels are less effective looking). Try slightly softer skirt shapes rather than anything close to the body. Invest in a few light-weight dresses with one neutral linen blazer. Opt for sleeveless or short-sleeved blouses. And pack a spray bottle of perfume in your tote but be sure to keep it in its original box so you have no spill problems.

"Can I wear sweaters to work?"

Not if they're collegiate Fair Isles or preppy crewnecks. Turtlenecks and cowlnecks can be overdone. Your best bet is a cardigan or a cardigan-collared cashmere slipover. Wear it as additional finishing (as a jacket or over a silk blouse).

COLOR

Defining conservative color options as either navy or grey is depressing to most women. While no one expects to be taken seriously in neon orange or metallic mauve, the search is always on for appropriate alternatives. Certainly colors from the classic palette (wines, camels, deep greens and blues) are entirely acceptable. Newer are the quiet neutral tones (taupe, charcoal, mauve, lavender and celery). And there's nothing wrong with adding either a brighter or a stronger shade for the blouse. It provides a focal point. If you find yourself tiring of a single color strategy, stay away from solids. Don't go off on a new color tangent, or you'll instantly outdate your entire wardrobe. But do look for interesting flecks, textures and weaves to break up the solid shade monotony. Or add a patterned blouse in a small, all-over print.

"Are there colors that aren't appropriate in certain parts of the country?"

Regional dressing went out with the old country. The myth that the South favors yellow, the East adores blue, the West likes who-knows-what must have originated in the days before business days began in New York and ended in Los Angeles. With bi-coastal and international hoppings a common corporate phenomenon, the professional look that's appropriate where you came from is your best calling card. If you have any doubts at all, the more conservatively colored the suit, the more instantly acceptable it will be on a world-wide basis. Stop worrying about regional color preferences and pay more attention to fabric and cut!

"Can I wear colored pantyhose?"

As our executive interviews indicated, a color-toned leg is gaining greater acceptance at the executive level. In general, sheer, see-through colors, such as wine, navy or black, that coordinate with both the outfit and the shoes are preferable to anything opaque, tweedy or thick.

CARE

With time at a premium, many executive women are concerned with the upkeep of a garment. Sending everything to the cleaners is the simplest solution for some; others object to being taken to the cleaners! Enormous monthly dry-cleaning bills have caused many to cast an appraising eye at natural fabrics. Linens, silks, woolens and cottons feel better on the body, but more and more professional women want to know the bottom line on care.

"Can I wash silk?"

The surprising answer is yes, with warm water and a mild detergent. Expect a silk blouse to wrinkle like crazy and shrink a little the first time you wash it. If you buy it a size larger, and keep a cool iron at the ready, you'll have a fresh blouse for pennies.

"I travel a lot. Do I need polyester?"

Not unless you're worried about wash and wear. That's the statement obvious synthetics make—hardly appropriate for a woman in an executive position. A blend of polyester with silk or cotton does make care easier, but you really shouldn't be washing out clothes in your hotel room, anyway. Depend on the hotel's valet service or plan to pack two shirts/blouses per day; one for business hours, one for evening entertainment.

DAY FOR NIGHT

What to wear when office hours are over is an important concern for the many women who don't take the time to go home before they go out. Executive lives are too busy and commuting distances are often too great to allow enough time for a complete transformation. As a result, more and more business suits are being seen in the best restaurants.

"How can I dress up a suit to go out?"

Fashion magazines are full of quick-change ideas to turn day looks into evening looks. But the simplest, easiest way to perk up is to slip a thin silk camisole into your briefcase (or keep one in the office). After hours, replace your business blouse with it, add a rhinestone or jeweled lapel pin, change your earrings, and you're set. It takes two minutes, and it's very effective with a suit. Don't try it with pinstripes, tweeds or heathery flannels, however. A soft camisole under a buisnesslike jacket creates a subtly glamorous look, so you'll need to play it up by heightening your makeup as well. Add brighter cheek and lip colors, and as much eye makeup as you like.

BITS AND PIECES

How to finish a professional look comes up as often as the basic components are decided upon. It's a good idea—right then—to pick up the exact pieces you'll need to complete the look. If you're in a store that has appropriate belts, jewelry, stockings and shoes near the professional clothing area, it will make shopping much easier for you.

"I can't seem to put accessories together."

Let a professional do it. You can't be expected to have expertise in all fields! Trying to pick the best accessories if you haven't the knack is like trying to answer a legal question if you aren't a lawyer! Know the kinds of things you are looking for, then listen to professional advice.

"What about hats?"

It's never necessary to wear one. Very few people feel comfortable in structured, tailored hats. Berets or soft head-hugging shapes serve when it's cold. If you like the effect of a "serious" hat, by all means wear one, but avoid masculine-looking brims. Even if it's the best style for your face, it'll come off as an imitation.

"Do I really need a navy blazer?"

The good old standby of the man-at-leisure isn't an automatic wardrobe-builder for women. While it looks classic over a man's grey flannel pants, it could look like an afterthought over a feminine silk dress. An occasional jacket is better if it's less tailored and structured than a traditional blazer. Look for lapel-less cardigan collars, shorter shapes, softened textures.

OPTIONS

Whether or not women have a real choice when it comes to selecting their professional clothes is a debate that's going to continue until more and more women are evident in positions of authority. With more role models, more peer influence, the following questions may finally cease to be asked. Right now, however, women still want to know:

"Are dresses appropriate for business?"

We've brainwashed ourselves into thinking that executive wear is synonomous with a suit, and it's going to take time to convince women that the right dress is equally acceptable. Men already know it. If you doubt it for a minute, re-read the executive interviews in Chapter 3.

"Should there be a uniform look for women?"

Absolutely not. Men have accepted it, and admittedly simplified their lives with it, but it just doesn't work for women. We tend to see clothes as expressive of individuality. Even the most un-clothes-conscious among us is not likely to want to wear the same looks in the same way as the other executives in the office.

That's why we rely on accessories to personalize the way we wear clothes more than men do. Boredom is another big factor. A too methodically plotted wardrobe will wear *us* out before we wear it out. There is a basic difference between the way clothing affects men and women, and we've got to allow for it. The minute you deny your need for expressive dressing is the time you're going to select clothes you won't be comfortable wearing.

"Do some women dress for failure?"

Contrary to this popularly expressed opinion, no woman consciously or sub-consciously puts herself into destined-for-failure looks. Of course it is possible to buy the wrong look for the wrong time—everybody's done it. But the more you arm yourself with information, the less chance you have of making costly mistakes.

"Why do retailers ignore the needs of the executive woman?"

The smart ones don't. And more will catch up as this market segment makes its economic influence felt. At the same time, the fashion industry's economics revolve around change. A 5-year wardrobe plan would strike fear into any manufacturer's heart. Their business is to convince you to buy something new every year, need it or not.

BIG MISTAKES

There are a million things that can betray a correct professional look, from the most obvious to the tiniest detail. Put them all together, and they'll change your overall impression drastically. You're not going to go wrong several ways at once, but do check out the danger points on the following pages. If you're guilty of making any one of these mistakes, correct it and notice the big difference it can make in your personal presentation.

NECKLINES

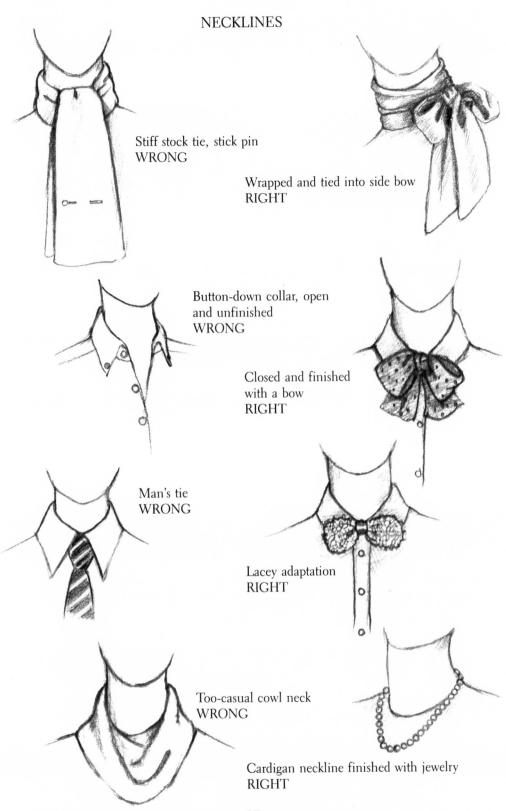

Stiff stock tie, stick pin
WRONG

Wrapped and tied into side bow
RIGHT

Button-down collar, open
and unfinished
WRONG

Closed and finished
with a bow
RIGHT

Man's tie
WRONG

Lacey adaptation
RIGHT

Too-casual cowl neck
WRONG

Cardigan neckline finished with jewelry
RIGHT

Unmatched blazer and skirt
WRONG (For interview)

Matching jacket and skirt
RIGHT

Jacket too long for skirt
WRONG

Right proportion
RIGHT

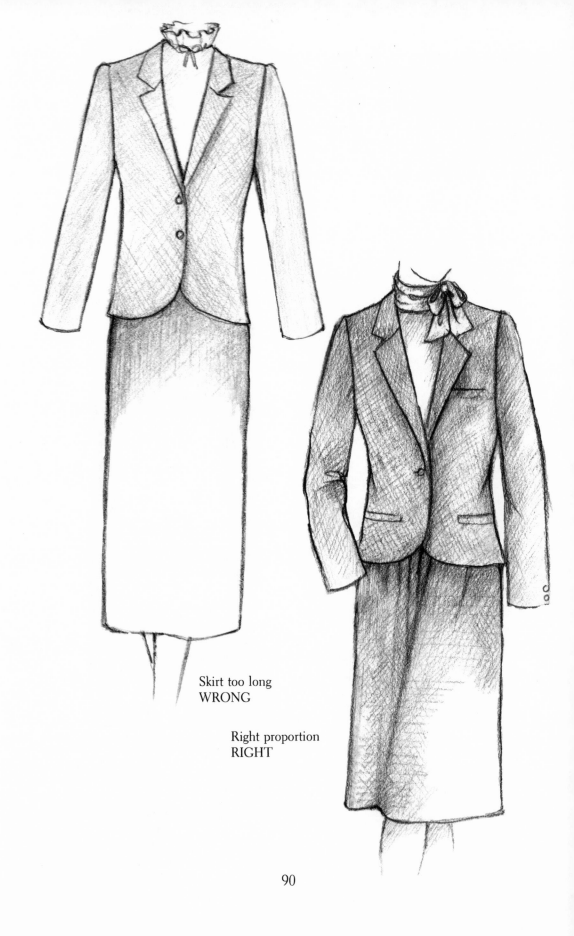

Skirt too long
WRONG

Right proportion
RIGHT

90

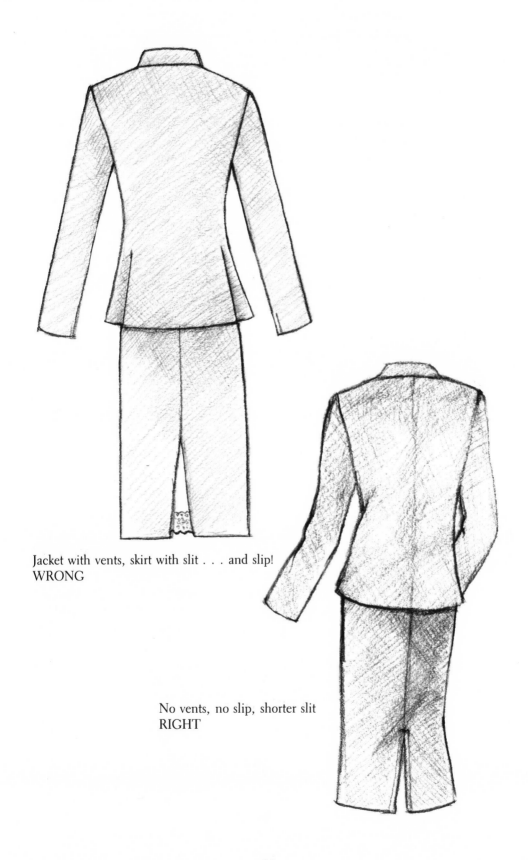

Jacket with vents, skirt with slit . . . and slip!
WRONG

No vents, no slip, shorter slit
RIGHT

See-through
WRONG

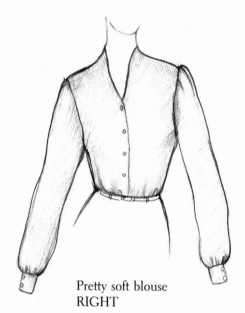

Pretty soft blouse
RIGHT

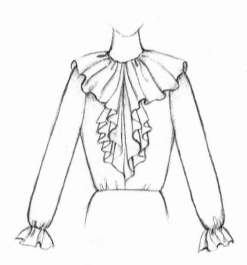

Ruffles, ruffles everywhere
WRONG

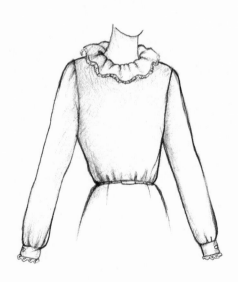

Feminine, but tailored
RIGHT

Peasant or country looks
WRONG

Businesslike blouse
RIGHT

Back-porch plaids
WRONG

Small, geometric prints
RIGHT

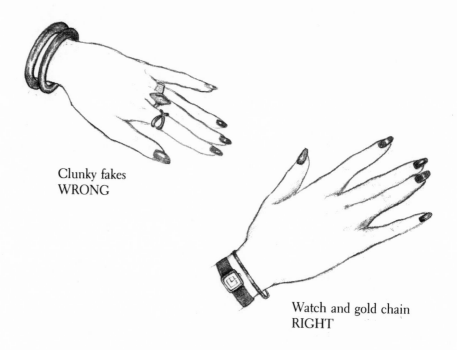

Clunky fakes
WRONG

Watch and gold chain
RIGHT

Attention-attracting earrings
WRONG

Neat, classic shapes
RIGHT

Cleopatra neck looks
WRONG

Small chains, pearls
RIGHT

Empty belt loops
WRONG

Thin, classic belt or cumberbund
RIGHT

Fishnets and sexy straps
WRONG

Chanel sling, pale leg
RIGHT

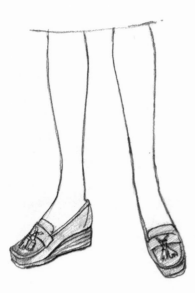

Clunky loafers and
sheer stockings
WRONG

Tailored classic pumps
RIGHT

Sporty tie-ups and
textured legs
WRONG

Dressy ghillies and
toned legs
RIGHT

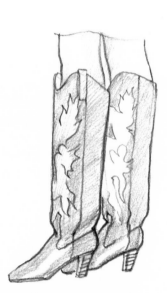

Cowboy or trendy boots
WRONG

Weather boots
RIGHT

CHAPTER

7

A Question of Quality:
How to Spot It

"Part of a professional appearance is a certain prosperous look. You
have to demonstrate that you are used to handling your own money in
a quality way."

It's easier for the untrained eye to spot items of obviously inferior quality than it
is to instantly recognize the reverse. Shiny polyester, for instance, stands out like a
sore thumb; the difference between varying grades of silk is far more subtle.
Knowing how to differentiate clothing of high calibre is simply easier if you're
used to it. Nothing is as apparent as quality to those who set their standards by it.

Still, there are certain giveaways that make it possible for even the uninitiated
to identify hallmarks of quality. If you don't know them, it will be worth your
while to learn them; the appearance of quality can make all the difference in the
impression you create. If you simply haven't thought about the distinguishing
characteristics lately, review the following checklist. As more and more manufacturers appear to be cutting corners in their construction of garments, it
will help to remind you of what to watch out for. With the escalating cost of
clothes, you owe it to yourself to make sure what you're getting is worth the price
tag!

FABRIC—THE ESSENTIAL INDICATOR

The most obvious characteristic of the quality of a garment is the stuff it's made
of. It's got to feel good, wear well, and be comfortable—even before aesthetic
evaluations enter into it! Judge the "hand" (the appeal to the sense of touch) of a
fabric by grabbing it and crinkling it in your hand. It should feel supple, not stiff;
firm, not limp; pliable, not inflexible. Release it and see if the wrinkles remain. If
a fabric bounces back the minute you open your hand, beware of it. It's too full of
chemicals to ever lie softly or drape naturally. Check for wear by rubbing your

thumb and second finger vigorously over a seam allowance. If the fabric has a propensity for pilling, this trick will bring them out.

Natural fibers have the edge when it comes to equating them with quality. Although second and third generations of generic man-made fibers have resulted in exceptional improvements over the originals, synthetics continue to be thought of as poor cousins to wool, silk, cotton and linen. Polyester, in spite of its remarkable attributes, has received such bad press that whole advertising campaigns have been planned solely to upgrade its image. It is finally gaining acceptance among fabric purists, but only in very discreet blends with natural fibers. If it really looks like the fabric it's mixed with, it's okay. If it has even a slight shine, however, it doesn't fool anyone. At the end of this chapter, we will give you a brief glossary-at-a-glance of the fabrics you'll most likely consider for your professional clothing, plus definitions of weaves you might have wondered about. If you're not positive you can spot the difference between a worsted covert, a Cheviot tweed or a wool serge, this quick guide will provide the clues. But, for now, on to other easy-to-spot attributes of quality.

STITCHING—LESS IS MORE

A lot of obvious overstitching going on cheapens the look of any garment. What you're looking for is stitching you can't see. Overstitching is always less expensive than subtle pick stitching. Check around the edges of jacket lapels, especially, for pick finishing. While you're looking at threads, make sure the manufacturer hasn't used the clear plastic kind. Besides being somewhat sharp, it unravels easily. Hems don't stay in a minute. And it's always a sign of cost corner-cutting.

Barely noticeable pick stitching.

SEAMS—A PERFECT MATCH

Any obvious pattern—plaids, stripes, bold prints—must meet its match at every seam. Nothing says more about you when your back is turned than a plaid that doesn't line up down the center seam. It takes a little extra fabric on the manufacturing end, and that will add to the cost of the garment. Expect it, and pay it. Unmatched seams are one of the quickest indicators of inferior quality. Whether the fabric is patterned or not, check all seams for smoothness. They must lie perfectly flat. A pucker is a sign of poor construction.

LINING—NOW YOU SEE IT, NOW YOU DON'T

There is a time and a place to have a lining on view, and it's never when it's peeking out from underneath! Expect jacket linings to be seen (especially if you never button your jacket), and judge the lining fabric accordingly. If it looks the least bit sleazy, it will undermine any impression the outside of the jacket makes. Watch where the lining ends in both jackets and skirts. If it stops just above the hem, there's less chance of it dropping into sight after repeated cleanings. A skirt lining will fit a little closer than the outside garment. If it is even a bit too tight, it will throw off the fit entirely. Since many lining fabrics tend to shrink if washed, allow for an easy enough fit if you intend to wash the item youself.

Comfort is the only reason for a lining today. There was a time when everything had to be lined, or the quality was in question. That just isn't so anymore. Some designers prefer the way fabrics fall when they aren't lined. Others advocate

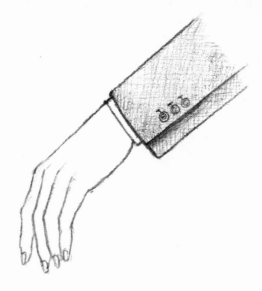

The look of buttonholes on a split cuff.

a natural, wrinkled effect. And the garments are every bit as expensive—with or without a lining. The rule to go by is comfort. When linings do appear, they are often to shield skin from a rough or scratchy fabric.

DETAILS—LITTLE THINGS MEAN A LOT

If there is something out of sync with the way you look, it instantly becomes a focal point. And if that detail is a dead giveaway of inferior finishing, you've automatically forfeited any impression of quality. Things to watch for:

Buttons: Try to avoid plastic buttons on jackets. If it's all but impossible, pick ones that look like they could be bone or tortoise. Notice if the sleeves of the jacket have buttons. Then check for the detail of buttonholes. They won't be real, but the look of a finished buttonhole around a stitched-on button is a quality touch. The sleeve should also be split at a button cuff, not stitched together.

Pockets: A double bizon pocket is always more formal than a flap pocket. You'll find it on jackets of better quality. If a pocket does have a flap, lift it. If the indentation of the flap shows, the jacket has been too hard pressed (The same thing can flatten lapels and make the fabric under them shiny and puckered. Inspect!)

A double bizon pocket.

Finishing: Give a garment the once-over for durable, smooth-working zippers, solidly sewn closures, and clipped threads. Threads hanging out of sleeves, or not cut off at the waistband are sure signs of shoddy workmanship.

CARE—PRESERVING A QUALITY IMAGE

Whether you spend a fortune on clothes, or stick with a few items of really good quality, the way you care for them is going to determine how others perceive you. The most expensive silk blouse with a soiled collar band is just a dirty shirt. A $400 blazer with a button missing is simply a sloppy jacket. A designer skirt with the hem hanging is only a good excuse to stay behind your desk! Clothes in need of repair—even minor repair—should go to a special section of your closet where they won't get worn again until they get fixed.

When we surveyed our executive customers, a slight majority (56%) said they were concerned about easy-care fabrics, yet they overwhelmingly preferred natural fabrics. While this may seem like a contradiction, the two are not necessarily mutually exclusive. With a little extra care (and a little larger size), most cottons, silks and woolens can be hand laundered. But remember to watch for shrinkage. Pay particular attention to anything that is lined. The lining is usually acetate, and will shrink more than the outside garment. Our best advice is to avoid washing anything with a lining.

Although dry cleaning sometimes seems like the safest alternative, you can overdo it. Repeated cleanings take the face off such fabrics as flannel and mohair. This can also cause others to go limp or weaken. The solvents used can sometimes change fabric colors or break down fibers. Resist the urge to dry clean after only one or two wearings. Often you can freshen a garment significantly by hanging it in the bathroom and turning on the shower. The steam will remove smoke odor, pollution—and wrinkles! If you have a soiled area, try spot cleaning. But be sure to test on an inside seam first for color fastness, and spread fluid cleaners over a wide area to avoid spotting.

MATERIAL GAINS—RECOGNIZING FABRICS

The Federal Textile Fiber Products Identification Act of 1960 went a long way toward demystifying the consumer about the material content of a garment. But even with the fabric or blend spelled out, it sometimes still isn't easy to know exactly what you're getting. If you saw crepe on a label, for instance, would you think you were getting silk, wool, or something synthetic? Does broadcloth automatically mean cotton? Can you assume a worsted is wool? If you're not certain of fabric terminology, browse through the following FIBERFINDERS before you look at a label. Knowing what to expect in terms of characteristics and care is the first step to getting exactly what you want in a fabric.

FIBERFINDER: WOOL

Perhaps the most important fiber for professional clothing, wool can be woven, knitted or felted in a variety of weights and textures. Its characteristic covering of minute overlapping scales gives wool a felting property which makes it an ideal fiber for blends. In general, wool is a comfortable, durable fiber. It can be stretched as much as 30% beyond its length and still hold its shape. It can absorb up to 50% of its weight in moisture and still not be saturated. Its interlocking outer scales trap air pockets for insulation. Although all of these qualities are important features when you're considering outerwear, you're looking for lesser degrees of warmth when you're shopping for something to sit behind a desk in. Why wool at all? Because it tailors beautifully, resists shine, and wears well. Although, like any natural fiber, wool does wrinkle, it gives a much softer look than a cardboard-stiff, wrinkle-free synthetic. You'll find wool in many different constructions. Some of the more common ones:

Angora. Angora goat hair (or mohair) is classified as a specialty wool fiber, and may be called wool under the Wool Labeling Act. Angora rabbit fur must be termed "hair." The fleece from an angora goat contains fine hairs of great strength and elasticity. It is comparitively coarse and its pile will stand erect. *Uses*: Upholstery pile fabrics, coats, linings, imitation furs, dresses.

Cashmere. A downy wool undergrowth produced by the cashmere (Kashmir) goat. The hair is fine, soft, silky and strong. Durability is increased when it is blended with sheep's wool. *Uses*: Shawls, dresses, coats, sweaters.

Cheviot. A rough woolen or worsted fabric with a hairy nap (man-made fibers, wool blends and reused wool and cotton may substitute). A harsh fabric, it does not hold a crease and sags with wear. It is similar to serge, but not as quick to shine. The highest grades of Scotch and British Cheviot suitings and overcoatings contain Cheviot wool.

Cheviot tweed. A loosely woven woolen tweed, shaggy in texture, in a variety of weights and colors. The quality may differ widely in that all Cheviot tweeds may not be made of Cheviot wool.

Flannel. A light- to medium-weight woolen fabric with a slightly napped surface. Woven with either woolen or worsted yarns or with wool combined with cotton, rayon and other man-made fibers. Heavier weights lend themselves to suiting, pants, coats.

Gabardine. A non-faced, tightly woven fabric with a distinct diagonal rib. May be worsted or in cotton, silk and synthetic fabrications, in dress and suiting weights. Wears well, but tends to be less supple than other wool weaves. Gabardine can look very drab, so watch for tailoring accents.

Melton. A heavy, tightly constructed woolen, finished to be completely smooth. It has the shortest nap of all face-finished woolens. May be all wool or blended with synthetic fibers.

Tropical. Lightweight, year-round worsted (although tropical suitings may be made in a variety of weaves and synthetic fibers). Tightly twisted yarns permit porosity, making this a cooler wool to wear all year through. Perfect for suits and jackets. This is your best choice for a suiting fabric that travels to any destination, any climate.

Wool Crêpe. A plain weave wool fabric used for coating and dress material. Generic use of the word "crêpe" indicates a silk material, unless it is preceded by a modifier (wool crêpe, polyester crêpe, etc.) Wool crêpe is produced in a variety of weights and crêpe effects.

Worsted. Tightly woven fabrics from yarn spun from combed wool. May also refer to worsted weight fabrics: gabardines, serges, tropical suitings. Generally, fabrics with a crisp hand.

FIBERFINDER: SILK

The most versatile of fibers for your professional wardrobe, silk can go from blouse to pants to jacket to skirt and to dress with the greatest of ease. Whatever way you wear it, silk looks soft, sensuous, elegant—and serious enough for the office. Many executive women now see it as the most desirable alternative to heavy suiting up.

It's a myth that silk hasn't got the strength to take it. Why do you think jockeys wear it? True, it's the lightest natural fiber, but silk also has more tensile strength than steel, compared weight for weight. It also has more give than cotton, and can absorb almost as much of its weight in moisture (30%) as wool, and eight times as much as nylon. Because silk is such a poor conductor of heat that it was once used to insulate electric wiring, it is both cool enough for summer and warm enough to keep in body heat in winter.

The care of silk varies with the quality. Generally, better silks will hold their dye and finish. A poorly dyed fabric will retain stains or lose color when anything containing alcohol is spilled on it. Check for lustre and a smooth silky feel when shopping for quality silk fabrics.

Although manufacturers' labels caution "dry clean only" for their own protection, you can carefully handwash silk broadcloth, crêpe de chine, shantung or pongee. One don't: never rub a spot with a damp cloth. This breaks the surface fibers and some silks will show water spots. Best to send taffeta, georgette, crêpe-y fabrics and brightly colored solids to the cleaners. Below, some of the best silk constructions for businesslike blouses, dresses and suitings.

Broadcloth. A stiffer woven silk that reveals a slight weave upon inspection. It has a lustrous, smooth surface that is somewhat crisper than crêpe de chine. It doesn't drape as well, but holds its shape better. The most common weave for shirts, blouses, some dresses.

Charmeuse. A satin-weave fabric with a semi-shiny, lustrous surface and a dull back. It is lightweight and drapes well. May also be in synthetics. Best for soft, dressier-looking blouses and cocktail clothes.

Crêpe de Chine. A thin, lightweight silk crêpe with no noticeable weave (although there may be a self-pattern jacquard effect). May also be made with worsted fillings or cotton yarns. The term is also used for rayon. Silk crêpe de chine drapes well, but does not hold its shape. It is best for blouses, two-piece dresses, evening wear.

Doupione. An irregular, rough silk fabric containing stubs and unevenness of color and weave. It is the result of double cocoons spinning side by side and interlocking at intervals. A knobby, thick-and-thin yarn is produced that is made into lightweight, textured fabrics. A good doupione tailors beautifully, takes to colors when dyed, and looks expensive. Doupione has a stiffer hand to it than other silks and can wrinkle considerably. *Uses:* Jackets, pants, skirts, suits.

Italian silk. Raw silk of high quality. It is strong, flexible, and has virtually no imperfections. *Uses:* Dresses, knits, lingerie.

Pongee. A light to medium weight plain-woven silk, characterized by nubs and uneven yarns. (May also be made from combed cotton, but this bears little resemblance to silk pongee.) The textured surface gives a hand-loomed effect. Often left in its natural ecru to tan color. *Uses:* Dresses, jackets.

Shantung. An uneven textured silk, retaining all knots, lumps and imperfections. Heavier than pongee. May also be used to describe synthetics or blends with a similar texture. Its crisp hand makes it ideal for suiting.

FIBERFINDER: COTTON

Cotton is one of the few vegetable sources of fibers, along with roots, stalks and leaves of other plants. It is a seed fiber with a high spirality or twist and exceedingly fine hairs. Cotton's natural color is light to dark cream, brown or green. It provides an extremely versatile and comfortable fabric with a variety of apparel and furnishings uses. When combined with other natural or synthetic fibers, cotton provides breathability and the advantages of easy care.

Batiste. A sheer, combed, mercerized muslin. May also be made in polyester and cotton blends, spun rayon, light-weight wool, or sheer silk. *Uses:* Shirts, handkerchiefs, nightgowns, slips.

Broadcloth. Cotton broadcloth is traditionally a shirting fabric, with a soft, firm finish. It is a closely woven, lustrous fabric with many of the same qualities as silk. However, it is more comfortable on the body because it is airier and absorbs better. Watch for wrinkles, shrinkage. Anything in cotton broadcloth must be carefully pressed. *Uses:* Shirts, some dresses.

Oxford Cloth. Combed cotton yarns made with a basketweave effect. The fabric is soft and porous with a lustrous finish. It may be white or woven with colored yarn and white filling for chambray or stripe effects. *Uses:* Shirting, suiting, sportswear.

Poplin. Similar to a broadcloth, but somewhat heavier. A durable, plain weave fabric that can be made of cotton, silk, synthetics, wool or a combination of these fibers. Cotton broadcloth in the U.S. is known as poplin in Great Britain. *Uses:* Heavier-weight raincoats, suiting, sportswear.

Sea Island Cotton. The finest grade of cotton. Superior in strength, lustre, fineness and uniformity. The length of the fiber requires several combings and is difficult to manipulate. *Uses:* Only the best cotton goods.

Seersucker. A weave of cotton that is permanently channeled or crinkled in stripes. Can also be made in rayon, acetate or other synthetic fabrics. Generally striped, but also available in plaids or checks. A lightweight, cool summer fabric that launders well and doesn't show wrinkles. *Uses:* Sportswear, suiting, dresses.

FIBERFINDER: LINEN

One of the oldest fibers known to man, linen's been around for at least 4,000 years. Woven from flax, linen was originally used for Lisle, chintz toile and damask fabrics now primarily made of cotton and man-made fibers. Linen is a fine, strong, durable cloth used for apparel and household articles. It also lends improved strength and resiliency when combined with other fibers for knitwear. Good linen has a luxurious feeling, but wrinkles considerably. It is not practical for packing and demands constant care. Designer claims that linen looks better when wrinkled are not understood by the majority of people who will wonder why you didn't take the time to press your skirt.

Butcher. A bleached linen fabric in a heavy, plain weave. When made of cotton or cotton and rayon spun of uneven thickness to resemble linen, the proper terminology is butcher cloth. *Uses:* Aprons and table linen.
Handkerchief. A fine, sheer linen fabric. Can also be rayon or cotton lawn. *Uses:* Handkerchiefs, lingerie, neckwear, dresses.
Irish. Designates point of origin only for apparel, handkerchief and domestic linens. The linen industry was founded in Ireland at the start of the 18th century by French textile workers.

FIBERFINDER: SYNTHETICS

This fifth fiber group originates not with the animal or vegetable sources of the others, but in the chemistry lab, with solutions based on cellulose, petroleum or natural gas, water, air, and certain minerals. The urge to improve on the intrinsic properties of natural fibers led chemists to create new molecular structures in search of specific qualities. As a result, the new technologies combine the best in aesthetics with the easy-care capabilities of synthetics. Blends which retain the appearance of a natural fiber are your best bets in the business world. Obvious synthetics are for those who spend their time worrying about wash and wear.

Acetate. Not technically a synthetic, since it is derived from cellulose. Still, a man-made silk-like fiber. A bit crisper than silk. *Uses:* Dresses, lingerie, sleepwear, sportswear.
Acrylic fiber. A generic name for man-made fibers such as Orlon®, Acrilan®, Zefran®, Creslan® and Zefchrome. Characteristically, acrylic fabrics have a soft, wooly hand. They're also wrinkle-resistant, sunlight-resistant, show stability to repeated launderings, and can take brilliant and high-shade colors. Their performance qualities make them good and durable for clothing.

Polyester. A minimum-care fiber, manufactured under the trademarks of Dacron, Kodel, Fortrel and Vycron. It is wrinkle resistant, abrasion resistant, shrink resistant. Polyester fibers are also noted for their resilience, strength, and shape retention. When blended with cotton, rayon or other man-made fibers, polyester passes on its easy-care attributes, plus balances the poor qualities of many natural fibers. It tends to stain and shine easily, however. And because it was at one time in inexpensive garments, it is still thought of as a low-status fabric.

Rayon. A man-made fiber made from cellulose derived from trees, cotton and woody plants. It can have the texture of many different fabrics, but most often it resembles the lustrous quality and feel of silk. Rayon drapes beautifully, yet it is very strong and durable. It resists wrinkles better than silk, and it is sometimes mixed with silk to add this quality. Rayon has a high absorbency and can take on brilliant color dyes.

WEAVES TO WATCH

It is easy enough to confuse a weave with a fiber—especially because it is sometimes easier to see and touch. You can quickly identify taffeta or velvet at a glance, but you still may not have a clue as to what fibers these fabrics are made from. The whole matter becomes simplified when you remember that there are only five basic fiber groups: wool, silk, cotton, linen and synthetics. Any other terminology applies to the construction (or the weave) of the fabric. You'll find that many commonly used descriptions apply to several fabrics across the board. Below, some names you should know:

Basketweave. A rather loosely constructed mat effect, similar to plaited-cane basket work. A variation of a plain weave, in which two or more threads weave alike in both directions. Also known as hopsacking.

Bouclé. A looped or knotted surface fabric made from rough, curly bouclé yarns. Bouclé yarns may alternate with plain yarns, and the fabric itself may be wool, rayon, cotton or a combination. You'll see it in sportswear, jackets, coatings.

Cashmere silk or rayon. A soft, thick fabric, finished to resemble cashmere on one side—but not the real thing. Watch for it in rayon, silk, or silk/worsted combinations.

Cavalry twill. Can be wool, worsted, cotton, spun rayon or other man-made fibers. It is a rugged, durable fabric with a definite twill, or coarse rib effect. Used for active sportswear (riding habits, skiwear) and uniforms.

Chalk stripes. White stripes of varying widths printed or woven on a dark ground. Usually broader than pin stripes. Commonly seen on suits or outerwear.

Challis. Originally made of a silk and worsted blend, this soft, lightweight fabric can be anything from wool to cotton to polyester blends. You'll find it most often in small floral or paisley patterned two-piece dresses, dresses and skirts. A good year-round weight.

Chambray. Plain-weave cotton, synthetic or blend fabrics with a colored warp and a white filling. Available in both solids or striped, checked and figured prints, all with characteristic white threads running through. Lighter weights are used in shirtings; heavier weights in workclothes, sportswear and children's playclothes.

Chenille. This is derived from the French word for caterpillar, and that's a pretty fair description of the yarn effect. Through weaving and taping groups of yarns, a special yarn is produced with pile protruding on all sides. Most commonly found in bathmats and bedspreads, Chenille every so often surfaces as a fashion fabric for tops, sportswear, jackets.

Covert. This medium- to heavyweight sturdy worsted or cotton fabric is usually found in suiting or coating variations, although lighter weights may be used for sportswear and workclothes. Wool coverts are closely woven with dark/light yarns creating a mixture effect usually in tan or brown shades. Cotton coverts have a mottled or flecked appearance in grey, tan and blue shades. They often are given a firm, starched mill finish.

Crepe. A general classification of fabrics with a range of crinkled or grained surface effects. May be silk, rayon, acetate, cotton, wool, synthetics or a combination.

Faille. A plain-weave fabric with a slight luster and a flat rib. Because of its body and tailoring capabilities, it is often used for spring coats and suits.

Georgette. A silk or silk-like fabric with a fine crepe surface. Sheer and lightweight for blouses, evening apparel.

Ottoman. A heavy, horizontally corded fabric, with larger ribs than faille. It has a lustrous surface and may be made of wool, silk or man-made fibers. You'll see it in evening wraps, upholstery, draperies, suits and coats.

Serge. Originally made of silk, serge is now woven in many weights and fibers: wool, cotton, rayon, silk and combinations. All have a characteristic flat diagonal wale. Most often, the designation applies to a staple, clear-finished worsted suiting fabric. It drapes well, and holds a crease, but watch for eventual shine.

Twill. A general term for a firm, durable fabric made with a twill weave, characterized by a diagonal rib.

8

The Time Factor: An Organization and Shopping Strategy

"What I need most in my wardrobe is organization and coordination. The last thing I have time to do in the morning is play mix and match."

The most precious commodity to any executive woman is time. There's barely enough of it to allow for essential activities, and certainly *never* enough of it for leisurely personal pursuits, like getting to the dry cleaner. Unfortunately, your appearance does come under the personal category, and hours spent on its care and maintenance are usually the first to be cut from a hectic schedule. Maybe some women can replenish their wardrobes on their lunch hours. You can't get away from your desk. Maybe others have time to create magazine-inspired looks in the morning. You spend most of your waking hours commuting. And to all those who look as if they were *born* coordinated, you say you simply haven't got the time. After all, your day will hold more important decisions to be made than what goes with what.

While that may be true, nothing is going to give you a professional edge more than an effective, organized appearance. The important word here is *organized*. With a little extra pre-planning, the crucial minutes between the time your alarm goes off and you dash for the door needn't involve either a hit-or-miss dressing strategy or a lot of time-wasting decision-making. Everything hinges on accessibility. If your clothes are arranged in a way that invites coordination, they'll practically pull themselves together. Take one Sunday a season to really think through the organization of your closet, and you'll be able to select the exact professional look you want in far less time than you think.

THE LOGICAL CLOSET

First and foremost, no closet is ever going to be organizable with a lot of leftover clothes stored away in it. We're not talking about bringing order out of chaos here. You've got to eliminate all the non-essentials before you can even begin. If you haven't already edited your clothing so that it is totally appropriate for your professional life, re-read Chapter Two right here and now. Then pitch. In fact, even if you have already mercilessly discarded most of your wrong-for-work clothes, it's a good idea to hold a pitch session once a season, as you're packing away winter clothes for spring/summer ones; or gearing the closet up for fall. (Keep only one season at a time hanging in your closet. Any dry cleaner will store out-of-season clothes, if you haven't the storage space.) It's best to get rid of anything you haven't worn that season before you automatically put it into storage. One woman we know applies a two-year test before deciding to discard something. If she wears an item infrequently during one season, she'll keep it in her wardrobe for one more year. If the second year shows little or no wear, out it goes. Obviously, it's something she didn't feel comfortable wearing in the first place. You usually do know right away if you like wearing something. But if you feel terribly wasteful parting with a mistake immediately, the two-year test will at least prevent you from keeping something forever.

Inventory what's left in your wardrobe before you put it away for a season. Don't think you'll remember what you've got. You won't. Use the Wardrobe Planner checklist in Chapter Four, and note the colors and/or fabric patterns of each item. Update the list by removing all items you've discarded, and adding new purchases. See where the holes are in your wardrobe. Get an idea of what you'll be looking for when the clothes start coming out for that particular season. Then, put the card away in a place you'll remember. When you're ready to look for wardrobe replacements, don't dare go shopping without taking it with you! We'll give you tips on how to use your limited shopping time more effectively later on in this chapter. But, for now, back to the closet.

Make space: If you're really serious about getting more space, architecturally, from your closet, remove everything that's in it. Top to bottom. Including shelves, rods—even doors. Carefully measure the shell that remains. Then plan new ways for maximizing every inch. You may need to work with a consultant on this if figuring out the width of furring strips isn't exactly your calling. Some ideas to consider:

- Combine double and single rods. Divide the hanging area in two. On one side, a single rod (placed higher than usual—you'll gain extra space underneath) will hold dresses, coats, pants, bathrobes, and other full-length items. On the other side, hang upper and lower rods. Again, keep the topmost rod higher than usual. Use it to hang blouses, jackets, tops. Use the lower rod for skirts—only. Do not fold your pants over hangers in this space. They will always show the crease.

- Get rid of folding doors. They may be standard equipment, but they're the worst for storage possibilities. Think of what you could hang on the back of a "real" door: belts! scarves! jewelry! bags! shoes! A pegboard-and-basket system could hold a myriad of drawer-fillers. Just make sure your closet is deep enough so the doors close securely without hitting what's hanging. Hollow-core doors are fine to replace folding ones, or you may consider solid-core doors if you're thinking of storing heavy items on them.

- Add vertical storage space. Move in a tall, narrow bureau to hold panty-hose, lingerie, belts, jewelry, scarves, gloves, etc. If there's just no room for a bureau, extra shelves holding slip-in-slip-out baskets will hold many of the same things.

- Go underground. The floor is no place for shoes! They only pile up and get messy there. Clearly marked shoe boxes on an upper shelf is really

THE LOGICAL CLOSET

Take advantage of new fixtures to create upper and lower level space. Find storage areas where they never existed before.

your best bet for instant identification. And the bonus is you get *both* shoes of the pair with one easy reach. Think of the time you'll save! Meanwhile, you free up the floor space for more storage. Think tall boots, tennis rackets, laundry baskets. If your clothing rods are at a new height, this space can really amount to something.

Put your clothes on display: Part of what makes some stores more appealing than others is their visual merchandising. The way they present what they have to offer must initially attract a consumer, and also make it easy for her to make a selection. If there is too much going on, the customer can quickly become confused and give up. Display directors must set a balance between high drama and merchandise accessibility.

If you think of your closet in terms of a retail store, would you want to shop there? Is everything easy to find? Can you tell what "department" you're in? Does it make any sense at all? If you've answered no to even one of those questions, it's time you went into the display business. Clothes that you can grab-at-a-glance will get you to your office faster in the mornings than an express train. Here are some ways to get everything out in the open:

- Hang clothing by classification. All suits should be hung together; all blouses; all pants; all skirts; all shirts. Silk ones should go on hangers with foam coverings. Cotton ones can even be folded into a drawer—if you don't mind the crease. (If you do, and you send your shirts out to be laundered, just request they be returned to you on hangers.) The next step is to group by a color rotation within each classification. For instance, navy might be your first color in each category, followed by burgundy, followed by beige. It helps, if for no other reason than to give your closet a sense of visual order. It's also a good way to inventory. You'll know at a glance which colors you're strongest in, which colors you only have once, which colors you don't need another thing in (do you really have *four* beige silk shirts?).

  Some women prefer to group by coordinated outfits: the suit, followed by the blouses that go with it, followed by the skirts that can work with the suit jacket, and so on. Organization is purely a personal choice. If you have little time or limited coordination possibilities, this may be your best system.

- Pick the proper hangers. Nothing throws the line of a jacket off quicker than hanging it up carelessly so one arm and shoulder hang lower than the other, or using a thin wire hanger. Invest in some good padded or plastic hangers. A man's wooden suit hanger is generally too wide for the shoulders of a woman's jacket, so don't rely on borrowing his. What you can use, however, are men's wooden trouser hangers. They're the best for hanging pants either from the waist or the hem. You want to avoid metal clip pant hangers. They make marks. And never buy the double-over metal bar kind. First of all, they're a nuisance; they swing open the minute you touch one of the bars. And even more important, you'll end up with a permanent crease in your pants—the wrong way! Skirt hangers are inevitable. They've got to have those metal clips. But try to avoid them whenever you can by using the loops on a skirt to hang it up. They'll hook around a plastic hanger (not a wire one) and stay. Sequential pant and/or skirt hangers do save space by hanging one item on top of another vertically, but only use them if you're really cramped. They keep visibility low, and the bottom rung lets pants hang too close to the floor.

DO use a padded or plastic hanger.

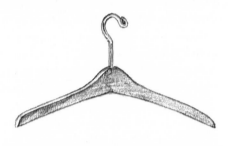

DON'T stretch out shoulders with a man's wooden suit hanger.

DO use a man's pant hanger for one-at-a-time alignment.

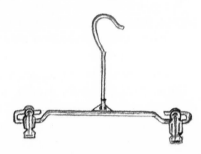

DON'T crease skirts or pants with metal clips. If you must use this hanger, a single is better than a sequential.

- When you're reaching for clothes in the morning, what you get is usually what you see. The most important idea is to keep everything as visible as possible. Hang belts and bow ties from hooks. Store sweaters in see-through boxes. Use a series of towel racks to drape scarves over. Take a trip through the housewares/hardware section of a dime store to see just how many different ways there are to hang things; then opt for the ones that will keep your clothes and accessories on full display. Choose wire baskets over prettier wicker ones. You can't see through those. Take plastic boxes over wood-grained cardboard ones. And never hang hooks in the back of your closet. Once you store something in an inaccessible area, it's the next best thing to losing it.

- Let there be light. If you've never dashed out the door wearing one blue shoe and one black shoe, you might not recognize the importance of a well-lit closet. But it can happen. With little organization, and even less light, you run the risk of turning your morning into a frenzied search for anything that goes with anything. Without a logical closet, enough light won't give you one second more time, but it will help you to be more confident in your choices.

What you're really striving for is instant identification. You should be able to see—at a glance—what you have and what goes with it. If it takes you one day per season to sort things out and turn your closet into an organized, logical presentation of the clothes you want to wear, you'll more than make up for the time every workday morning. Once you can see what your options are, you'll also improve your clothes rotation and give your whole wardrobe a longer life. You'll find you won't rely on the same wardrobe solutions time and time again just because they're there. With a logical closet, everything will be within reach—within seconds!

THE ONCE-A-SEASON SHOPPING STRATEGY

When it does come time to add a few things to your wardrobe, you're going to need a gameplan if you expect to get in and out of stores with a reasonable degree of efficiency. The majority of executive women we questioned dreaded the whole ordeal of shopping enough to confine it to a once-a-season excursion. Over 65% of them found that was ample time to spend scouting for the items their wardrobes lacked, although virtually all of them expressed varying degrees of frustration with the anticipated store-to-store chase. Very few retailers are making life easy for the over-scheduled, after-hours executive woman. Either the hours aren't convenient enough, the services aren't extensive enough or the merchandise isn't businesslike enough.

Shop First for a Store

You're not going to find personalized attention or custom-designed services in a large department store. After all, they can't alter their schedule to suit yours. Although the mix of merchandise may be better, you're still going to have to hop from one department to another coordinating it. And, very often, you can't borrow a blouse from one floor to match it with a suit on another. Sometimes even items on the same floor can't be tried on in the same dressing room if they're from different departments. Although, at first glance, a larger store seems like one-stop shopping, it often isn't.

Your time and energy will be better spent in a smaller specialty store that has a broad-enough merchandise mix to be able to offer you suits, separates, dresses, blouses, and the accessories necessary to finish each look. Search for a store that reflects your clothing point of view (don't waste your time going into the ones

The Time Factor: An Organization and Shopping Strategy   115

with leather minis in the windows). Once you've narrowed down the field, investigate services. A store with an in-house tailor, personal wardrobe consultant, messenger delivery service and eight o'clock evening hours is going to uncomplicate things for you.

Don't Be Anonymous—Get Acquainted

When you find a store that meets all of the above qualifications, begin to develop a relationship with it *immediately*. This doesn't take hours of browsing. Just a quick introduction to the owner or manager. In smaller stores, the relationship between sales personnel and management is a close one. If the owner isn't around, it's relatively easy to spot the other key people. Explain your clothing needs, ask if there is a customer file card you should fill out, and find out when the best time is to come in for some serious shopping. If there is a wardrobe consultant on staff, book an appointment with her. Be sure to plan on the better part of a day. If all the sales people are trained to work with customers, get the name of a specific one. Then call ahead, ask for her, and tell her when you're coming in and the types of things you'll be looking for. If she knows her business, she will have pre-selected several items for you before you arrive. Always remember, when you can book appointments, do. It will save your time and also let the store know you're a serious customer who expects efficient service. This takes you out of the leisurely browser category instantly.

SPECIAL ARRANGEMENTS? IT DOESN'T HURT TO ASK

Once you've developed an on-going relationship with a store or a particular salesperson, you might be allowed to come in very early before they open, or after the shop has closed to do your selecting. This is the only way some high-powered female executives can squeeze any shopping into their schedules. The store that accommodates them is the store that gets the business.

Help! Personal Shoppers and Image Consultants

If you're not at the strata where stores stay open for you, you can still take advantage of many personalized services. Many of the executive women we surveyed expressed interest in letting a professional guide them in their purchasing decisions. There are two ways to go with this. A personal shopper may, or may not, be employed by a store. Many larger stores have one on staff, although her services are frequently not advertised. Don't be afraid to ask. In most cases, a store's personal shopper's services are free, although some stores may require a minimum expenditure. If you're a dedicated department store shopper, this service can be a godsend. The personal shopper can do what the ordinary customer can't. She'll be able to pull merchandise from all departments store-wide and bring it into a single dressing room. She should also be able to write up everything you buy on a single ticket, and not send you back to each individual department to purchase each item. And she can also have everything delivered at the same time. A personal shopper can cut through a lot of retail red tape! Plus, between visits, she'll be your scout in the store. Shoppers who know their customers' needs and preferences should constantly be on the lookout for items they intend to buy, and call them the minute anything comes in. Keep in mind that you can develop the same relationship with a knowledgeable salesperson in a smaller store.

If you feel you need "outside" help, or a shopper to scour every store in town for you, you'll have to hire one. The advantage to this is not being locked into one particular store's merchandise. The disadvantage is the price tag. Some charge a flat fee, some an hourly rate, some a percentage of your purchase costs. Depending on where you live, standard rates may range from $50 an hour to a flat $600 per day. Add that to the cost of a season's wardrobe and you could practically pay for a whole new suit instead!

A personal shopper will put her expertise to work in the marketplace. She should know every store, every department, every off-beat boutique in town. If she can't find exactly what you have in mind—in a minimum of time—chances are it doesn't exist. The services of an image consultant combine a bit of analysis along with a shopping excursion (and you'll go along). More along fairy-god-mother lines, a good consultant will come to your home, go through your closet, and come up with your best looks—head to toe. Hair and makeup suggestions are often part of the image "makeover." Expect to pay one a set fee for the initial analysis, then an hourly rate for time spent taking you all over town. Rates vary, of course, in different parts of the country, and services sometimes cross over. But, in general, expect a personal shopper to be strongest in doing just that—shopping; and an image consultant to be best at advising you of the most workable wardrobe and look for your lifestyle. You can find a national listing of image consultants in any library.

If you decide to tough it out and take on your seasonal shopping yourself, arm yourself with all the information you'll need beforehand. To re-cap:

1.   Select a store that carries a sufficient merchandise mix.
2.   Know their services.
3.   Find out the name of a qualified salesperson, consultant or coordinator who can work with you.
4.   Book an appointment, if possible.
5.   Take a wardrobe inventory before you leave home.
6.   Bring your wardrobe planner with you.

You can't be expected to put together a logical, thought-through wardrobe in much less than a day. If you're only picking up a few pieces, you might get away with a few hours. But if you plan never to enter a store again until you need to buy for the *next* season, you better take enough time to be thorough. Even down to buying 52 pairs of pantyhose, if need be. Now is the time to buy everything that will pull each look together, as well. Wandering around town looking for just the right lizard belt later will only waste your time. Whatever you think you need to finish a look (a bar pin for a lapel; a silky pocket square, something for the neck), simply stick with it until you get it. *That day.*

Don't Be Distracted

There is such a thing as overdoing it, however. It will happen if you allow yourself to be distracted by something you had absolutely no intention of buying. Either be firm and resist it, or apply the same shopping strategy to this item as you use for all others: make sure you buy everything you need to go with it. If a sensational blouse doesn't really fit with anything else in your wardrobe, you better buy a suit or a skirt and jacket—right then—to go with it. When distractions begin to add up and throw your clothing budget out of whack, they suddenly cease being irresistible. If you don't make sure you have something to wear with an unplanned purchase, you'll be searching all season through. This can lead to a lot of unrelated buying that has nothing to do with your wardrobe needs. Avoid it, if you can.

Timing makes all the difference in the success of your mission. If at all possible, plan your stock-up day for any day *other* than Saturday. That's when a store is bound to be its busiest. Weekday mornings can be as quiet as a tomb in some stores—a good time to go. When the crowds are light, you'll be able to think clearly and get the attention you need. Selection is also easier if you shop just slightly ahead of the season. Don't wait until the mad dash is on the first day the weather changes. And don't count on waiting for end-of-season bargains. True, the prices may be better, but you'll have to take what you can get. And it will take much more time to pull your outfits together when there's slim pickings on the shelves. You'll find the best selections, of course, when merchandise is at its peak during each selling season. But if you know what you're looking for, you can catch the first deliveries of the latest looks. Everything that will be coming in later has its predecessor a good four-to-six weeks earlier. Plan to scout for fall/winter harbingers in late June or early July. By August, everybody's buying. Look for dressy holiday clothes as early as October. By the time November rolls around, the best will be already snapped up. See the first signs of spring in February, and don't wait a day past May to grab up all the casual summer clothes you'll need. Times when you *don't* want to be anywhere near a store: during the July/January inventory sales or any time in December.

WHAT HAPPENS WHEN YOU GET IT ALL HOME?

Don't put a thing away until you've had a try-on session. The trick is to mix old clothes with new, integrating recent purchases with old standbys. See how well they work together (or if you've missed by a mile). Experiment with combinations you wouldn't have time to try in the morning. You may surprise yourself. Some of your new things—accessories included—may go with clothes you never considered. Take the time now to get the feel of each new look. Sit in it; move around in front of a mirror in it; personalize it. Push up the sleeves. Try the collars buttoned up, bowed, or open. Tie on a sash instead of a belt. Wear a silk shirt as a jacket over another shirt. Make each addition to your wardrobe uniquely you. Then relax. Put your feet up and your clothes away. You've devoted all the time you need to organize your wardrobe for another season.

CHAPTER
9
The Business Trip:
A City-By-City Guide

"I need comfortable clothes with good looks that can take a travel beating. They have to be able to adapt to changes, but still project a professional image."

As more and more businesses are operating on a bi-coastal or international basis, the all-expense-paid ticket to an out-of-town meeting has become almost inescapable for the executive. And women executives are no exception. According to research recently conducted by Westin Hotels, about 3 million businesswomen spent 33 million nights on the road. Seventy-one percent selected their own hotels. Although women business travelers accounted for only 16% of the market at that time, their ranks began growing at triple the speed of men's.

Conducting a client meeting, attending a conference, presenting a proposal or negotiating new terms in a strange city with comparative strangers is known as the business trip. Glamorized by all those who never go on them, and scrutinized by superiors who must approve them, these out-of-town treks are usually more exhausting than exciting, and sometimes more hectic than effective. Still, if you accomplish the purpose you went for, represent the best interests of your company at all times, and bring back information you can act upon, your trip will be judged a success. What you don't want to do—ever—is visibly suffer from jet lag; not have all the information you need with you; insist on staying in for room service instead of accepting a business-related invitation; and wear the wrong clothes at the wrong time. You'll show an obvious lack of judgment if you do any of the above. But the last is possibly the worst. You can cover an error of omission. You can plead headache instead of fatigue. You can excuse preferring to spend time alone with the need to go over piles of briefs. But you can't hide if you show up at a company cocktail party in much more than a silk dress, or go before the CEO in much less than a suit. Coast-to-coast, the same rules of professional dressing seem to hold, although knowing how to adapt them to the style of a specific city will show you've done your research. When you can go in with some knowledge of the customs of the city you're visiting, you won't seem so much the stranger. Familiarize yourself with as many particulars about a place as you can find beforehand. The people you'll be dealing with will be impressed that you took the time, and they'll be more likely to listen to your business proposals if you're conversant with local concerns. Later on in this chapter we'll give you a Trip Tip Guide to the major cities most often traveled to by the executive women we surveyed (and 79% of them do travel for business). You'll find packing suggestions, places to book reservations for lunch, a seasonal weather re-cap, and other acclimation information. No matter what your destination, however, there are a few realities common to every business trip. If you review them now, you'll stand less chance of overlooking them later.

GETTING THERE IS HALF THE JOB

Whether your company has a corporate travel department, or books exclusively through one agent, there are undoubtedly certain specifications that must be followed. If you don't know them, find out. Nothing is worse than having to justify why you stayed at a certain hotel after the fact. Or, worse yet, having to pay out of pocket the difference between your first-class fare and the customary coach costs. The policy dictates of even the bluest chip organization can make it risky to assume that all senior officers naturally fly first class. Sometimes, even the presidents don't!

Once you know the company's "rules of the road," don't rely on either your secretary or your booking agent to work out the details. Know in advance which flights are available, and at what times. It helps to have your very own official flight guide for this. These pocket-sized monthly editions list all flights on all airlines, so you can pick and choose according to *your* timetable. Tuck one in your briefcase and take it with you. If you need to switch flights fast, you'll have all the information you need in front of you. It's also a lifesaver if you must keep track of clients coming in on various arriving flights. There's a world of information in the hande *Official Airlines Guides*, both domestic and international. You'll have to subscribe on a yearly basis (the pocket guides run around $40 for 12 issues), but if you travel at all frequently, they're an invaluable aid. Write to: Official Airlines Guides, 2000 Clearwater Drive, Oak Brook, Illinois, 60521, if you wish ordering information.

Secondly, don't leave your setting to chance. During peak travel periods, airlines often overbook, and it's first-come, first-serve at airport check-in counters. This makes things especially difficult if it's going to be nip-and-tuck between your last meeting of the day and lift-off, or if you're traveling with an associate and absolutely, *positively* need to sit together to work out some last minute details. Don't count on anything, much less a window seat in non-smoking, unless you've confirmed a seat assignment along with your reservation. It takes a lot of last minute stress out of business travel if you accomplish as much as you can in advance:

1. Pre-order a special meal. "Vegetarian" ones are always easier on the stomach than the standard starch-heavy entrees. The fruit salads look like heaven next to soggy, sticky canneloni. But you won't get it if you haven't asked in advance.

2. Request the seat you like the best. If you're more relaxed next to an emergency exit, admit it.

3. Arrange for your ticket to be delivered by messenger at your desk. No sense standing in line at a ticket counter while they're calling your flight.

Belonging to an airline "club" can simplify the booking process for you. Often club members are promised special attention to accommodate seating preferences. Private, unlisted reservations numbers provided to members also facilitate matters. And extra services, such as check cashing privileges, free local phone service, a message desk, luggage identification and special travel assistance can make these clubs worth more to the frequent traveler than just a comfortable place to relax and have complimentary beverages between flights. Although they are that, too. The atmosphere of an airline club is more conducive to continuing a business conversation than the more heavily trafficked airport areas. Can you seriously wind up last minute details standing up at the "Sidecar Bar"? The private quiet of an airline membership club does say a little bit more about the way you do business. Expect to pay a nominal annual fee for these services, or invest in a lifetime membership. Some clubs offer three- or five-year membership options as well. The one you eventually select may depend on which airline you use most often—or which airports. Check club locations before you decide. If you're interested in obtaining a membership application, ask your travel agent, or write to the following:

American Airlines
The Admiral's Club
P.O. Box 61616
Dallas/Fort Worth Airport, Texas 75261
Cost: $25 Initiation fee, $50 Annual fee, $600 Lifetime membership

British Airways
The Executive Club
Dept. BT—Accounts
245 Park Avenue
New York, New York 10167
Annual membership: $100

Delta Airlines
Crown Room
1 Pennsylvania Plaza
11th Floor
New York, NY 10119

(212) 239-0700
Annual fee: $85, 3-year fee: $200

Eastern Airlines
The Ionosphere Club
The Ionosphere Club Administrator
Miami International Airport
Miami, Florida 33148
Initiation fee: $25, Annual fee: $50, Five-year fee: $200, Lifetime membership:
$500

Northwest Airlines
VIP Top Flight Lounge
537 Fifth Avenue
New York, New York 10017
Membership is free, but you must complete an application.

Pan Am
Clipper Club
Pan American World Airways, Inc.
Clipper Club Membership Dept.
P.O. Box 2782
Boston, Massachusetts 02208
Annual fee: $50, Three-year fee: $135, Senior Lifetime fee: $300, Lifetime membership: $500. Courtesy card available for spouses at no extra cost.

TWA
Ambassadors Club
Two Ambassadors Club
P.O. Box 20287
Kansas City, Missouri 64195
Initiation fee: $25, Annual fee: $45, Annual fee with spouse: $75, Lifetime membership: $600, Lifetime membership with spouse: $750

United Airlines
Red Carpet Club
JFK Airport
Jamaica, New York 11430
Initiation fee: $50, Annual fee: $60, Lifetime membership: $900

Before you take off for the airport, check two things. One: Make sure you've left a complete itinerary with hotel addresses and all phone numbers (day and night) with both your secretary and superior. People tend to get unnecessarily nervous if they don't know how to get in touch with you. Two: Examine all luggage for inside and outside identification. Outside tags should have your business address, not your home address. (Thieves have been known to case airports for addresses of people leaving home.) If you can have your business card laminated into a luggage tag, so much the better. Inside identification isn't mandatory, but it's nice to know your suitcase may find its way back to you if the outside tags are torn off. You'll have less worry, of course, if you plan to carry all bags on board. Unless your trip looks like it's going to stretch beyond 10 days, there's really no excuse for carrying so much you have to check it through. You'll look much more efficient with the lightweight garment bag and carry-on tote described in Chapter 5.

Eliminate last-minute stress by avoiding the office altogether if your flight is anytime before noon. You won't get as much done in the morning as you think if you plan to go in for an hour then dash for the airport. And you may have enough distractions to make you miss your flight completely. It's better to go over what you need to review at home *quietly*, then allow yourself enough time to get to the airport *peacefully*. You'll be able to concentrate more easily on business matters when you're not worried about the traffic tie-up.

The most important thing is to be in control of as many of the uncertainties of your trip as you can be. From where you sit, to what you eat, to when you arrive and where you stay. You're going to have to be on top of every situation, so it's advisable to arrive as refreshed as possible. That doesn't necessarily mean to nap all the way. But you should take into consideration how altitude and pressurized air affect your body. It's a fact that some people suffer oxygen fatigue at higher altitudes. This is greatly increased by smoking. The effects of alcohol are also heightened by cabin pressure. One drink can feel like three or four, and slow down your body clock considerably. Stay away from anything that induces fatigue if you want to be fresh when you arrive.

Exercise can also help keep your energy level up, especially during long flights. We're not talking about stand-in-the-aisle calisthentics. There are things you can do in your seat to keep key joints flexible and circulation stimulated. You're going to be in for a lot of sitting on a business trip, in taxis, in conferences, in restaurants, and you'll be away from your usual workout routines. So you might as well start doing what you can to maintain fitness the moment your trip gets off the ground. You'll feel fresher and less fatigued if you devote at least 10 minutes a day to physical toning. Even if you use only 20% of muscle capacity, you'll be able to stay in condition. If you operate at 30% capacity, you'll actually be able to increase muscle strength.

For invisible, in-flight toning, try alternately flexing and relaxing different muscle groups from head to toe. Start with the left calf muscle, then the right. Tighten the left thigh, then the right. (Exercising leg muscles gives you a double bonus of helping to support the return of blood to the heart. This is especially important when you've been sitting for several hours.) Move up to the abdomen. Tighten and hold for a count of seven, then relax. Repeat in rhythm seven times. Tense the left buttock, then the right, hold both and release. Do the same tightening/relaxing procedure for arm muscles (squeeze the armrest if it helps), shoulders and back muscles. Then work on joint flexibility by rotating ankles, wrists and neck first four times to the left, then four times to the right. Practice isometrics by shaking hands with yourself and pushing against the palm of one hand with the opposite one. And, finally, leave your seat from time to time. A brief walk to the back of the plane will do wonders to relieve that cramped, cooped-up feeling.

Once you get to the privacy of your hotel room, add a few bending and stretching exercises. Increase isometrics by pressing against walls, door frames or desk chairs. Twist your torso, rotate your shoulders, use the stairs instead of an elevator every once in a while, and you'll find typical business trip fatigue vanishes—and a lot of tenseness with it.

YOUR HOME AWAY FROM HOME

Even if your very best friend from fourth grade lives in the town you'll be traveling to, never *ever* make arrangements to stay with friends for the duration of a business trip. The connotation is more vacation, no matter how hard you intend to work. You need to be near the center of activity, and you don't need to trouble yourself or your associates with special transportation arrangements to get you there. You also need a reliable message center. Your friend's husband (or child) answering their home phone might cause a great deal of confusion on the part of the caller—just who are these people, anyway? It would also be natural for associates to assume your evening hours are spoken for. Possibly beneficial business dinners just won't happen.

It's better form to book a hotel room as close to your meeting place as possible. If you wish to get recommendations from the people you'll be working with, show them you mean business by asking for the name of a nice hotel near their offices. There's a world of difference between that and saying "What's the best hotel in town?" It has to do with efficiency—and the way your firm spends money.

Make sure you have a guaranteed reservation at the hotel you do choose, and ask that a confirmation slip be sent to your office in advance of your departure. Bring this with you. It is also a good idea to make advance arrangements for billing. Don't automatically assume that a hotel will bill your company, even if it is a well-known, household name! If your firm has not done business with a particular hotel before, the desk clerk won't care how many business cards you wave in front of his face. He has his orders. And too often they say, "Without prior notification, on letterhead from a person in a position to authorize payment, no special billing arrangements will be honored." Even if the "person in authority" at your firm is *you*, some places are just not going to take your word for it as you're checking out. The trick is to get all necessary arrangements worked out in advance of your arrival at the hotel.

Once you have established billing procedure with a hotel, check out their check-out system. Knowing that they have express check-out (you drop your key in a box, they bill later) can save you peace of mind as the minutes of your last meeting tick off closer and closer to take-off time. You'll also want to know when to be out of your room. If you need a one- or two-hour extension beyond the hotel's check-out time, let them know in advance. Most hotels will try to accommodate you. If you don't ask, however, you're likely to get billed for an extra day.

ALONE AT LAST

The minute you've tipped the porter and the door closes behind you, unpack immediately. It may be the only ten minutes you'll have to yourself the entire trip. Plus, it gives you a headstart on getting the wrinkles out of your clothes. Hang really badly wrinkled garments over the shower rod and get the steam going. If you have the time, combine this with a quick shower. You'll feel fresher, less travel weary. If you've got to be someplace in twenty minutes, skip it for yourself, but do keep the water running to steam out wrinkles. The whole hang-up process will be a lot easier if you've carried a garment bag. Everything is already on hangers. If you carry a standard suitcase, always be certain to keep thin wire hangers and skirt hangers in the bottom of it. They should go with you on every trip. It's a rare hotel that provides enough hangers, and you can lose valuable time (sometimes even *days*) waiting for housekeeping to deliver extras.

You'll become more comfortable in your surroundings if you put everything in places similar to where you keep them at home. Fragrances on a dresser; body lotions, mouthwash, shampoos, hair dryer, etc., into the bathroom; cosmetics in drawers. Don't live out of a tote. It's too disorienting. Open a travel alarm, place it on a bedside table and get it ticking to the time zone you're in. Nobody wants to hear that you're still operating on your hometown time. And if you know that you don't sleep well in a strange hotel room, try bringing a small nightlight. It's better than trying to go to sleep with one room light on (as many traveling women admit to).

Get your professional papers in order, too. Set up a working area in your room, and get all business-related materials out. It's a good double-check to make sure you've brought everything you need: small calculator, files, extra tablets, reports, contracts, slides, etc. Organize all papers according to your meeting schedule, and you won't have to lug everything with you all the time. Some women we know prefer to do this before ever leaving the office, putting everything into separate legal-sized envelopes, clearly labeled with the day and the parties involved in each meeting: TUESDAY/10:30 A.M./SMITH & PARTNERS/1240 SOUTH AVENUE. It is a simple matter to organize the envelopes into chronological order upon unpacking. Then all you'll have to do is grab the right one at the right time, tuck it into your portfolio and go. Of course, if your week is going to be one long meeting with the same people day in and day out, count on lugging everything you brought with you all the time. With a freer structure, it's difficult to determine in advance exactly what you'll need when.

You can use your hotel for more than a place to retire to at the end of a long and wearying day. Take advantage of the services they may offer. Investigate any indoor recreational facilities: exercise equipment, jogging tracks, swimming pools, rooftop tennis courts. With the high priority many people place on maintaining physical fitness while traveling, the newer establishments (and some innovative older ones) have added excellent exercise accommodations. It doesn't hurt to throw a pair of jogging shorts and a T-shirt into your tote, just in case. An end-of-the-day workout will do more to rev your energy than a solitary 6:00 P.M. visit to the lobby's cocktail lounge.

Take a moment to glance at the list of other hotel services. It helps to know when the deadline is for valet cleaning (although a dry spot remover can take care of an unexpected stain or a soiled collar in an emergency. Always have an easy-to-use spot remover packed in your bag!) You might also be able to enlist the services of a secretary or translator, rent a typewriter, or have papers duplicated through your hotel. If these services aren't part of an official list, ask the manager anyway. At the very least, you may be permitted to use the equipment in the hotel's offices. The days of women guests only being interested in the hours of the beauty salon are long gone, and the hotel that caters successfully to the traveling business executive can usually come up with anything you need.

NO VISIBLE MEANS OF SUPPORT

Unless you travel with an entourage in tow (or at the very least, an assistant), you're on your own out there. Once you leave the security of your office support system, you need to be totally self-reliant. Nobody's going to be there to provide you with any more information than the facts you take with you. Nobody's going to be there to take care of annoying, minor details. And nobody's going to be there to handle arrangements, book appointments, make reservations. It's all up to you—as well as accomplishing the main purpose of your mission.

If you don't like dealing with details, and you can "borrow" the services of somebody's secretary, so much the better. But don't count on it. The best advice is the old Girl Scout motto: Be prepared. For *everything*. Travel with as much information as you think you'll need, then bring along a few extraneous files of information that is only slightly related. Analyze as many angles of inquiry as you can think of. Imagine several possible approaches to a problem, and bring along back-up material for every one. If you're giving an audio/visual presentation, bring along extras of key slides; a duplicate sound track; a second projector light; your own cassette tape recorder. Don't rely on the one they "think" they have somewhere around the office. Remember, too, that tapes break and projector bulbs burn out. Unless you want to repeat the entire script orally, be ready for any disaster. It can happen.

Be prepared to get yourself anywhere you need to go. Know in advance if it's advisable to rent a car. If it is, have one reserved and waiting at the airport. Study the map of the city for a few moments to familiarize yourself not only with the best route from the airport, but also where to turn the minute you hit the down-town area. If you need to, write key directions on a 3 x 5 card and tape it to the dashboard. You won't have a navigator sitting beside you to remind you of exit or street names. Even if you don't plan to rent a car, always carry a valid credit card and driver's license with you. You may find that you suddenly need a car. Don't ever put yourself in the position of having to rely on your working associates for any form of transportation. No matter how gracious they are, it's going to inconvenience someone to have to chauffeur you around from place to place. Plan ahead to know exactly the best way to get somewhere, and approximately how much time it will take. You'll simply sound uninformed if your excuse for arriving late is you didn't realize you had to *call* for a cab. (If you will be using this form of transportation, remember to have plenty of voucher slips or receipt forms ready for every cab driver to fill in.)

THE FOURTEEN-HOUR DAY

Because of the time constraints of a business trip, you're usually trying to accomplish your objective in less time than you would like to devote to it, but more time than you can afford to be away. The result: time telescoping. Normal eight-to-ten-hour days slide together into fourteen- or sixteen-hour marathons, with breakfast meetings, dinner appointments, or hotel room homework all squeezed in. You have to expect to be on-call and alert, even for those early morning calls from the home office when it's 10:00 A.M. their time, but only 7:00 A.M. where you are. If you've planned an excessively heavy schedule, the only "down-time" you may get could come when you're too tired to do anything with it except sleep. Don't count on sneaking away to see the sights of the city. Save touring for another time.

The reality of the situation after hours is often only room service and work. Although, in this chapter, we've included wardrobe tips on what to wear in case you're wined and dined, don't expect it. An invitation to a social function, even one related to business, is rare. You'll spend more nights staying in and preparing for the next day's meetings than you will at the best restaurants in town. So be sure to bring along something comfortable for late-night catch-up sessions in your room. If you do your best thinking in a ratty old robe, pack it!

WHAT TO WEAR . . . WHERE

Executive women living in the cities mentioned most often as business trip destinations give remarkably similar wardrobe advice. There is little difference between the best wardrobe to bring to Chicago, and the most appropriate clothes for Atlanta. Or Boston and Denver. Or Dallas and Washington, D.C. Although climate conditions do affect choices in fabric and color, there all distinctions end. Coast to coast and north to south, all women interviewed advocated very conservative, tailored travel wardrobes, with suits still the number one choice for business dealings.

In general, darker colors were preferred for formality and day-into-evening flexibility. Where colors were specified, navy led the field, followed by black, tan and grey. Fabric variations, such as tweed or seersucker, were considered too casual to be worth packing. "After all," one law partner noted, "nobody expects you to have an extensive wardrobe with you, so you might as well bring the fewest things that can give you the most mileage. And dark colors do just that."

Soft silk dresses were the number one choice for optional variety. Every executive surveyed said she would recommend packing at least two for days when you want to get out of a suit, or nights when you want to dress up a little. The versatility of a covered—not bare—silk dress seemed the answer for everything from cocktails through the dressiest evening. Although some women did differentiate between a silk "day" dress and a dressier cocktail style for the most formal occasions, all of them answered a resounding "NO" when asked if a woman need bring a long dress to their town. "In situations where other women may be wearing a long dress, a short cocktail dress is perfectly acceptable, where in the reverse situation, long wouldn't be," explained one executive. When it came to clothes for the more casual events that may occur during a business trip, having a sportier blazer along tied with packing a more relaxed skirt or a pair of pants. "It helps if you know what sort of occasion is being planned. Certainly, I'd pack pants if I knew I were going to a barbecue," a bank officer noted, "but, if I didn't know, I'd stick with a skirt. It's always safer."

All advocated carrying as few clothes as possible. "You have to remember, you'll probably be loaded down with papers, both in your briefcase and in your bag," a lawyer commented, "and you only have two hands. What goes by the board first is space for clothes." Other proponents of lightness pointed out that you have to be able to carry everything yourself *easily*. If you're traveling with a male associate, you don't want him to feel obligated to help you out with an obviously overweight bag. That puts you in a helpless position, and him in an awkward one.

Still, there are a few essentials that should always go with you, no matter how little space you have. Here's a quick checklist of the supplies travel-savvy professionals recommend packing:

TO TAKE

☐ Extra hangers	☐ Extra presentation equipment
☐ Travel alarm	☐ Emergency sewing repair kit
☐ Lightweight steamer	☐ Extra eyeglasses
☐ Small calculator	☐ Extra contact lenses
☐ Hair dryer	☐ Toiletries
☐ Fold-up umbrella	☐ Cosmetics
☐ Spot remover	☐ Small scissors
☐ Extra work materials	☐ Plastic bags
	☐ Nail polish remover pads

You can probably add a few personal items to this list that follow you everywhere, as well. Some women insist on taking their own radios, in case the hotel room is without one. Others take special exercise tapes and a recorder to play them on. Still others wouldn't go anywhere without a set of electric hair rollers. All of these items add weight—and you still haven't packed a thing to wear!

Another essential that takes up no space at all, but is literally worth its weight in gold is a credit card. You really shouldn't leave home without one. What you can leave without, however, in spite of what the commercials say, is travelers' checks. With a good credit card for a companion, you shouldn't need more than a couple hundred dollars *in cash*. Cashing endless $20 checks is too time consuming and totally unnecessary. Of course, if you feel you must carry large amounts of cash, for whatever reason, then travelers' checks would be advisable. Otherwise, our advice is to skip them.

Individual wardrobe Trip Tips follow for the major cities most often mentioned as destinations by the executive women we surveyed: Atlanta, Boston, Chicago, Cleveland, Dallas, Denver, Los Angeles, Miami, New York, Pittsburgh, San Francisco, and Washington, D.C. If your plans call for travel to any one of these places, here's the best advice on what to bring, where to stay and where to entertain from women professionals living—and working—in each of those cities.

WHAT'S THE WEATHER LIKE THERE

Even your best business look will wilt if you've packed the wrong fabrics for the weather conditions of the city you're visiting. And neglecting essentials like umbrellas, gloves and warm wool mufflers during certain seasons can make you wish you'd stayed at home. To help you know when to throw in the raincoat, included are average temperature and precipitation charts, month by month, for each of the cities in our Trip Tip Guides.

TRIP TIP GUIDE

ATLANTA

"Atlanta is not as casual as one might think. Business dressing is very conservative here; always suits, sometimes tailored dresses. On a professional level, there's nothing relaxed about our way of dressing. Even seersucker is considered too informal. The best colors to wear are navy, grey or tan. I'd wear a suit and a silk blouse for business, and the same business attire would work at all the good restaurants. Sometimes you will see long dresses at a concert, but you could still get away with a good suit and blouse for most evening events. If something is going to be really dressy, I'd advise a cocktail dress, but definitely a covered-up style. If you're going to a casual affair at someone's home, you could wear a sundress, or a blazer with either pants or a skirt.

"You don't see a lot of fur in the winter here. Even though it can get down to the forties, I'd still advise leaving your fur coat at home.

"It's best to depend on cabs for transportation. You do have to call them, but in the long run it's easier than renting a car. You can expect to pay about $13 from the airport to downtown."

Executive Accommodations

Atlanta Hilton (downtown)
255 Courtland & Harris Streets
Atlanta, Georgia 30043
(404) 659-2000

Colony Square Hotel (downtown)
Peachtree at 14th Street NE
Atlanta, Georgia 30361
(404) 892-6000

Dunfey Hotel
1750 Commerce Dr. NW
Atlanta, Georgia 30381
(404) 351-6100

Guest Quarters
Perimeter Center 111 Perimeter Center West
Atlanta, Georgia 30346
(404) 396-6800

or

7000 Roswell Road NW
Atlanta, Georgia 30328
(404) 394-6300

Hyatt Regency (downtown)
265 Peachtree Street NE
Atlanta, Georgia 30021
(404) 577-1234

Omni International (downtown)
400 S. Omni International
Atlanta, Georgia 30335
(404) 659-0000

Peachtree Plaza
Peach & International Blvd. NE
Atlanta, Georgia 30303
(404) 659-1400

Sheraton Century Center
2000 Century Blvd. NE
Atlanta, Georgia 30345
(404) 325-0000

Best Bookings

Halpern's
3393 Peachtree Road
Lenox Square Mall
(404) 231-5050
Lunch: Monday–Saturday
Dinner: Monday–Saturday
Serving 11:00 A.M.–9:30 P.M. No reservations. Fresh seafood and American cuisine. Moderate to expensive.

Hedgerose Heights Inn
490 East Ferry Paces Road
(404) 325-3081
Dinner only, two settings, reservations required.
Monday–Thursday, 7:00 or 9:00 P.M.
Friday–Sunday, 8:00 P.M. or 9:30 P.M.
Small, intimate restaurant located in a mansion setting. International cuisine. À la carte menus. Moderate to expensive.

Herren's
84 Luckie Street, N.W.
(404) 524-4709
Lunch: Monday–Friday, 11:00 A.M.–3:00 P.M.
Dinner; Monday–Friday, 5:00 P.M.–9:30 P.M. (Saturday until 10:00 P.M.)
Reservations suggested for dinner. Steaks, seafood, American cuisine. Moderate.

Midnight Sun
Peachtree Center Garden Mall
Peachtree Plaza
(404) 577-5050
Lunch: Monday–Friday, 11:30 A.M.–2:30 P.M.
Dinner: Monday–Sunday, 7:00 P.M.–10:30 P.M.
Reservations required. International cuisine. Moderate to expensive.

Nikolai's Roof
Atlanta Hilton Hotel
255 Courtland & Harris Streets
(404) 659-2000
Dinner only: Monday–Sunday, 6:30 P.M. and 9:30 P.M. seatings (6:00 P.M. and 9:00 P.M. after Labor Day). Reservations required. French cuisine with Russian specialties. Five-course meal. Prix fixe.

	Average Temperature	Average Rainfall
December	43.5	4.24
January	42.4	4.34
February	45	4.41
March	51.1	5.84
April	61.1	4.61
May	69.1	3.71
June	75.6	3.67
July	78	4.9
August	77.5	3.54
September	72.3	3.15
October	62.4	2.5
November	51.4	3.43

Atlanta Chamber of Commerce (404) 521-8045

TRIP TIP GUIDE

BOSTON

"People make the mistake of packing ultra-conservative clothes when they're coming to Boston, although there's really no need for it. If you stick to well-tailored suits in conservative colors, you'll be set. You can't go wrong with one navy and one black suit with an assortment of dressy silk blouses. This will take you from a boardroom to a banquet. Simple, elegant suits will go everywhere, from day through dinner. Even if your plans include the theatre or a concert in the evening. Pants and a blazer are fine for casual occasions; I wouldn't recommend wearing a dress. You should bring along a cocktail dress if you know there's going to be a dressy event, but avoid the slinky, strappy styles.

"Getting around Boston can be confusing if you've rented a car. I'd opt for cabs. They're expensive, but very easy to get. A trip from the airport to downtown could run around $12, before tipping."

Executive Accommodations

Hyatt Regency
575 Memorial Drive
Cambridge, Massachusetts 02139

(617) 492-1234
(800) 228-9000

Parker House
600 School Street
Boston, Massachusetts 02107
(617) 227-8600
(800) 228-2121

Ritz Carlton
15 Arlington Street
Boston, Massachusetts 02117
(800) 225-7620

Best Bookings

Bay Tower Club
60 State Street
(617) 723-1666
Lunch: Members only
Dinner: Monday–Saturday, 5:00 P.M.–9:30 P.M. (10:00 P.M. weekends).
Continental cuisine. Moderate to expensive.

Cybelle's on the Waterfront
240 Commercial Street
(617) 523-1126
Lunch and Dinner: 11:00 A.M.–11:00 P.M. Reservations required on Saturday and
Sunday only. Northern Italian and French cuisine. Moderate.

Lockobers
3 Winter Place
(617) 542-1340
Lunch and Dinner: Monday–Saturday, 11:00 A.M.–10:00 P.M.
Reservations required. Continental cuisine. Moderate.

Maison Robert
45 School Street
(617) 227-3370
Lunch: Monday–Friday, 11:30 A.M.–2:30 P.M. Reservations required.
Dinner: Monday–Saturday, 5:30 P.M.–9:30 P.M. Reservations required.
French cuisine. Moderate.

	Average Temperature	Average Rainfall
December	33	4.24
January	29.2	3.69
February	30.4	3.54
March	38.1	4.01
April	48.6	3.49
May	58.6	3.47
June	68	3.19
July	73.3	2.74
August	71.3	3.46
September	64.5	3.16
October	55.4	3.02
November	45.2	4.51

Boston Chamber of Commerce (617) 426-1250

TRIP TIP GUIDE

CHICAGO

"Because the weather is variable in Chicago, I'd always make sure I packed a raincoat—summer or winter. When the weather turns, it can get pretty windy and raw. Conservative business looks work here, sometimes to the point of being severe. You'll see more polyester here than in the East. And the blouses for business are a bit more tailored. Ruffles haven't quite caught on as part of a professional image. Women here are going through an inconspicuous dressing phase. They'd never wear pants or culottes, and the ubiquitous suit goes just about everywhere—out to dinner, out for the evening. Cocktail looks are pretty conservative, too. A dress is fine as long as it's not too bare. For casual dressing, I'd wear a skirt and sweater, maybe a blazer or dress, but no pants.

"Cabs are easy to get everywhere. You wouldn't want to rent a car. The fare from the airport to the loop is about $20.

"Breakfast meetings are more the norm in Chicago than dinner engagements. Commuters would rather get in earlier than stay in later at night. A lot of entertaining goes on at luncheon clubs. This doesn't exclude the out-of-town visitor entirely. One of the nicest ones for instance, the Lake Shore Tower Club, is open to all United Red Carpet Club members."

Executive Accommodations

Ambassador East
1301 N. State Parkway
Chicago, Illinois 60610
(800) 228-2121

Ambassador West
1300 N. State Parkway
Chicago, Illinois 60610
(312) 621-8090

Drake
140 East Walton
Chicago, Illinois 60611
(312) 787-2200
(800) 223-1146

Raphael
201 East Delaware Place
Chicago, Illinois 60611
(312) 943-5000

Ritz Carlton
160 East Pearson Street
Chicago, Illinois 60611
(312) 266-1000
(800) 828-1188

Tremont
100 East Chestnut Street
Chicago, Illinois 60611
(312) 751-1900
(800) 621-8133

The Whitehall
105 East Delaware Place
Chicago, Illinois 60611
(312) 944-6300

Best Bookings

The Cape Cod Room at the Drake
Michigan & Walden Streets
(312) 787-2200

Lunch and Dinner: Monday–Sunday, 12:00 noon–11:00 P.M.
Reservations required. Seafood and steak. Moderate to expensive.

Chez Paul
660 North Rush
(312) 944-6680
Lunch: Monday–Friday, 11:30 A.M.–2:30 P.M.
Dinner: Saturday and Sunday, 5:30 P.M.–10:00 P.M.
Reservations required. French and Continental cuisine. Moderate.

Le Français
269 South Milwaukee
Wheeling, Illinois
(312) 541-7470
Dinner only: Tuesday–Sunday, 6:30 P.M., 9:15 P.M. or 9:30 P.M.
Reservations required. French cuisine. Expensive.

The Palm
181 East Lake Shore Drive
(312) 944-0135
Lunch: Monday–Friday, 12:00 noon–3:00 P.M.
Dinner: Monday–Saturday, 5:00 P.M.–10:00 P.M.
Reservations required. Steaks, lobster, some Italian dishes.
Moderate to expensive.

Perroquet
70 East Walton Street
(312) 944-7990
Lunch: Monday–Friday, 12:00 noon–3:00 P.M.
Dinner: Monday–Saturday, 6:00 P.M.–10:00 P.M.
Reservations required. French cuisine. Prix fixe: $38.50 for dinner, $15.75 for
lunch, drinks and gratuities extra.

The Pump Room
Ambassador East Hotel
1301 North State Parkway
(312) 266-0360
Breakfast, Lunch and Dinner: 7:00 A.M.–11:00 P.M.
Reservations required. French nouvelle cuisine. Moderate.
Special Sunday Brunch 10:00 A.M.–2:30 P.M., $10.95 for five courses.

	Average Temperature	Average Rainfall
December	29.3	2.10
January	24.5	1.93
February	27.2	1.80
March	36.5	2.70
April	47.9	3.14
May	58.3	3.49
June	68.4	3.69
July	73.8	3.43
August	72.5	3.15
September	65.6	3.13
October	54.4	2.59
November	40.4	2.32

Chicago Chamber of Commerce (312) 786-0111

TRIP TIP GUIDE

CLEVELAND

I'd avoid the grey pinstripe "power" look, and just wear a nice conservative suit or a dress and jacket. There's no stigma against synthetics, especially in blouses, although a silk blouse with a suit is as dressy as you need to get. I'd wear this to give a presentation in, or to go out to dinner in. You might want to bring a conservative dress for evening activities, and a casual skirt to wear for informal events.

I think a high-pressure, perfectly accessorized look might intimidate a lot of professionals here. At least they'd be concentrating more on what you were wearing, rather than on what you were saying. If you look more conservative than fashionable, you'll do better.

Taxis have to be called for, and the fare from the airport is about $15. It's easier to get around if you rent a car."

Executive Accommodations

Airport Marriott
4277 W. 150th Street
Cleveland, Ohio 44135
(800) 228-9290

Cleveland Hilton South
1-77 Rockside Road
Cleveland, Ohio 44130
(216) 447-1300

Marriott Inn East
3663 Park East Drive
Beachwood, Ohio 44122
(216) 464-5950
(800) 228-9290

Stouffer's Inn on the Square
24 Public Square
Cleveland, Ohio 44113
(216) 696-5600
(800) 362-6100

Best Bookings

Au Provence
2195 Lee Road
(216) 321-9511
Dinner only: Monday–Saturday, 6:30 P.M. or 9:15 P.M. seating. Reservations required on Saturday only. French and American cuisine. Moderate to expensive.

French Connection
Stouffer's Inn on the Square
24 Public Square
(216) 696-5600
Lunch: Monday–Friday, 11:30 A.M.–1:30 P.M.
Dinner: Monday–Saturday, 6:00 P.M.–9:30 P.M. Reservations required. French and American cuisine. Moderate to expensive.

Giovanni's
255 50 Chagrin Blvd.
(216) 831-8625
Lunch: Monday–Friday, 11:30 A.M.–3:00 P.M.
Dinner: Monday–Friday, 5:30 P.M.–9:45 P.M., Saturday until 10:30 P.M. Reservations required. Northern Italian cuisine. Moderate to expensive.

Wagonwheel
131 14 Woodland
(216) 561-6900
Dinner only: Monday–Friday, 6:00 P.M.–10:00 P.M. Saturday until 11:00 P.M.

Reservations suggested. Necessary on weekends. French cuisine. Moderate to expensive.

	Average Temperature	*Average Rainfall*
December	30.5	2.34
January	28.3	2.67
February	28.4	2.33
March	35.1	3.13
April	47.0	3.41
May	57.9	3.52
June	69.7	3.43
July	71.8	3.31
August	70.4	3.28
September	64.1	2.90
October	53.4	2.42
November	41.2	2.61

Cleveland Chamber of Commerce (216) 621-3300

TRIP TIP GUIDE

DALLAS

"Although you will have to bring lighter-weight clothes if you're coming from the north, don't sacrifice formality. In Dallas, a navy blue suit with a silk blouse is always safest for business meetings. Silk dresses will do, too, but I'd definitely wear a suit if I were giving a speech or a presentation. Whatever you wear to work is fine for going out to dinner, although you can be more casual at some places. Casual here means a skirt or slacks. Leave the tweed blazers at home! You can wear strappy cocktail dresses and dressy shoes to more formal evening occasions, but the invitation really has to say dressy. Otherwise, you'll be too fussy for most places. And you'll never need a long dress!

"Take a taxi from the airport ($22), and then rent a car to get you to your daily appointments. It's very hard to get a cab.

"No matter what time of year you come to Dallas, the best tip is to always pack a raincoat."

Executive Accommodations

Fairmont Hotel
Akard at Ross
Dallas, Texas 75201
(214) 748-5454

Hyatt Regency
300 Reunion Blvd.
Dallas, Texas 75207
(214) 651-1234
(800) 228-9000

Loew's Anatole
2201 Stemmons Freeway
Dallas, Texas 75207
(214) 748-1200
(800) 223-0888

Best Bookings

Calluaud's
2619 McKinney Avenue
(214) 823-5380
Dinner only: Monday–Saturday, 6:00 P.M.–10:00 P.M. Reservations suggested, required on weekends. French cuisine. Expensive.

Jean Claude's
2404 Cedar Springs (corner of Maple Street)
(214) 653-1823
Dinner only: Monday–Saturday, 6:00 P.M. and 9:00 P.M. Reservations required: 2–4 weeks in advance for Fridays, 4–6 weeks in advance for Saturdays. Prix Fixe: $29.00. French nouvelle cuisine.

Pyramid Room at the Fairmont Hotel
Ross & Akard Streets
(214) 748-5454
Lunch: Monday–Friday, 11:30 A.M.–2:00 P.M.
Dinner: Monday–Sunday, 6:00 P.M.–11:00 P.M.
Reservations required. Continental cuisine. Moderate to expensive.

	Average Temperature	Average Rainfall
December	47.9	1.82
January	44.8	1.80
February	48.7	2.36
March	55.0	2.54
April	65.2	4.30
May	72.5	4.47
June	80.6	3.05
July	84.8	1.84
August	84.9	2.26
September	77.7	3.15
October	67.6	2.68
November	55.8	2.03

Dallas Chamber of Commerce (214) 651-1020

TRIP TIP GUIDE

DENVER

"All you need to survive here are suits and silk dresses. Depending on the length of your stay, one or two suits, a change of silk blouses, and two silk dresses should do it. I'd wear the dresses in the evening, although suits are perfectly acceptable at any restaurant. If you know in advance that something casual is planned, you might want to pack an extra blazer and skirt, or a pair of pants. Cocktail dresses are about as dressy as anyone gets, but they're worn for specific events, never just out to a nice restaurant, or to a concert.

"Getting around in downtown Denver can be a bit tricky. It's best to cab or limo to and from the airport (cabfare is about $8), but once you get in, it's more convenient to have your own car, even if parking can sometimes be a problem.

Executive Accommodations

Brown Palace Hotel
321 17th Street
Denver, Colorado 80202
(303) 825-3111

Denver Hilton
1550 Court Place
Denver, Colorado 80202
(303) 893-3333

The Denver Marriott City Center
1701 California Street
Denver, Colorado 80202
(303) 825-1300

Best Bookings

Cafe Giovanni
1515 Market Street (downtown)
(303) 825-6555
Lunch: Monday–Friday, 11:30 A.M.–3:00 P.M.
Dinner: Monday–Saturday, 5:30P.M.–11:30P.M. Reservations required. Continental cuisine, á la Carte menu. Moderate

Manhattan Cafe
1620 Market Street
(303) 893-0951
Lunch: Monday–Saturday, 11:00A.M.–3:00 P.M.
Dinner: Monday–Thursday, 5:30 P.M.–11:00 P.M., Friday and Saturday, until 11:30 P.M. Reservations required. Seafood and steaks. Moderate.

Marquis Room at the Fairmont
Fairmont Hotel
1750 Welton Street
(303) 571-5825
Lunch: Monday–Sunday, 11:30A.M.–2:00 P.M.
Dinner: Monday–Sunday, 6:00 P.M.–11:00 P.M. Reservations required. French cuisine. Considered by some to be the "best restaurant in town". Expensive.

The Plum Tree Cafe
92 South Pennsylvania
(303) 722-4556
Lunch: Tuesday–Saturday, 11:30 A.M.–2:00 P.M.
Dinner: Tuesday–Thursday, 5:30 P.M.–10:00 P.M. Friday and Saturday, until 10:30 P.M. Reservations required for lunch only. American cuisine, seafood. Moderate.

Refresher Courses

The following facilities are available for out-of-town visitors, although you may have to call ahead to make a reservation.

International Athletic Club
(303) 623-2100
Racquetball courts, weight machines, running track, sauna, whirlpool, fitness classes, steam room, rooftop sun deck, pro shop, massages, beauty salon. Open to guests of several hotels; check to see if yours is included. $10.

International Health Club
(303) 696-9313
Heated pool, gym, jogging track, racquetball and squash courts, weight machines, steam and whirlpool baths, sauna. Open to guests of Ramada Renaissance (800 228-2828) for $10.

Sheraton Denver Technological Center Recreation Center
(800) 325-3535
Indoor pool, whirlpool, steam, sauna, weight room, racquetball courts, pro shop, aquanastics classes. $6.00

Stapleton Plaza Hotel and Athletic Center
(303) 321-9043
Rooftop sundeck and jogging track, weight machines, racquetball courts, sauna, co-ed steam room, whirlpool, heated outdoor pool, aerobics classes, pro shop. Hotel guests, $3. All others, $8.50.

Yoga & Fitness Center
(303) 320-6310
Classes for $5.50, or private sessions in your hotel room for $20/hour.

	Average Temperature	Average Rainfall
December	33	0.43
January	30	0.61
February	33	0.67
March	37	1.21
April	48	1.93
May	57	2.64
June	66	1.93
July	73	1.78
August	72	1.29
September	63	1.13
October	52	1.13
November	39	0.76

Denver Chamber of Commerce (303) 534-3211

TRIP TIP GUIDE

LOS ANGELES

"Although the same principles of business dressing hold true in Los Angeles, the style is somewhat more relaxed. It's more of a blend of conservative and sporty. If we wear suits, they're softer, not man-tailored at all. Fashion enters into our choices a little more. I think I'd bring more dresses than suits to L.A. Nobody wears suits to restaurants or out to evening concerts or plays. You'll need a silk dress for this. And you can wear a dress with equal confidence to all your business activities, too. Bring along a neutral blazer or jacket that works with everything, however. Depending on the season, mornings can be cloudy and cool, and once the sun goes down, it cools off fast. Be sure your dresses for evening activities are coordinated with some sort of cover-up.

"Casual wear here can mean anything from very informal to a very put-together look. For casual business occasions, I'd feel safest bringing a good pair of slacks, maybe silk, and a dyed-to-match, coordinated silk top. Or a cotton or linen skirt with a soft, string knit sweater. We tend to "dress up" a little more casually, too. The best cocktail dress to bring—if you know there's going to be a special event—is something strappy with a shawl for the cool night air or the air conditioning. Covered-up velvets or conservative crêpes are just not the right mood for out here. And be sure to bring strappy heels to wear with this look. Don't count on daytime pumps to go with everything. You'll stick out like a visiting fireman!

"You've got to rent a car to get around in Los Angeles. Everything is spread out, and at least a half an hour away on the freeway. Your best bet is to just pick one up at the airport. A cab ride from there could run between $20 and $30 plus tip, depending on which part of town you're going to."

Executive Accommodations

Beverly Hills Comstock Hotel
10300 Wilshire Blvd.
Los Angeles, California 90024
(213) 275-5575 (call collect)

Beverly Wilshire Hotel
Wilshire Blvd. at Rodeo Drive
Beverly Hills, California 90212
(213) 275-4282
(800) 421-4354

Bonaventure
Fifth & Figueroa Streets
Los Angeles, California 90071
(800) 228-3000

Century Plaza
Avenue of the Stars
Los Angeles, California 90067
(800) 228-3000

Hyatt Regency
Broadway Plaza
711 South Hope Street (downtown L.A.)
Los Angeles, California 90017
(800) 228-9000

Best Bookings

Chasen's
9039 Beverly Blvd.
Los Angeles, California
(213) 271-2168
Dinner only: Tuesday–Sunday, 6:00 P.M.–11:00 P.M. Reservations required. Continental cuisine. Moderate to expensive.

La Scala
9455 Little Santa Monica Blvd.
Beverly Hills, California
(213) 275-0579
Lunch: Monday–Friday, 11:30 A.M.–2:30 P.M.
Dinner: Monday–Friday, 5:30P.M.–10:30 P.M., Saturday, 5:30 P.M.–12:00 Midnight. Reservations required. Northern Italian cuisine and fresh fish. Moderate to expensive.

The Bistro Gardens
176 N. Cannon Drive
Beverly Hills, California
(213) 555-3900
Lunch: Monday–Saturday, 11:30 A.M.–3:00 P.M.
Dinner: Monday–Saturday, 6:00 P.M.–12:00 P.M. Reservations suggested. European and Continental cuisine. Moderate.

Jimmy's
201 Moreno Drive
Beverly Hills, California
(213) 879-2394
Lunch: Monday–Friday, 11:30 A.M.–3:00 P.M.
Dinner: Monday–Saturday, 6:00 P.M.–12:00 P.M.
Reservations necessary. French and Continental cuisine. Moderate to expensive.

Refresher Courses

The following facilities are available for out-of-town visitors, although you may have to call ahead to make a reservation.

Biltmore Hotel Health Club
(213) 477-8231
Heated swimming pool, steam room, Nautilus equipment, masseur, hair dryers and private showers. Open to guests of the Biltmore weekdays, from 6:30 A.M.–8:00 P.M. Saturdays, 10:00 A.M.–6:00 P.M.

Jane Fonda's Workout
(213) 652-9464
Single classes for visiting businesswomen. Slow stretching to strenuous jazz. $6.50 each.

	Average Temperature	*Average Rainfall*
December	57.5	2.66
January	55.9	3.4
February	56.9	3.4
March	58.5	2.5
April	60.7	1.1
May	63.2	0.31
June	66.9	0.07
July	71.3	0.01
August	72.2	0.03
September	70.6	0.21
October	66.5	0.52
November	62.2	0.32

Los Angeles Chamber of Commerce (213) 629-0711

TRIP TIP GUIDE

MIAMI

"The weight of the clothes you bring to Miami is an important consideration. It can get very hot and sticky here, especially in the summer months. And the humidity doesn't go down, even at night. If you're going to bring suits, go for lightweight fabrics and lighter colors. They're good all year 'round. I'd definitely recommend dresses for going to restaurants or out for the evening, but a suit is still the best thing to wear for business. We tend to dress down a little here, however. You don't have to wear the buttoned-up, bow-at-the-throat look. Even for cocktail occasions, you wouldn't want anything too flashy or décolleté. A silk dress is fine. For a casual look, I'd pack a blazer and polo shirt with either a skirt or khaki pants. No jeans. Sports are extremely popular here, and it may be a way some business associates entertain. I wouldn't come to Miami without a swimsuit, tennis dress or golf skirt. You never know when you'll get an invitation to participate in an outdoor activity. The one item to always bring with you, at least from September through May, is an umbrella. We have a lot of rain here, no matter what the travel agents say. Usually, it comes and goes quickly, but you still wouldn't want to get caught in a pre-hurricane downpour!

"Taxis must be called for, so it's best to simply rent a car right at the airport. If you do cab it to downtown Miami, plan to spend around $12 for the ride."

Executive Accommodations

Doral Hotel & Country Club
4400 NW 87th Avenue
Miami, Florida 33178
(305) 592-2000
(800) 327-6334

Fontainebleau Hilton
4441 Collins Avenue
Miami Beach, Florida 33140
(305) 538-2000

The 4 Ambassadors Hotel
801 South Bayshore Drive
Miami, Florida 33131
(305) 377-1966
(800) 327-5708

Hyatt Regency
400 SE 2nd Avenue
Miami, Florida 33138
(305) 358-1234
(800) 228-9000

Omni International
1601 Biscayne Blvd.
Miami, Florida 33132
(305) 374-0000
(800) 241-5500

Best Bookings

Brasserie de Paris
250 N.E. Three Street
Miami
(Everglades Hotel)
(305) 374-0122
Lunch: Monday–Friday, 11:30 A.M.–3:00 P.M.
Dinner: Monday–Saturday, 6:00 P.M.–11:00 P.M. Reservations required. French cuisine. Moderate to expensive.

La Maison
1601 Biscayne Blvd.
Miami
(Omni Hotel)
(305) 374-4399
Dinner only: Tuesday–Saturday, 6:00 P.M.–11:00 P.M. Reservations required. French cuisine. Expensive.

Reflections on the Bay
310 NE Mia Marina
(305) 371-6433
Lunch: Monday–Friday 12:00 Noon–3:00 P.M.
Dinner: Monday–Saturday, 6:00 P.M.–10:00 P.M.
Brunch: Sunday, 12:00 Noon–4:00 P.M. Reservations required. American gourmet and seafood. Moderate to expensive.

The Two Dragons
350 Ocean Drive
(Sonesta Beach Hotel)
Key Biscayne
(305) 361-2021
Dinner only: Monday–Saturday, 6:00 P.M.–11:00 P.M. Reservations required. Chinese and Japanese cuisine. Moderate to expensive.

Victoria Station
7541 North Kendall Drive
Miami
(305) 667-3010
Lunch: Monday–Thursday, 11:00 A.M.–4:00 P.M.
Dinner: Monday–Sunday 5:00 P.M.–10:00 P.M. Reservations required for dinner. Steaks, seafood, Continental cuisine. Moderate.

	Average Temperature	*Average Rainfall*
December	67.7	1.85
January	66.6	2.13
February	67.2	2.04
March	70.5	2.22
April	74.4	3.26
May	77.3	5.66
June	83.2	8.53
July	81.8	6.48
August	82.2	6.36
September	81.1	8.76
October	77.3	8.61
November	71.8	2.58

Miami Chamber of Commerce (305) 350-7700

TRIP TIP GUIDE

NEW YORK

"Dark suits are going to take you most places in New York, daytime to evening. For a five-day stay, I'd pack at least two and wear one. Anything in the navy, grey (charcoal to medium) or black range would be both businesslike and versatile, particularly if you bring several different styles of blouses. In the summer months you might wish to lighten the color scheme a bit, switching into beiges, lighter blues or medium pastels, but avoid Easter egg colors. They have "tourist" written all over them! What's really seasonless and good for almost any situation in New York is a black crêpe suit. It's conservative by day, and can be dressed up with a lace or satin blouse and a gold belt for any evening function. I'd wear this to restaurants, the theatre, a cocktail party. Of course, silk dresses can serve the same purpose. Although you can get as fashionably dressy as you like in this town, I'd leave the lamé knickers at home for business-related events! And don't bring your barest cocktail dresses, either. Stick to fairly conservative, covered silks. You might add a livelier blazer and skirt for casual plans, but no cullottes or pants, unless you know the people you'll be with. You could also opt to replace one of your suits with a good gabardine skirt and tailored blazer, for more informal business hours.

"Unless it's the middle of winter or the middle of summer, save enough space in your bag to bring along some survival essentials: like a fold-up umbrella, a trench coat and wool beret. Always be prepared for a raw or cold snap, as early as September, and sometimes as late as April! You'll walk a lot in New York, and the street is a terrible place to be stranded in the middle of a downpour! Don't expect a cab to save you. They disappear at the first sign of rain. A beret can fold up flat, tuck into a trenchcoat pocket, and save your appearance (not to mention your health) while you're rushing to your next appointment. A comfortable pair of shoes you can walk in is also essential, no matter what the season! It's so important in New York that I'd plan the color scheme of my travel wardrobe around one pair of black and one pair of navy (or other-colored) shoes. Do bring two pair, and make sure one works for evening. I'd also tuck a small black clutch into my bag if I expected to go out at night. Your classic leather shoulderbag can look out of place.

"It is easy to get around in Manhattan, whether by foot or by cab. The last thing you'd want is a car; parking can be a problem and driving can be unsettling. Cabs can be hailed everywhere, all the time. The fare from LaGuardia airport to midtown can run around $15–$20; from JFK airport, around $25–$30 before tipping."

Executive Accommodations

Carlyle Hotel
35 East 76th Street (on Madison Avenue)
New York, New York 10021
(212) 744-1600

Halloran House
525 Lexington Avenue
New York, New York 10017
(212) 755-4000

The Helmsley Palace
455 Madison Avenue
New York, New York 10022
(212) 888-7000

Hotel Inter-Continental
111 East 48th Street
New York, New York 10017
(212) 755-5900

Nova-Park Gotham
700 Fifth Avenue
New York, New York 10019
(212) 247-2200

The Plaza
768 Fifth Avenue
New York, New York 10019
(212) 759-3000

The St. Regis Sheraton
2 East 55th Street
New York, New York 10022
(212) 753-4500

UN Plaza Hotel
1 UN Plaza
New York, New York 10017
(212) 355-3400

The Waldorf
301 Park Avenue
New York, New York 10022
(212) 355-3000

Best Bookings

Christ Cella
160 East 46th Street
(212) 697-2479
Lunch: Monday–Friday, 11:45 A.M.–2:30 P.M.
Dinner: Monday–Saturday, 5:00 P.M.–10:30 P.M. Reservations necessary for lunch, suggested for dinner. Steaks, Continental cuisine. Moderate.

Le Cirque
58 East 65th Street
(212) 794-9292
Lunch: Monday–Saturday, 12:00 Noon–2:30 P.M.
Dinner: Monday–Saturday, 6:00 P.M.–10:15 P.M. Reservations required. French cuisine. Expensive.

La Côte Basque
5 East 55th Street
(212) 688-6525
Lunch: Monday–Saturday, 12:00 P.M.–2:30 P.M.
Dinner: Monday–Saturday, 6:00 P.M.–10:30 P.M. Reservations required. French haute cuisine. Expensive.

The Edwardian Room at the Plaza
Plaza Hotel
768 Fifth Avenue at 59th Street
(212) 759-3000

Lunch: Monday–Sunday, 12:00 Noon–3:00 P.M.
Dinner: Monday–Sunday, 5:30 P.M.–12:30 P.M. Reservations suggested. French and Continental cuisine. Moderate to expensive.

The Four Seasons
99 East 52nd Street
(212) 754-9494
Lunch: Monday–Saturday, 12:00 Noon –2:30 P.M.
Dinner: Monday–Saturday, 5:00 P.M.–11:00 P.M. Reservations required. International haute cuisine. Expensive.

Le Madrigal
216 East 53rd Street
(212) 355-0322
Lunch: Monday–Friday, 12:00 Noon–2:15 P.M.
Dinner: Monday–Saturday, 6:00 P.M.–10:15 P.M. Reservations required. French cuisine. Expensive.

The Palm
837 Second Avenue
(212) 599-9192
Lunch: Monday–Friday, 12:00 Noon–5:00 P.M.
Dinner: Monday–Saturday, 5:00 P.M.–10:45 P.M. (Saturday until 11:00 P.M.) Reservations for lunch only. Continental steak house, giant lobster, casual atmosphere. Moderate to expensive.

Le Perigord
405 East 52nd Street
(212) 755-6244
Lunch: Monday–Friday, 12:00 Noon–3:00 P.M.
Dinner: Monday–Saturday, 5:30 P.M.–10:30 P.M. (On Sunday after Labor Day) Reservations required. French cuisine. Prix fixe: $23 for lunch, $36 for dinner; drinks, wine and gratuities extra.

Le Trianon
The Helmsley Palace
455 Madison Avenue
(212) 888-7000
Breakfast: Monday–Sunday, 7:00 A.M.–11:00 A.M.
Lunch: Monday–Sunday, 12:00 Noon–2:30 P.M.
Dinner: Monday–Sunday, 5:30 P.M.–10:00 P.M. (a light supper menu is available from 10:00 P.M.–12:00 Midnight) Reservations required for lunch, suggested for dinner. Continental cuisine. Moderate.

The "21" Club
21 West 52nd Street
(212) 582-7200

Lunch: Monday–Friday, 12:00 Noon–3:00 P.M.
Dinner: Monday–Friday, 5:30 P.M.–11:00 P.M. (On Saturday, after Labor Day)
Reservations required. International Cuisine. Moderate to expensive.

Meet-To-Eat Places between Lunch and Dinner

When you don't want to meet in a bar, suggest taking tea at one of the following places. You'll have a selection of light sandwiches and pastries to sustain you.

The Helmsley Palace
455 Madison Avenue
(212) 888-7000
Tea is served in the Gold Room from 2:30 P.M.–6:00 P.M. Make reservations. Cocktails are served from 6:00 P.M.

The Plaza Hotel
768 Fifth Avenue
(212) 759-3000
Tea is served in the Palm Court from 3:30 P.M.–7:00 P.M. Cocktails are served from 8:00 P.M.–12:30 A.M. Reservations are not necessary.

Refresher Courses

The following facilities are available for out-of-town visitors, although you may have to call ahead for a reservation.

Hudson Health Club
(212) 586-8630
Heated pool, jogging track, universal gym, table tennis, exercise classes, sauna/steam room. Fee $5. For $10 more, you will get a 3-month storage locker for frequent visitors.

New York Health & Racquet Club
(212) 683-9800
Swimming pool, sauna/steam room, whirlpool, jogging machines, sunlamps, classes in calisthenics, yoga, aerobics. Open to guests of members at $25/day. $10 more an hour for squash and racquetball courts.

Rivereast Health Club
(212) 689-4043
Swimming pool, whirlpool, sun rooms, exercise classes, health bar. $10.

	Average Temperature	Average Rainfall
December	36	3.0
January	33	3.0
February	33	3.0
March	46	4.0
April	50	3.0
May	61	4.0
June	70	4.0
July	74	4.0
August	73	4.0
September	67	4.0
October	58	3.0
November	47	3.0

New York City Chamber of Commerce (212) 561-2020

TRIP TIP GUIDE

PITTSBURGH

"The strictly tailored look seems to be softening up a little in Pittsburgh. Suits are still the best bet for business, but the style and color can be a little more relaxed. I'd suggest bringing something to soften a very severe look; like a more feminine blouse, a scarf for a neckline, a less traditional color. Anything too stiff looks like overkill. For alternatives, silk or soft wool dresses work well, especially if you're going from all-day appointments to cocktails or dinner. You don't have to get overly dressy to dine in the best restaurants in town; business clothes are fine as long as they are somewhat feminine. Casual here can mean pants or a pants skirt. A skirt and jacket would be equally appropriate, if you didn't know the degree of casual dress expected.

"There's no need to rent a car in Pittsburgh, although the ride to and from the airport is a fairly long one. It should cost around $20. Cabs in the city usually have to be called, except around the hotels."

Executive Accommodations

Hilton Hotel
2 Gateway Center
Pittsburgh, Pennsylvania 15222
(412) 391-4600

Sheraton Motor Hotel
Station Square
Pittsburgh, Pennsylvania 15219
(412) 261-2000

William Penn Hotel
530 William Penn Place
Pittsburgh, Pennsylvania 15230
(412) 281-7100

Best Bookings

Grand Concourse
Station Square
(412) 261-1717
A showplace of a restaurant in a converted railroad station.
Lunch: Monday–Friday, 11:30 A.M.–3:30 P.M.
Brunch: Sunday, 10:30 A.M.–2:30 P.M.
Dinner: Monday–Sunday, 5:00 P.M.–10:00 P.M. Continental cuisine, specializing in seafood. Reservations suggested. Moderate.

Hugo's at the Hyatt
112 Washington Place
(412) 288-9326
Lunch: Monday–Friday, 11:00 A.M.–2:30 P.M.
Sunday brunch: 11:00 A.M.–2:00 P.M.
Dinner: Monday–Sunday, 5:30 P.M.–10:30 P.M. Continental cuisine, seafood buffet Friday night. Reservations suggested. Moderate.

La Plume
William Penn Hotel
William Penn Plaza at Mellon Square
(412) 553-5065
Breakfast: Monday–Sunday, 7:00 A.M.–11:00 A.M.
Lunch: Monday–Sunday, 11:30 A.M.–2:30 P.M.
Dinner: Monday–Sunday, 5:00 P.M.–10:00 P.M. Reservations suggested. French cuisine. Moderate to expensive.

Top of the Triangle
U.S. Steel Building
600 Grant Street
(412) 471-4100
Casual elegance with a spectacular view of the city.
Lunch: Monday–Saturday, 11:30 A.M.–3:00 P.M.
Dinner: Monday–Saturday, 5:30 P.M.–10:00 P.M. Continental menu. Moderate.
Reservations suggested.

	Average Temperature	Average Rainfall
December	30.5	2.48
January	28.1	2.79
February	29.3	2.35
March	38.1	3.60
April	50.2	3.40
May	59.8	3.63
June	68.6	3.48
July	71.9	3.84
August	70.2	3.15
September	63.8	2.52
October	53.2	2.52
November	41.3	2.47

Pittsburgh Chamber of Commerce (412) 392-4500

TRIP TIP GUIDE

SAN FRANCISCO

"You have to remember that San Francisco is always chillier than you would expect. We wear wool here even in the summer months. There's a continuous fog until about 11:00 most mornings and that keeps the temperature down and the air a little damp. Other than that, the weather is absolutely perfect, all year long. But that doesn't mean hot. If you dress as you would for fall in the East, you'll be comfortable. Although we're in the same state as Los Angeles, we're worlds apart when it comes to dressing. People here are much more formal. For a business trip, I'd definitely bring suits. If you prefer dresses, always remember to pack coordinated jackets, for warmth, as much as for formality! What you wear to work can go to the theatre or to restaurants, but if you have the chance to change, do. We tend to get more dressed up in the evening. A cocktail dress can even be worn to special evening events. Of course, if you know you're going to the opening of the opera, you should pack a long gown! Keep pretty pulled together for casual occasions, too. I'd bring a Harris tweed blazer and gabardine pants or a sporty dress for informal plans.

"It's easier to call a cab than rent a car for getting around to most business appointments. Cabfare from the airport is between $25 and $30."

Executive Accommodations

Fairmont
Nob Hill
San Francisco, California 94106
(415) 772-5000
(800) 527-4727

Four Seasons Clift Hotel
495 Geary Street
San Francisco, California 94102
(415) 775-4700
(800) 828-1188

Hyatt Regency
5 Embarcadero Center
San Francisco, California 94111
or
Union Square (downtown)
345 Stockton Street
San Francisco, California 94108
(800) 228-9000

Mark Hopkins Hotel
999 California Street
San Francisco, California 94102
(800) 327-0200

Sir Francis Drake
Powell and Sutter Streets
San Francisco, California 94101
(800) 223-1818

Best Bookings

Blue Fox
659 Merchant Blvd.
(415) 981-1177
Dinner only: 6:00 P.M.–10:15 P.M. Reservations required. Continental cuisine.
Moderate.

Ernie's
847 Montgomery Street
(415) 397-5969
Dinner only: Monday–Sunday, 6:30 P.M.–10:00 P.M. Reservations required.
French cuisine. Moderate to expensive.

Le Castel
3235 Sacramento
(415) 921-7115
Dinner only: 6:00 P.M.–11:00 P.M. Reservations required. French cuisine. Moderate.

L'Etoile
1075 California Street
(415) 771-1529
Dinner only: Monday–Saturday, 6:00 P.M.–11:00 P.M. Reservations required. Classical French cuisine. Expensive.

Trader Vic's
20 Cosmo Place
(415) 776-2232
Lunch: Monday–Friday, 12:00 Noon–2:30 P.M.
Dinner: Monday–Sunday, 5:30 P.M.–11:00 P.M. Reservations required. Chinese, Polynesian and Continental cuisine. Moderate to expensive.

Caravansary
310 Grand Sutter Street
(415) 362-4640
Lunch: Monday–Saturday, 11:00 A.M.–3:00 P.M.
Dinner: Monday–Saturday, 5:00 P.M.–10:00 P.M. Reservations required. Middle Eastern cuisine. Moderate.

Le Central
453 Bush Street
(415) 391-2233
Lunch: Monday–Friday, 11:45 A.M.–3:30 P.M.
Dinner: Monday–Saturday, 5:30 P.M.–10:30 P.M. Reservations required. French provençal cuisine. Moderate to expensive.

The Greens
Fort Mason Center
Marina Blvd. and Buchanan Streets
(415) 771-6222
Lunch: Tuesday–Saturday, 11:30 A.M.–2:30 P.M.
Dinner: Friday and Saturday only, 6:30 P.M.–8:00 P.M. Reservations required for dinner, suggested for lunch. Vegetarian, French provençal cuisine. Moderate.

Mary Gullis
3661 Sacramento Street
(415) 931-5151
Lunch: Tuesday–Saturday, 11:45 A.M.–2:30 P.M.
Dinner: Tuesday–Saturday, 6:00 P.M.–10:00 P.M. Reservations required. Continental cuisine. Moderate.

	Average Temperature	Average Rainfall
December	53.7	5.35
January	51.0	3.37
February	55.0	0.19
March	53.2	2.12
April	53.8	0.01
May	53.4	0.22
June	57.8	0.57
July	58.9	trace
August	60.0	0.01
September	62.4	trace
October	63.1	1.90
November	55.3	3.99

San Francisco Chamber of Commerce (415) 392-4511

TRIP TIP GUIDE

WASHINGTON, D.C.

"You have to look businesslike in this town, but our interpretation of that is more fashionable than conservative. Certainly, I'd bring an all-occasion navy suit, but I'd also pack a less stuffy one, perhaps a soft glen plaid. A stylish look counts. You'll have some use for feminine-looking dresses too, if you're going out to dinner or out for the evening. And if your plans include a dressy event, bring along a cocktail dress. And not necessarily a demure, conservative one! Women here just don't wear that mannish, "safe" look. A blazer isn't required for casual dressing. You'd be fine in just a skirt and sweater or possibly slacks. Comfort is an important consideration when you're deciding what to pack. The summers here can get very hot and very muggy. Spring and fall can also be rainy; be sure to bring a raincoat.

"Taxis are plentiful and reasonable in the Washington area. Figuring out the traffic flow would be more of a problem if you rented a car! From the airport, a taxi ride will cost about $10."

Executive Accommodations

Four Seasons
2800 Pennsylvania Avenue
Washington, D.C. 20007
(202) 342-0444
(800) 828-1188

Guest Quarters
801 New Hampshire Avenue
Washington, D.C. 20037
(202) 785-2000
(800) 424-2900
                or
2500 Pennsylvania Avenue
Washington, D.C. 20037
(202) 333-8060

Hyatt Regency
400 New Jersey Avenue NW
Washington, D.C. 20001
(800) 228-9000

L'Enfant Plaza
480 L'Enfant Plaza SW
Washington, D.C. 20024
(202) 484-1000
(800) 223-0888

Stouffer's The Mayflower
1127 Connecticut Avenue NW
Washington, D.C. 20036
(202) 347-3000
(800) 321-6888

Best Bookings

Clyde's
3236 M Street NW
(202) 333-0284
Breakfast, Lunch and Dinner: 7:00 A.M.–11:00 P.M. Continental cuisine. Casual and reasonable.

The Four Seasons
2800 Pennsylvania Avenue
Georgetown

(202) 342-0444
Lunch: Monday–Sunday, 12:00 Noon–2:30 P.M.
Dinner: Monday–Sunday, 7:00 P.M.–11:00 P.M. Reservations required. French nouvelle cuisine. Moderate to expensive.

Prime Rib
2020 K Street
(202) 466-8811
Lunch: Monday–Friday, 12:00 Noon–2:30 P.M.
Dinner: Monday–Saturday, 6:00 P.M.–10:30 P.M. Reservations suggested. Steaks, lobster, chops. Expensive.

Refresher Courses

The following facilities are available for out-of-town visitors, although you may have to call ahead for a reservation.

Congressional Fitness Center
(202) 544-4500
Exercise classes, weight machines, sauna, steam and whirlpool bath. $10.

Nautilus Fitness Center
(202) 887-0760
Exercise classes, weight machines, sauna, steam/whirlpool bath. $7.

Saga Club
(202) 298-8455
Classes, weight machines, pool, sauna, steam and whirlpool bath, facial massage, body treatment. $13 visit; $95 for a day package. Waxing, manicure, makeup and lunch extra.

Washington Hilton Racquet Club
(202) 483-3061
Outdoor pool, tennis courts, weight machines, classes, bicycling and jogging escorts, whirlpool, sports clothes provided. $4 to hotel guests only. Massage and beauty services extra.

Watergate Health Club
(202) 298-4460
Indoor pool, steam cabinets, sleep room, sun rooms, classes, weight machines. $12. Massage and beauty services extra.

YWCA
(202) 638-2100
Swim and slimnastics class. $4 to members.

	Average Temperature	*Average Rainfall*
December	45.2	3.04
January	43.5	2.62
February	46	2.45
March	55	3.33
April	67.1	2.86
May	76.6	3.68
June	84.6	3.48
July	88.2	4.12
August	86.6	4.67
September	80.2	3.08
October	69.8	2.66
November	57.2	2.90

Washington, D.C. Chamber of Commerce (202) 347-7201

INTERNATIONAL ARRANGEMENTS

The details involved in making arrangements for a trip to a foreign country can go far beyond the where-to-stay and how-to-get-there considerations. You'll need a visa to conduct business in many countries, a shot or two to enter some, and a passport to get into all of them. Embassy and State Department regulations can vary dramatically, depending on where you're going. And sometimes requirements can change with the tide of foreign affairs. There are certain countries, for instance, that will not allow you to enter even with a valid visa, if your passport bears an airport stamp from a country they are not on friendly terms with. This is particularly true in Middle Eastern countries. In some, you won't be issued a visa if your passport shows an Israeli entry or exit stamp.

There are, of course, ways to resolve restrictive regulations. One way is to apply for two passports, keeping one for world travel and one valid only for restricted countries. Other ways to expedite matters is to know in advance the particular peculiarities of the embassies who process applications. Sometimes, use of a paper clip instead of a staple can make all the difference between acceptance or rejection of a visa request.

Visa agencies are your best bet for cutting through international red tape. Not only do they know the details a first-time traveler might miss, they also can avoid unexpected delays caused by embassy shutdowns, national holidays and the like. Most major cities do have visa agencies, although the majority of transactions are funneled through the several agencies in Washington, D.C. Because many visas can only be issued from an embassy, and not from a consulate, Washington is the only place to obtain proper documents from certain countries.

Visa agencies can also offer other travel services: securing passports, arranging for translations of applications, obtaining proper State Department documentation, duplicating forms, and arranging for express mail delivery. Fees are usually minimal, and well worth it in time saved during the working day! Ask your travel agent to recommend several visa companies, then call the embassy in question to confirm each agency's track record. You're looking for efficiency and reliability.

Most doctors have current vaccination requirement information, but you can also call your state or local health departments, the US Public Health Service, and the embassies of the countries you plan to visit to find out if you need inoculations before entering the countries. Make sure you clear your *entire* itinerary. Some countries require vaccinations only if you arrive from an infected area. If you do need cholera, smallpox and/or yellow fever shots, have them validated with an official health department stamp on an International Certificate of Vaccination. If your doctor does not have this stamp, have the shots validated at city hall or at a county or state health department. Yellow fever vaccinations can only be given at special vaccination centers in major U.S. cities. And you can't take it within ten days of a smallpox or cholera shot. Take this into consideration when you're planning your pre-trip timetable.

CHAPTER

10

Professional Maintenance: Staying in Peak Condition

"Sometimes being successful has a lot to do with *feeling* successful. What it all boils down to is having the proper levels of self-esteem and energy."

There's no question that life in the executive lane can take its toll—both physically and emotionally. The one-two punch of long hours combined with responsibility overload can create enough professional stress to rob you of sleep, vitality, enthusiasm. Unrelieved pressure situations negatively affect performance, appearance, and, eventually, health. Unless there's some escape. More and more women in management positions are discovering that, without time out for personal attention, it would all be impossible.

Taking the best possible care of yourself isn't something you reserve for weekends or once-a-year retreats. It's got to be an ongoing, carefully calculated maintenance program designed to circumvent the fatigue factor before the effects become obvious. And it begins with something as simple as putting your best face forward every morning of the working week. Chicago skin care and makeup expert Marilyn Miglin attributes a 40–50% growth in business over the past eighteen years to the increase in the number of working women needing her salon's instructive services. "We offer classes in makeup application and home skin care, and professional women are intensely interested. They are more concerned with putting themselves together, both to look prettier and as a function of competition."

Greater day-to-day need of products and services designed to polish up a professional appearance has beauty marketers targeting businesswomen as their most sought-after customer. The $3.6 billion cosmetics industry is expected to grow into $21.7 billion in shipments by 1985, according to the Department of Commerce. And it's the heavy users—the women who need makeup more often than the ones who apply it only to go out to a party or on a date—who are going to push the sales figures up. Although some experts feel that the impact working women have had on the beauty industry has reached its peak and both the market and the industry have "matured," there can be little doubt that both goods and services will have to be geared to the busy, demanding customer who's life is at least equally as active outside the home. It's no coincidence that, in the last decade, when the number of women in the work force jumped from 31 million to 43 million, total growth of cosmetic sales increased at an unprecedented rate. According to Supermarket Business Expenditures Studies, increases (in all outlets) were up 42.4% for face makeup; up 213.5% for eye makeup; up 101.1% for face creams and lotions; up 189.8% for skin creams; up 102.7% for lipstick; and up 111.1% for nail color. That's a lot of image-creating going on. And the woman who is most concerned about her looks is the woman who wants her appearance to be a reflection of her professionalism. Most working women, in fact, don't believe it's the least important aspect of performance. A *Cosmetics & Skin Care* survey found out that 89% of all working women use moisturizers; 70% use toners and astringents; 67% use cleansers; 41% use night creams; 54% use foundation daily; 83% use some form of cheek color; 74% use mascara; 44% use eye shadow; 48% use eye liners. Not important? Don't kid yourself.

The impact of this market has gone far beyond total sales volume. What's important to a working woman has influenced everything from product development to distribution. Pipe dreams have become passé. Enter the era of efficient cosmetics. A woman who does not have an hour to primp in the morning (or before every meeting) wants long-lasting, easy-to-apply products. They must do what they say they're going to do, or she won't waste her time on them. Because this is the message the busy professional woman wants to hear, advertising approaches have switched from pure fantasy to scientific fact. Products must be easy to buy as well. Despite all the claims for the great amount of discretionary income the working woman is supposed to be bringing home, studies have shown that, even if that were the case, she chooses not to spend it on cosmetics. Mid- to low-range lines are selling far better than more expensive brands. And if they're available in the supermarket, even better! With less time for leisurely shopping, the woman who works prefers to buy her cosmetics in stores that are multi-purpose. Although drugstores hold the title as chief dispensers of beauty aids, food stores are capturing an increasing share of the market.

Just as the "self"-conscious professional woman has been a bare-faced blessing to the cosmetics industry, she's cut the hair salon business somewhat short. Where women used to keep weekly appointments with their hairdressers, a study developed by *Modern Salon Magazine* discovered that women now only find time to check in every six weeks on the average, and chances are it's for a color touch-up. Almost 62% of all salon clients questioned who color their hair are working. As a response to the now-you-see-them, now-you-don't professional customer, salons have added soothing, rejuvenating services once reserved to spas. What seriously fatigued executive can resist a thermal-wrap pedicure while she's getting a trim? And, as long as she's there, why not ask for a waxing? It's all a question of scheduling salon hours to accommodate office hours. Beauty care centers that wish to attract an executive clientele are opening as early as 7:00 A.M., scheduling standing appointments and getting the lunch-hour customer in and out—on time.

SHAPING UP AN IMAGE

But beauty isn't only in the hands of the hair/cosmetic industry. For millions of women, a total maintenance regime takes in the total body. In fact, it is estimated that over half the adult population of the United States is actively participating in some sort of fitness program. Interestingly, the let's-get-physical boom has exploded in the same decade that saw gains in women's entry into the work force and increased use of beauty products. Undoubtedly, working goes hand in hand with the need to look and feel good. The $30 billion-a-year it takes to keep us in shape for a sedentary, desk-bound daily existence is channeled into everything from at-home workout gear to do-it-yourself exercise and diet programs, to correct suiting-up attire, and all the foods, drinks, vitamins and gadgetry required to keep us going on the path to health.

SWEATING OUT EXECUTIVE STRESS

Beating executive stress by the sweat of one's brow is not necessarily a solitary pursuit. Included in the total annual cost for fitness is $5 billion spent in health clubs and corporate fitness centers. "There has been a tremendous growth in the involvement of women with fitness over the past five years," according to Jerry Zuckerman, PhD, one of the founders and developers of Cardio-Fitness Systems, Inc. As President of this executive-oriented fitness facility (with three locations in New York and planned expansion to other urban areas such as Chicago, San Francisco, Boston and Philadelphia), he has watched the percentage of women participants nearly double in the five years since the first center opened. "Women are much more knowledgeable now as to the value of exercise and proper nutrition. Plus, it's no longer unfeminine to be physical." Since 95% of the female members of the Cardio-Fitness Centers are employed at the executive level, Dr. Zuckerman feels there is an important correlation between women perceiving the dangers of the corporate stress style, and doing something about it. "There's no difference between male and female motivations. It's a case of the same pressures and the same response. This generation of executives has seen far too many victims of heart trouble in the previous generation. They want to actively do what they can to avoid it. As they find themselves moving up the corporate ladder, it suddenly becomes more and more relevant. The sad correlation between the fact that more women are working, more women are smoking and more women are developing heart disease, while just the opposite is true for males, clearly illustrates that women are succumbing to the pressures of professional stress. The forward-thinking female executives are doing something about it."

HEALTH—THE NEWEST "PERK"

Between 60% and 65% of the members of Cardio-Fitness have some, if not all, of the annual fee bankrolled by their employers. In fact, it was in response to the demand for in-house cardiovascular fitness facilities by such corporations as Exxon, Mobil, Chase Manhattan Bank, AT&T and Western Electric that the Cardio-Fitness system was developed. Although the purpose of this venture was to provide a convenient, separate facility (saving the corporation the investment and staffing expenses of establishing their own), many companies are doing just that. Indoor physical fitness labs, complete with weight-training equipment, treadmills, rowing machines, stationary bicycles, running tracks, sports courts, swimming pools and personal counseling services have been installed at many major corporations, from Alcoa to Xerox. Where logistics permit, outdoor recreation areas are developed as well. Jogging trails, tennis courts and exercise par-courses attract many a lunch-hour devotee. Awareness by corporations of the long-term economic benefits of an employee fitness program began taking shape in the mid-1970s. The advantages of improved alertness, reduced absenteeism, increased performance, lowered fatigue levels, and heightened stress resistance made sense to chief executive officers concerned with the bottom line effects of mental and physical stress. It became apparent that spending millions in company fitness facilities was a crucial investment in employees, and a partial solution to the escalating costs of directly paying medical expenses. Where companies could not install their own fitness centers, assuming the costs of membership in a monitored fitness program became a highly valued perquisite of the total corporate benefits package.

WORKING IN WORKING OUT

A weekly regime of cardiovascular/aerobic/and flexibility exercising is so critical to peak performance that an increasing number of executive women see it as absolutely essential to their success. "I'd never unwind if I didn't have my six o'clock squash game," claims a financial management V.P. "If I didn't stretch my tensions away, I'd be totally tied up in knots," adds another marketing executive. "I don't think I could make it through the week if I didn't do something to work up a sweat," insists a product manager. In fact, 73% of the women we interviewed do engage in some sort of exercise. Although sports participation is the most popular route to fatigue relief (jogging, skiing, sailing, bicycling, swimming, walking, playing tennis), nearly 66% of them also work out regularly at a fitness facility. And those who don't cite time, not unwillingness, as the chief culprit. "Health clubs are usually too busy at peak hours when I can go, and I don't have time to wait for the equipment," complained an investment broker. Her solution? Join a limited-size exercise class, like aerobics, dancing, stretching. "At least you know you'll be in and out by a set hour."

"If the facility is not over-enrolled, there should be a workable distribution of participants at any given time," according to Cardio's Zuckerman. The Centers, who keep time-in, time-out track of all members, record a fairly equal spread of the hours male and female members sign in. "We're starting to see a higher percentage of pre-work exercisers. There is also a significant percentage during the lunch hour. Women's attendance tends to drop away in the late afternoon hours, probably because they feel the pull of family/dinner responsibilities." While the women we interviewed prefer before and after work workouts to doing anything on their lunch hour, this also reflects their preference for sports as an exercise medium. It's hard to go skiing or swimming and be back at your desk by two! A lot of women also find it both inconvenient to shower mid-day, and impossible to return to work without one!

THE SECRET ENERGIZER

Yet, whenever they do it, overtense, overtired executives find exercise means more than a muscular blitzkrieg. It's the secret energizer that propels you to meet challenges head-on. It's the physical resilience builder that lets you level stress when you need to most. Exercising provides you with stamina, strength, self-confidence. In fact, the more you do, the more energy reserves you create, enabling you to tackle additional activities. Increased vitality and better command of your body lifts your spirits like nothing else. Of course, it's essential for professional effectiveness, but even more importantly, proper exercise gives you enough energy to live the life you want outside of work. There's no sense in having six o'clock fade-out when you can be taking your pulse to whole new highs. A sedentary jobstyle is the worst treatment you can give your body. You've got to compensate by stretching, strengthening, and building cardiovascular efficiency. It's not enough to do one—or two—out of three. And it's not enough to take one quick class a week. To keep your desk-bound body in healthy condition, experts advise that you get physical at least three times a week (preferably on alternating days), for no less than 30 minutes a crack. The secret to selecting an exercise program you will stick with is to find one that accomplishes the stretching, strengthening and aerobic aspects of conditioning. Then look for ways to incorporate it into your day when your energy levels are at all-systems-go. You don't have to carve out blocks of time where they don't exist. Try, instead, to add exercise to your daily activities: *stretch* as part of your wake-up routine; *walk* at a brisk clip—or *bicycle*—to work; *tone* with a fitness training program at lunchtime or after work. Whenever you can squeeze in a few minutes of exercise during the day, it's going to leave you feeling less tense, less tired, more on top of everything.

LET'S GET AWAY FROM IT ALL

Apparently, executive women are doing just that—sneaking off to sybaritic retreats, where the emphasis has shifted, over the past years, from pampering to pushing to the limits. Exercise as a way of life is intensive enough to be the invigorating shot-in-the-arm many desk-weary women find they need. When it's combined with in-depth beauty attention—bubbling baths, hot wraps, head-to-toe mud packs, stimulating scrubs, deep massages, vitalizing showers, and face/hair/nail services—so much the better. It's the ultimate refresher, both physical and spiritual, for many women who feel the amount of rejuvenation is worth the sky-high price tag. Although a week at a health and beauty retreat can easily run into thousands of dollars, repeated annual visits have become a priority for women who want to be totally reconditioned. "I feel as worn-out as an old car after a particularly hectic period," explained a publishing executive. "If I didn't feel there was a place to go to concentrate on the signals my body was sending, I'm afraid I'd just run down!"

Here are some of the best perk-up places in the country. To find the one that's right for you, make sure their emphasis is going to give you what you need. Know first if you place greater importance on serenity or activity. Although most places offer a bit of both, there's no sense finding yourself stuck in the middle of a Hatha-yoga class when you'd rather be out climbing a mountain. Each of the spas below will be happy to send you a complete brochure showing special areas of concentration, as well as current rate information.

The Ashram
P.O. Box 8
Calabasas, California 91302
(213) 888-0232

Don't look for deluxe accommodations or luxurious pampering when you commit yourself to a one-week stay at the Ashram. You're allowed to bring only Spartan-like essentials (toothbrush, swimsuit and hiking or jogging shoes). The Ashram supplies you with everything else—including a tube of Ben-Gay! Be prepared for breathtaking hikes, morning and afternoon, killer calisthenics, exhausting exercise, and vegetarian sustenance. The Ashram's rigorous schedule (in which only eight to ten guests participate at any one time), gives no sense of regimentation. The focus is on a reunion of inner self and nature. Evening yoga classes integrate the body and the mind in a "new sense of aliveness." A pre-interview determines whether you can take it or not.

Bonaventure Spa
Ft. Lauderdale Inter-Continental Hotel
250 Racquet Club Road
Ft. Lauderdale, Florida 33326
(305) 474-3300

Five hours of exercise a day awaits guests at the new Bonaventure Spa. Three fitness plans are available to custom-tailor the amount of aerobics, calisthenics, muscle toning, yoga, jogging, running and water exercises that will be right for your improvement goals. Before arrival, a computer will help analyze your responses to a health questionnaire. A total fitness test, taken once you get to Bonaventure, helps to complete your health profile and structure a seven-day fitness program, and a follow-up maintenance "living plan." The underlying emphasis is to design a schedule of activity, nutrition and rest that you can live with for the rest of your life. The goal at Bonaventure is to provide both the impetus and the professional help most people need to get them started on a proper fitness regimen.

La Costa Hotel & Spa
Rancho La Costa
Carlsbad, California 92008
(714) 438-9111

You can tone up or wind down at La Costa. Take your pick of exercise and relaxation activities for a Personalized Spa Plan. A minimum four-night stay puts you on the Spa plan, where you can select from daily exercise classes, makeup classes and specialized beauty treatments. A personal diet, exercise and beauty care program will be developed for you by the La Costa Medical Director and Spa Dietician. A typical schedule includes Stretch & Flex, Spot Reducing, Water Exercises, Dance, Yoga, Fitness Class, Co-ed Dance and Beach Walks. Include tennis, golf and/or horseback trail riding to turn it into more of a vacation experience. In the evening, there are activities ranging from spa cooking demonstrations to disco dancing and duplicate Bridge. Forty-five minutes from the San Diego airport (and you can arrange to be picked up by their chauffeur), La Costa offers luxurious hotel, cottage, villa or executive home accommodations.

The Golden Door
Box 1567
Escondido, California 92025
(714) 744-5777

Serenity and removed-from-it-all relaxation are the attributes of a visit to The Golden Door. Mental unwinding is totally possible in an idyllic atmosphere with Japanese gardens and teahouse-like buildings. Tucked away in the California hills, The Golden Door sets the stage for quiet reflection and restoration. Orchards, greenhouses and gardens provide most of the natural foods served in elegant Japanese tradition. But it's not all peace and quiet. The emphasis is on a combination of high- and low-energy activities. After a sunrise hike (6:30 A.M.), the day stretches into water and aerobic exercising, beauty breaks, stretching, walking, biofeedback techniques, acupressure massages and pre-sleep tub sessions. Thirty-two guests, attended by three times that many staff members, are divided into Novice, Experienced and Expert in Movement categories for individual goal-setting. Each guest receives a personalized exercise tape with spot toners for particular problem areas to take The Golden Door experience home with her.

Gurney's Inn
Montauk, Long Island, New York 11954
(516) 668-2345 or (212) 895-6400

Overlooking the Atlantic, with its own private ocean beach, Gurney's Inn offers a European-oriented spa facility in the midst of a corporate conference center. Two separate spa pavilions (one for women and one for men) offer Finnish rock saunas, Russian steam rooms, Swiss showers. Much is made of the therapeutic powers of healing sea water in special treatment services: thalasso (immersion in a large tub for massage) and fango (mud/paraffin packs for muscle relaxation) therapy; French vichy treatments combined with salt glow rubs or mint loofah scrubs; herbal and kelp wraps; Swedish and Shiatsu massages, Scotch hosings and Roman baths. Aerobic, aquatic, calisthenic, isometric and cardiovascular exercises are available. Go for either the Seven-Day Rejuvenating Plan or the Four-Day Executive Fitness Program, concentrating on proper responses to distress, exercises to combat a sedentary lifestyle, and healthier eating habits. Facilities are open to non-resident guests as well.

Maine Chance
Phoenix, Arizona 85018
(602) 947-6365

A mountain oasis created by Elizabeth Arden in 1945, Maine Chance is acres of pink and turquoise elegance. Don't come here to rough it. You'll be surrounded by Impressionist masterpieces, marble floors and antique furniture. Personal maids will pamper you with everything from breakfast in bed to unpacking aid. Guests never number more than 50 to 60, and participate in four exercise sessions daily. Heat treatments, facials and nail and hair attention are all part of the Maine Chance beautifying regime.

The Spa at Palm-Aire
Pompano Beach, Florida 33060
(800) 327-4960

Sports and spa facilities keep guests active here. You can play on any one of five golf courses or thirty-seven tennis courts, or stick to vigorous, pound-shedding workouts. Jogging, gymnastics, water exercises and obstacle course run-throughs are some of the ways they have of working up a healthy sweat. Afterward you can soothe soreness with daily whirlpools, herbal wraps, facials and massages. Ask for the Seven-Day Renaissance Spa Program.

INSTANT ENERGIZERS

"Whenever I feel a little depressed," a New York law partner confessed, "I think the best way out of it is to go and have a facial—whether I need one or not!" At the risk of being deep cleansed and declogged to death, more and more high-powered executives are turning to pampering beauty treatments as a way of coping with the depersonalizing demands of their jobs. External self-improvement has become the antidote to internal turmoil. There are all sorts of relaxation techniques—from free-as-the-air deep breathing exercises to a day-long orgy of self-indulgence—but they all add up to the same thing: a megadose of TLC for the work weary. Below, some of the best de-stressers we know.

Facials. Although any salon worth its scrubbing grains will have developed its own unique facial technique, most follow a deep cleansing, declogging, stimulation, toning and moisturizing procedure. Look for a thorough skin analysis and between-visit home treatment recommendations as well. Special plusses: herbal steamings, tingling gel masks, vitamin and collagen treatments, skin sloughings, galvanic stimulation, neck and shoulder massage. Allow about one hour for a facial and schedule your first one after work (your skin could turn more red than glowing.) And, no matter how sensational a thorough cleansing makes you feel, never schedule more than one facial a month. The more elaborate treatments (peels, sloughings, ionizations) are things you do only every three to six months.

Swedish massage. Muscle tensions glide away under the hands of a trained Swedish masseuse. A combination of five basic strokes manipulates and stimulates muscles all over the body. Beginning with the front of your legs and moving up to the back and neck, your masseuse will use firm rolling and kneading movements. Mineral oil provides the glide for long, smooth stroking. Tapping and vibration is also used to stimulate the nervous system. Don't try to squeeze an hour's worth of this total relaxation into the middle of a hectic day. You won't feel a thing like working afterward!

Shiatsu. This traditional Japanese massage technique is like acupuncture without needles! Using gentle to strong hand manipulation, pressure is applied to trigger points along the energy pathways of the body. By slowly exerting and releasing pressure, a Shiatsu therapist eliminates energy blockages and reduces the effects of stress. Don't be surprised if your masseuse goes for a walk—on your back! Although much more rigorous than a Swedish massage, this technique leaves the same deep feeling of calm.

Hot tubs. Women have known the care-easing benefits of soaking in a tub ever since bubble bath and scented oils were invented. With the advent of tubs big enough to invite the neighbors in, soaking in deliciously warm water has gone public. Sitting in gallons of 100°F water with a built-in whirlpool mechanism is a thirty-minute way to unwind. As long as you don't become drowsy, dizzy or drunk! Alcohol and hot tubs don't mix. You must also use precaution if you're pregnant, under medication or have a heart problem. Once only a West Coast phenomenon, these redwood, fiberglass or tile tubs are now standard equipment at many health clubs and hotels. Meeting after work for a soak has become, for some, a better "happy hour" than the cocktail kind!

Isolation tanks. Being "in the tank" used to imply a less-than-healthy condition. Today, it describes a return to a womb-like watery environment. Floating in a dark Epsom-salt buoyancy, with all outside sensory stimuli removed, your mind is left free to wander into weightless oblivion. You'll be totally enclosed in 175 gallons of 93°F water for about an hour, until all tensions slip away.

Deep breathing. The anytime, anywhere energizer. Whenever anxiety or tension threaten to tie you into knots, take a moment to concentrate on oxygenating tired muscles (and a tired mind)! When you get to the point of heart-racing nervousness, chances are shallow breathing is responsible. If you've heard "take three deep breaths" all your life, now is the time to try it. Collapse your body and force yourself to exhale deeply. Inhale and hold for five counts, exhale slowly for five counts. This "cleansing breath" exercise will make you more aware of the energizing benefits in slower, fuller breaths. During the deep breathing exercise, force yourself to focus on only the counting, or fix a point of concentration across the room. When you're walking, time your breathing to your strides. The trick is to fill your lungs to capacity, then expel every bit of air. The physical effect? Less waste carbon dioxide and more oxygen in the bloodstream. You'll feel refreshed, better able to handle tension.

Reflexology. This little piggy went to market and turned into a revival of an early Chinese technique. Therapists use pressure and massage at specific points on the feet that correspond to organs of the body. Blockages are released by rubbing and pulling reflex points as energy flows are re-established.

Saunas. An after-exercise, pre-shower treat. Dry heat, 165°–175°F, is made temporarily humid by ladling water onto heated rocks, resulting in a skin-tingling sensation. A good way to coddle tired muscles, cleanse impurities. But don't plan to spend the day. Start with only five minutes and build up to no more than fifteen minutes. Close pores and bring down body temperature by following sauna-sitting with a cool shower.

Steam rooms. Moist heat (100% humidity) has its purifying powers, too. The combination of humidity and heat in a steam room opens pores, peripheral capillaries and lubricates the upper respiratory tract. Stay five minutes at first, then cool down and close pores with a follow-up shower.

Day-of-beauty. Many local salons provide complete head-to-toe pampering "packages" which take the better part of a day, and the better part of $100–$300 dollars. Think of it this way: it's going to be more expensive than your usual quick trip to a salon, but less expensive than escaping to a spa. And some of the services can be just as lavish. You can be herbal-steamed; henna-packed (all over!); massaged from scalp to toes; Scotch-hose showered; given a facial, mask, manicure and pedicure; waxed; hair-conditioned, shampooed and styled; and taught a whole new makeup strategy, designed just for you. Taking a one-day "vacation" inside the beautifying environment of a local salon may be just the ticket to restore a frazzled self-image. And you can't consider it total indulgence. After all, the package price of each "miracle makeover" is usually less than if you requested each service separately. Investigate "Day-of-Beauty" programs at your favorite local salons, or check out the special attention you'll receive at these coast-to-coast hosts:

Elizabeth Arden

MAINE CHANCE DAY: Exercise, steam cabinet, massage, hairstyling, manicure, pedicure, face treatment, makeup, plus a light lunch. Approximately 5 hours for $130.

MIRACLE MORNING: Massage, hairstyling, manicure, face treatment, makeup. Approximately 4½ hours, $93.

VISIBLE DIFFERENCE DAY: Face treatment, hair consultation and styling, manicure, makeup application and lesson. Approximately 4½ hours, $98.

P.M. PICK-ME-UP: Massage and steam cabinet. 90 minutes, $35.

(Note: prices will vary slightly across the country due to sales tax differentials.)

LOCATIONS:

Beverly Hills, California
434 North Rodeo Drive
(213) 273-9980

Chevy Chase, D.C.
5225 Wisconsin Avenue N.W.
(202) 362-9895

Chicago, Illinois
717 North Michigan Avenue
(312) 266-5750

Coral Gables, Florida
340 Miracle Mile
(305) 445-5443

Fort Lauderdale, Florida
2457 East Sunrise Boulevard
(305) 565-0359

New York, New York
691 Fifth Avenue
(212) 486-7900

Palm Beach, Florida
351 Worth Avenue
(305) 655-7270

Phoenix, Arizona
Biltmore Fashion Park
24th St. & Camelback Rd.
(602) 956-1500

San Francisco, California
230 Post Street
(415) 982-3755

Southampton, New York
(June-Sept.)
14 Main Street
(516) 283-0871

Surfside, Florida
9592 Harding Avenue
(305) 865-3586

Washington, D.C.
1147 Connecticut Avenue
(202) 638-6212

Georgette Klinger

FULL DAY OF BEAUTY: Facial–deep cleansing, herbal steaming, body massage, scalp treatment, makeup application, manicure, pedicure, lunch. Approximately 6½ hours, $150.

HALF-DAY OF BEAUTY: Facial, body massage or scalp treatment, mini-makeup lesson. $80.

LOCATIONS: New York, Beverly Hills, Chicago, Bal Harbour, Palm Beach.

Christine Valmy

DAY OF BEAUTY: Consultation with dermaspecialist, facial, massage, manicure, pedicure, makeup application, lunch. Approximately 8 hours, $160.

LOCATIONS:

Boston, Massachusetts
114 Newbury Street
(617) 266-1221

Natiek Towne Mall
Route 9 & Speen Street
(617) 235-7575

New York, New York
767 Fifth Avenue (G.M. Plaza)
(212) 752-0303

153 West 57th Street
(212) 581-9488

Forest Hills, New York
107–27 71st Avenue
(212) 793-0222

Manhasset, New York
1360 Northern Boulevard
(516) 627-7067

Massapequa, New York
4131 Merrick Road
(516) 541-8130

Paramus, New Jersey
409 Bergen Mall Shopping Center
(201) 843-4180

Philadelphia, Pennsylvania
Rittenhouse Regency
225 South 18th Street
(215) 546-5660

Wilkes-Barre/Scranton, Pennsylvania
Narrows Shopping Center

Edwardsville
(717) 288-6972

Washington, D.C.
79 Woodmont Avenue
Bethesda, Maryland
(301) 652-3840

Miami, Florida
The Falls Shopping Center
8888 Howard Drive
(305) 255-0665

Fort Lauderdale, Florida
3307 N.E. 33rd Street
(305) 565-6500

Las Vegas, Nevada
157 The Fashion Show
3200 Las Vegas Boulevard South
(702) 369-8411

Scottsdale, Arizona
4400 North Scottsdale Road
(602) 994-8584

Houston, Texas
2630 Sage Road—Galleria West
(713) 840-8888

Midland, Texas
39 Plaza Center
(915) 683-9891

San Francisco, California
77 Maiden Lane
(415) 986-8377

Los Angeles, California
140 Main Street, El Segundo
(213) 322-6699

9675 Wilshire Boulevard
Beverly Hills
(213) 273-3723

562 Washington Street
Marina del Rey
(213) 821-8892

24450 Hawthorne Boulevard
Torrance
(213) 373-0792

3431 Via Opporto
Lido Marina Village
Newport Beach
(714) 675-5700

Toronto, Ontario, Canada
11 Hazelton Avenue
(416) 964-6216

Tokyo, Japan
Patio Building 7F 13-23
Miami Aoyama 3chome Minatoku
03/408/3651

THE NEW REGIME

Developing a personal maintenance schedule should be a top priority for every working woman, and absolutely essential for time-confined executives. It's more important than ever to keep your appearance polished and your health in good working order. And you don't have to turn into a salon "groupie" to do it! Devising your own system to accomplish all of the above in the least interruptive manner is simply a case of concentrating on the three "R's": Repair. Rehabilitate. And *Relax!* If you stick to a weekly, monthly and quarterly beauty tune-up program, you'll be able to stop minor trouble spots from turning into major disaster areas. You'll be able to correct the more serious ravages of your workstyle. And you'll be able to re-energize yourself before the only alternative is total collapse.

Practice "preventative" maintenance by establishing—and following—a regular, efficient regime. And don't think twice about doing things for yourself. It's perfectly healthy to be a little selfish. You've earned it, and you need it. Part of being professional about what you do is the ability to take total responsibility for yourself. And that includes keeping yourself in the best condition you can be! When you think of personal time planning in the most positive sense, it will be a simple matter to come up with an easy-upkeep schedule that works for you. Take a tip from our suggestions, below, or organize your own program. The important thing is to do it.

Weekly

Aside from determining wash-when-ready shampoo times, many executive women rely on "Sunday Night Specials" to get themselves into shape to greet the week. A national marathon of tweezing, waxing, manicuring, masking and hair conditioning goes on in homes across the country. It's not a bad idea if you have a blank slate from 9:00 on every Sunday night. But if you're still winding up the weekend, or organizing for the week ahead, our advice is not to let everything go until the last free minute.

- Run a clear topcoat of polish over your nails every other night. The topcoat re-applications add longevity to your undercolor and should keep your manicure going at least a week, sometimes longer. Start from scratch when the chips can no longer be camouflaged. If you can find an hour's time (ask for an 8:00 A.M. appointment, if you must), book a professional to do your nails once a week. It's the no-fuss way to keep your nails in display-able condition, and it will take less time than doing them yourself. All you'll have to worry about are two-second topcoat touch-ups between visits.

- Pluck stray eyebrows as they appear. The best time to find them is when you're applying your morning eye makeup. Take them out there and then. You won't get all red and blotchy if you're only removing one or two misfits. Now is not the time for a major re-arching!

- Deep-clean skin with cleansing grains, a thorough steaming and toner application. Follow-up with a moisturizer. While this can wait until the weekend, it's a wonderful treat at the end of a long working day. Try the luxury of indulging in a 7:00 P.M. mask on a dull Wednesday night.

- Special care for hair could mean slapping on a henna pack, wrapping steamy towels around conditioned or oil-treated ends, or simply using an extra-rich once-a-week body builder. Don't neglect this tender treatment (hair dries out especially fast at the end of summer and in winter heating), but if your hair becomes too limp or lifeless, wait two weeks between conditioning sessions.

Monthly

- Prevent sebum build-up by taking your face to a professional once a month. A stimulating facial will unclog pores, improve circulation, and deep cleanse skin. Take the time during your appointment to go over your daily home-care regime. If your skin condition is going through a change, the products you use and the way you use them may have to change as well. Never rely on the same old cleansing system season in and season out. Your skin responds to environmental variables; your method of taking care of it should, too. Any good esthetician should educate you to things you can do to properly take care of your skin between visits. A facial without such a discussion is a waste of time.

- Shape up your hair (including touching up color if the clock has run out on the roots). You'll find your style will fall into place faster when the ends aren't longer than they should be. Sometimes even a half inch gone awry in the wrong place can make all the difference between an easy-to-care-for style and one that needs constant fussing.

- Wax any body hair you don't want once a month (including bikini line and lip line). When you have a professional waxing done, new hair growth doesn't return as rapidly as it does with daily shaving.

- Treat your feet to a little attention. A professional pedicure will instantly take the tiredness out of your step. Look for one that follows a vibrating water bath with hot wrapping. It's absolutely therapeutic! Your feet will be beautified via creamy massage, callus and cuticle removal, and nail polishing. It's something you wouldn't do as well for yourself at home, and once a month is all you need to keep your feet well-cared-for.

Quarterly

- Re-evaluate your total maintenance regime with the experts. Discuss your hairstyle/lifestyle correlation. Is it working, or is it time to devise a less time-consuming cut/color? Investigate optional techniques for adding a bit of color without worrying about re-growth line. Try a body wave, or re-perk your perm. Experiment with a totally different hair shape.

- Are you presenting your best face to the world? Even if you've got your skin glowing, is your makeup defeating the effect? Maybe it's time to learn a few new techniques. As seasons and colors change, it's better to know what to do with them. Automatically applying deep new wine shades to the same places you used to put peach may throw your natural effect off entirely. Treat yourself to a "how-to" makeup application session at a department store's cosmetic counter, or schedule a private visit with an esthetician. It's not frivolous. Nothing dates you faster than clinging to outdated makeup techniques.

- Skin sloughing, a mildly abrasive rubdown to remove dead skin cells can leave you tingling and glowing, as fresher, younger cells reform the surface layer. It's especially effective to remove fading summer tans or flaking winter skin. Some places do sloughings only on the face, others do a wonderful total-body treatment.

Naturally, the more elaborate the treatment, the less often you should do it. But it's not smart to ignore the long-term benefits of professional services. Executive women who pride themselves on doing everything they need at home—from hair coloring and perming to manicures to skincare procedures—are probably not as efficient at it as an expert would be. The result? They spend twice as much time trying to save time, and the effects may be noticeably inferior. There's nothing wrong with the do-it-yourself school of beauty maintenance, as long as you feel that nobody else can do it better. But you won't know unless you investigate the new beauty services available. Today's techniques are geared more to scientific problem-solving, less to non-essential, time-wasting rituals. One of your main objectives in seeking professional services should be to learn the most result-producing ways to take care of yourself on a regular maintenance schedule.

NINE MONTHS AND COUNTING

Pampering is even more important to the pregnant executive. If you're among those women who choose to work straight through, rather than sit home and wait, the evolution of your self-image into something quite unexpected can seem threatening, if not frightening. "Everyone said I had this great 'glow'," said the president of a retail firm, "but I certainly didn't feel it. The word for the way I felt was ugly."

The clothes you choose have a lot to do with making you feel confident in your appearance. Trying to hide behind skirts that are inching up in front, or jackets that obviously pull when buttoned is only going to make things more obvious—and uncomfortable—for you. It's ridiculous to try to cover up the fact that you are pregnant. Those who don't know will soon guess, and it will become a matter of speculation. It's best to break the news and get on with things. Although you won't need to move into maternity clothes until around your fourth month, you'll feel better about yourself if you switch from skirts to loosely fitting dresses as soon as too-tightness sets in. Look for them in non-wool fabrics (your skin will tend to be dryer than usual, and wool may feel scratchy), and dark colors. Always keep your professional image in mind. Many pregnant women fall prey to frilly little-girl smocks and Baby Jane jumpers at this pre-nursery stage of their lives, but this simply won't carry much clout in a client meeting! Remember, you're having a baby, you're not turning into one! Expect to pay a good price for sophisticated, well-made maternity clothes. Many non-working women balk at spending $150 on a dress that has less than a year to live. When you consider that you'll wear each item much more frequently than clothes in your normal wardrobe, you'll see that the cost balances out. You will get your wear out of a dress you buy to see you through the waiting period, so it's wise to pay for the best quality you can afford.

Use scarves or bows at the neck to vary basic looks, and draw attention upward. If your legs tend to bother you, look for graceful shoes on a lower heel. Don't think it's okay to switch into clunkers just because your doctor told you to avoid high heels. If you don't maintain your image now, when you need to most, you'll be the one who won't like yourself. And it will show. Ease any day-to-day dissatisfaction with be-nice-to-yourself beauty treats. A pedicure will feel twice as good to you now, a facial will relax you like never before. It's important to continue maintenance treatments post-partum, too. Your skin and hair may be totally different for the first six months after your baby is born. And at that point, you'll need them to be fuss-free. Get a no-bother hairstyle and a quick new makeup and cleansing system started right away. Don't slip into disorganization just because there are more demands on your time. If you're organized pre-baby, you can be organized post-baby. All it takes is correcting what doesn't work with your new lifestyle before it turns into a constant source of irritation. Don't wait. Take the first day you can find for yourself and fix whatever's troubling you about the way you look and feel.

BEST BEAUTY SERVICES CITY-BY-CITY

BOSTON

Hair

John Dellana Salons
33 Newberry Street
Boston, Massachusetts 02116
(617) 267-5100

623 Commonwealth
Boston, Massachusetts 02215
(617) 262-8750

1236 Commonwealth
Boston, Massachusetts 02135
(617) 566-8719

1 Winthrop Square
Boston, Massachusetts 02110
(617) 482-5694

All open 6 days a week, 9:00 A.M.–9:00 P.M. You can walk in for an appointment. Great haircuts, full line of hair products.

Diego at the Loft
143 Newberry
Boston, Massachusetts 02116
(617) 262-5003

57 Boylston Street
Cambridge, Massachusetts 02139
(617) 661-7660

Monday, Tuesday, Friday, 9:00 A.M.–6:00 P.M. Wednesday and Thursday, 9:00 A.M.–7:00 P.M. Saturday, 9:00 A.M.–5:00 P.M. Probably the most famous salon in Boston. Chic, but low-key. Full service: hair, eyebrow waxing, face waxing, manicures and pedicures. Book standing appointments in advance. For a Saturday appointment, book one week ahead. For a weekday appointment, schedule it 2 or 3 days in advance.

Skin

John Dellana Salons
623 Commonwealth
Boston, Massachusetts
(617) 262-8750

New full skin care area at this location. Waxing, facials, make-up manicures, pedicures. Licensed estheticians.
Open 6 days a week, 9:00 A.M.–9:00 P.M.

Elizabeth Grady Face First
39 Newbury Street
Back Bay, Boston, Massachussetts 02116
(617) 536-4447

Skin analysis and consultation, education in proper at-home skin care, deep pore cleansing facial, sloughing facials, ionization treatment with collagen catalyst, acne treatment, complete makeup instruction.

Christine Valmy
114 Newberry Street
Boston, Massachusetts 02116
(617) 266-1221

Facial treatments, professional techniques and specialized apparatus, including skin vacuuming, toning sprays, use of Byogenic ® Skin Care Preparations, different types of biological masks. Development of daily home care routine.

Fitness

Fit-Corp
133 Federal Street
Boston, Massachusetts 02110
(617) 542-1010

Open Monday–Friday, 7:00 A.M.–8:00 P.M., Saturday, 8:00 A.M.–1:00 P.M. In the center of the financial district, a complete fitness facility with indoor track, Nautilus and Universal equipment, stationary bicycles, free weights, slimnastics. Classes in stress management, aerobics. Complete locker facilities. Full staff for fitness and cardiovascular testing. Guest fee: $12 a day. 2-month membership:

$115. Yearly: $500. Memberships permit unlimited use and unlimited classes. Co-ed.

Women's World
788 Boylston Street
Boston, Massachusetts 02119
(617) 267-4646

Open Monday–Friday, 9:00 A.M.–9:00 P.M. Saturday, 9:00 A.M.–3:00 P.M. Hourly classes in group exercise, yoga, jazz, stretch. Individual programs also available. 6-week membership: $25. Members may bring guests free, otherwise there is a $10 guest fee.

YWCA
140 Clarendon Street
Boston, Massachusetts 02116
(617) 536-7940

Drop-in exercise classes at 12:00 Noon and 5:30 P.M. at $1.75 per class. Call the phys ed department at Extension 130 for a guest pass. Other fitness facilities include the use of a pool ($2.50) and sauna ($3.00).

CHICAGO

Hair

Brady C'est Bon
920 North Michigan Avenue, 3rd Floor
Chicago, Illinois 60611
(312) 664-3600

Ambassador West Hotel
1300 North State Parkway
Chicago, Illinois 60610
(312) 337-3600

400 East Randolf
Chicago, Illinois 60601
(312) 861-0606

Complete service salon, with waxing, manicures and pedicures, massage, skin care, facials, body wraps. Private line of makeup and skin care products. Expert coloring (ask for Thelma). Complete makeup application (ask for José).

Dimitri Kermeli's
333 East Ontario Street
Chicago, Illinois 60611
(312) 944-0065

Open Tuesday and Thursday, 7:30 A.M.–7:00 P.M., Wednesday, Friday and Saturday, 7:30 A.M.–3:00 P.M., Monday, 12:00 Noon–6:00 P.M. Great hours for professional women. Will book even earlier morning appointments. Many early morning appointments are standing ones. They will also take later appointments on request until 8:00 or 8:30 P.M. on Tuesday and Thursday nights. Manicurist is there Wednesday to Saturday. Otherwise, exclusively hair services: coloring, tipping, perms, chemical relaxing, cuts, etc.

Skin

Face & Facials by Mila Brari
104 East Oak Street
Chicago, Illinois 60611
(312) 266-9506

Open Tuesday–Saturday, 10:00 A.M.–7:00 P.M. Exceptional European facials with deep pore cleansing, intensive moisturizing. Body massage which is a combination of Swedish and Shiatsu techniques. Acupressure, steam bath, corrective manicure and pedicure involving special massages and thermal treatment boots and gloves. Will devise home care routine.

Marilyn Miglin
112 East Oak Street
Chicago, Illinois 60611
(312) 943-1120

Skin and makeup consultations, although the emphasis here is on techniques, rather than treatment. They do not offer facials, but they do stress skin care. Makeup classes for all levels of interest. Have own makeup and skin care products. Will do a special makeup for special evenings: $25. Laboratory and chemist on premises.

Fitness

East Bank Club
500 North Kingsbury Street
Chicago, Illinois 60610
(312) 527-5800

A two-block, five-story total fitness club containing 10 tennis courts, a complete indoor golf facility, eight handball/racquetball courts, saunas, whirlpools, massage rooms, sleeping rooms, steam rooms, sunrooms, a library, a nursery, a card-room, an outdoor restaurant and an indoor jogging track.

Flash, Flash Fitness
59 East Oak Street
Chicago, Illinois 60611
(312) 787-9600

Classes taught at a variety of levels, limited to 15 in each class: Total fitness class, a total workout, using gymnastic, aerobics and a mini-trampoline for knees and back. This is the most advanced level. Physical contouring class, contouring and shaping, concentrating on problem areas. Deep conditioning class, involves no aerobics. Only stretching, flexibility and graceful moves to build up to an aerobic level. Classes are taught at 7:00 A.M., 8, 9, 10, 11 and 12, and again at 4:30, 5:30 and 6:30 P.M. A single class is $7.50. 5 classes: $35; 10 classes: $70; 15 classes: $105.

Lakeshore Centre
1320 W. Fulerton Street
Chicago, Illinois 60614
(312) 477-9888

An enormous fitness village on the east side of Chicago with indoor/outdoor pool, massage room, sauna and steam rooms, whirlpool and sundeck, volleyball/rac-quetball courts, running track with pacing lights, weight room, Nautilus equipment, exercise and aerobic programs, juice bars, snack bars, mechanical ski slope, large-screen television lounge, restaurant and board rooms for corporate meetings. A functional capacity test combined with an electrocardiogram, plus readings and strength and flexibility testing is performed on all new members before a general exercise program is prescribed. Both corporate and private memberships are available.

Rena
920 North Michigan Avenue
Chicago, Illinois 60611
(312) 944-6663

One of the best workouts in the country. Serious exercise classes (on the strenuous side!) are offered every hour on the hour. The maximum class size is six people. Owner Rena Ettinger suggests classes two to three times a week. There are no machines here ("The best machine is your own body."). Out-of-towners can take a class for $7.50. A series of nine classes: $49.50; a series of 13 classes: $69.50.

DALLAS

Hair

Ric Bishop Salon
8041 Walnut Hill Drive, Suite 810
Dallas, Texas 75231
(214) 692-5895

Open Tuesday, Wednesday and Friday, 9:30 A.M.–5:30 P.M., Thursday, 9:30 A.M.–7:00 P.M., Saturday, 8:30 A.M.–3:30 P.M. Design basic, workable cuts for professional, media and fashion people. Specialists in color and perms. Full services offered: cut and blow dry, manicure, pedicure, makeup, waxing. Own line of hair and makeup products. By appointment or walk-in. For a floating extra fee (depending on location), they will also make house calls to hotels, homes.

L'Image, Inc.
3128 Harvard Avenue
Dallas, Texas 75205
(214) 522-6230

5100 Beltline Road, Suite 520
Dallas, Texas 75240
(214) 934-8080

47½ Highland Park Village
Dallas, Texas 75205
(214) 526-6410

All shops open Monday–Saturday, 9:00 A.M.–6:00 P.M., Thursday, 9:00 A.M.–7:00 P.M. Haircut, styling, conditioning, perming, coloring, highlighting, fashion styling, waxing, eyebrow/lash dyeing. European facials, pedicures, manicures, body massage, reflexology and polarity foot massage. Full makeup consultation with image consultants. "Le jour de Beauté" full-day program includes facial, manicure, pedicure, haircut, styling, conditioning, makeup lesson, lunch. Tuesday and Thursday only: $100, other days: $150.

Skin

J.D. & WE
8141 Walnut Hill Lane
The Corner Shopping Center
Dallas, Texas 75302
(214) 987-0350

Open Monday–Wednesday, 9:30 A.M.–5:30 P.M., Thursday, 9:30 A.M.–6:30 P.M., Saturday, 9:30 A.M.–4:30 P.M. Specialty full-service salon. Body massage and stress therapist. Nutritionist. Skin care, esthetician cleansing, makeup application, pedicure, manicure. Specialists in hair coloring and color correction. Hair services include cutting, styling (new techniques). Body waxing, face, legs, bikini line. Total Day of Beauty includes haircut, facial, body massage, makeup application, manicure, pedicure, styling, lunch @ $250.

Paul Neinast
6632 Snider Plaza
Dallas, Texas 75205
(214) 369-5350

Full service salon for skin care, makeup, hair. Six varieties of manual facials. Makeup application, massage, eyebrow/lash dyeing, waxing. Massage, shower, steam sauna and whirlpool facilities. Hair services include color, perming, styling. It is suggested that you book your appointment about a week prior to the time desired.

Fitness

Cosmopolitan Lady
5511A Arapaho Road
Preston Wood Village Shopping Center
Dallas, Texas 75248
(214) 980-8009

or

9815 N. Central Expressway
The Corner Shopping Center
Dallas, Texas 75231
(214) 987-9778

Member IPFA. Hours: Monday–Friday, 7:00 A.M.–9:00 P.M. Saturday, 9:00 A.M.–6:00 P.M. Classes exclusively for women in aerobics, body contour, yoga, progressive resistance. Individual nutritional guidance. Whirlpool, sauna, steam, pool, cold plunge, indoor track, private dressing rooms. Professional massage department. Tanning salon. Boutique for nails and facials. Nursery for child care. All programs based on exercise, nutrition and stress reduction. Short-term non-resident memberships available for traveling people. No daily fee for classes. Individual fees for facials or massages.

President First Lady Health Club
1310 Elm Street
Dallas, Texas 75202
(214) 747-3707

There are a total of 13 other clubs in the Dallas/Ft. Worth area. Open Monday–Friday, 6:00 A.M.–8:00 P.M. Men/women dual facility. Facilities include pool, racquetball courts, Nautilus equipment, weights. Yoga and Aerobics classes. Memberships only. Guests may come with a member. If you have a membership with an affiliate club, you are welcome.

DENVER

Hair

Hair Cartel
209 Clayton Drive
Denver, Colorado 80206
(303) 333-8014

Open Monday–Saturday, 7:00 A.M.–7:00 P.M. And they will book later appointments, lunch and standing appointments. Services: hair, manicures, pedicures. Specializing in quick and good service.

InterHair
1000 South Gaylord Street
Denver, Colorado 80209
(303) 777-3245

or

8101 East Belleview
Denver, Colorado 80237
(303) 773-1152

Open 6 days, 8:00 A.M.–5:00 P.M. Mondays 9:00 A.M.–5:00 P.M. If requested a week to a week and a half in advance, they will book later hours or early morning appointments (ask for Neil or Harry). A full-service salon with facial and skin care, waxing, eyebrow tinting, sauna and massage, manicures and pedicures, hair sparkling (tipping using foil method). If you feel extravagant, ask for their "Rolls Royce treatment." For $350, you will be picked up in a Rolls and taken to a day of beauty, including hair styling, facial, manicure, pedicure, makeup application, and lunch. The Rolls will also take you home.

Skin

Ilona of Hungary
3201 East Second Avenue
Denver, Colorado 80206
(303) 322-4212

Open Monday–Saturday, 9:00 A.M.–5:30 P.M. Tuesdays, until 8:00 P.M. Skin care, manicures and pedicures, herbal wraps, scalp treatments (a specialty), massages, electrolysis. Appointments are relatively easy to book on a short notice. They will book lunch hour appointments. Own skin care and makeup line.

InterHair
1000 South Gaylord
Denver, Colorado 80209
(303) 777-3245

Total skin care at this location only. Facials, massage and sauna, eyebrows tinted, waxed, arched. Full body waxing. Makeup center, with own line of cosmetic and skin care products. Open 6 days, 8:00 A.M.–5:00 P.M., Monday, 9:00 A.M.–5:00 P.M. Will take later and early morning appointments if requested a day or two in advance.

Fitness

Cleo-Parker-Robinson Dance Ensemble
2006 Lawrence Street
Denver, Colorado 80205
(303) 893-2404

Exercise classes offered Monday–Thursday at 12:15 P.M., 12:45, 5:15 and 6:00 P.M., Saturdays at 12:00 and 1:00 P.M. All one level (advanced) classes which are a combination of aerobics and dance. Also offers dance classes—modern and jazz.

Denver Athletic Club
1325 Glenarn Street
Denver, Colorado 80204
(303) 534-1211

Members only, with reciprocal memberships at other Athletic Clubs around the country (among them, the Downtown Athletic Club and the New York Athletic Club). Squash courts, racquetball, pool, gym with running track, Nautilus equipment, free weights, sauna and massage for both men and women and co-ed whirlpool. Three restaurants, five rooms for out-of-town or reciprocal guests.

YMCA
25 East 16th Avenue
Denver, Colorado 80202
(303) 861-8300

The "Y" has great facilities here: two running tracks, pool, handball and racquetball courts, squash. Flexibility and conditioning classes are offered hourly between 7:00 A.M. and 5:45 P.M. Monday through Thursday. Stretch classes are available Monday–Thursday, 5:45 and 6:45 P.M. Also offer aerobics, gymnastic and trapeze classes. Daily membership: $5.00 all facilities. 2-month membership: $80. Annual membership: $292. There are eight other "Y's" in town.

HOUSTON

Hair

Gemelli and Pierre
5300 North Braeswood
Houston, Texas 77096
(713) 723-5129

Open 9:00 A.M.–5:00 P.M. Thursday, 9:00 A.M.–6:30 P.M. Wednesday, 9:00 A.M.–3:00 P.M., Saturday 9:00 A.M.–4:00 P.M. Closed on Monday. Full service salon with hair, facials, massages, body wraps, nails. You can book an early morning appointment (depending on the stylist) and a standing appointment.

Strands
24 Seventeen Drive
Houston, Texas 77005
(713) 526-7555

Open Monday–Saturday, 10:00 A.M.–6:00 P.M. Standing and lunch hour appointments are available, but all appointments must be booked in advance. Owner Jorge Enrique is formerly of Saks in New York.

Skin

Dermaculture
6415 San Felipe, Suite J
Houston, Texas 77027
(713) 974-8004

Open six days a week, 9:00 A.M.–5:30 P.M. Complete facial, waxing, body wraps and massages. Book at least a day or two in advance. Own line of skin care products.

Fitness

Body Design by Gilda
12520 Memorial Drive
Houston, Texas 77063
(713) 465-2950
or

5870 San Felipe
Houston, Texas 77047
(713) 977-4745

Open Monday–Saturday, 7:45 A.M.–8:00 P.M. Vigorous hourly classes are offered
every 1½ hours. Ten minutes of aerobics and flexibility are followed by 50 minutes of toning. There are no class levels, but you can work at your own pace. 1
class: $8. Monthly unlimited classes: $60. Showers and changing rooms. Men
and women.

Exercise to Music
P.O. Box 6507
Houston, Texas 77265
(713) 666-3212

Located in three convenient places throughout the city. Call for schedule and
locations. An aerobic and calisthenic workout to physically tone-up the body and
build cardiovascular strength. Classes are offered at 8:45 and 9:00 A.M. and 5:00
and 5:30 P.M. $6 a class, $60 a month for unlimited classes. In the works: plans for
a new studio with extended hours.

LOS ANGELES

Hair

Rumors
9018 Beverly Blvd.
Los Angeles, California 90048
(213) 550-5946

Specialists in "pretty hair"—soft, controlled, beautiful, but not particularly
trendy. Hair, makeup, and excellent nail services. Book 2 or 3 days in advance
unless you want owners Jim or Warren, then make your plans 2 to 3 weeks in
advance. Standing appointments can be arranged.

Vidal Sassoon
405 North Rodeo Drive
Beverly Hills, California 90210
(213) 553-6100

Lifestyle, image and bone structure all go into determining the best look for a
client. Most styles are classic. Hair, manicure and pedicure services. Can book a
standing early morning appointment, depending on your stylist. Open 6 days a
week, 9:00 A.M.–5:00 P.M. Best to book 1 to 2 days in advance.

Skin

Aida Grey
9549 Wilshire Blvd.
Beverly Hills, California 90212
(213) 276-4681

Full service salon. Special emphasis on skin and facials. All natural skin care products. Open Monday and Tuesday, 9:00 A.M.–6:00 P.M. Wednesday–Saturday, 8:30 A.M.–6:00 P.M.

Georgette Klinger
312 North Rodeo Drive
Beverly Hills, California 90210
(213) 274-6347

Open 6 days a week, 9:00 A.M.–5:30 P.M. Wednesday until 8:30 P.M. Facial, peeling, collagen treatments, manicures, pedicures, waxing, body massages and wrapping. Valet parking. Full-day and half-day programs available.

Visage
1100 South Beverly Drive
Beverly Hills, California 90035
(213) 552-0667

Facial electrolysis, waxing, makeup lesson and application, facials. Natural line of skin care products. Open Tuesday–Saturday, 9:00 A.M.–5:00 P.M. You can book a standing monthly appointment.

Fitness

Alex & Walters Gymnastics
3380 Motor Avenue
Los Angeles, California 90034
(213) 204-2250

Open Monday–Friday, 7:30 A.M.–8:00 P.M. Saturday, 7:30 A.M.–2:00 P.M., 90% of all classes are private, although group classes (no more than six people) can be arranged, as can semi-private half-hour instructions. Physical fitness class is based on gymnastics, with the level of difficulty being determined by yourself or the group. Most people book standing appointments. Many professional women. Half-hour private class: $20, 1 hour group class: $8, or $70 in advance for 10 classes. Semi-private class: 1/2-hour, $12.

Jane Fonda's Workout
369 South Robertson
Beverly Hills, California 90211
(213) 652-9464

Open 7 days a week, 6:00 A.M.–9:30 P.M. Beginning, Intermediate and Advanced classes in jazz, slow and intensive stretch, pregnancy and recovery exercises.

Miscellaneous Services

Jessica's Nails
8327 Sunset Blvd.
Los Angeles, California 90069
(213) 659-9292

Nail treatment, manicures and pedicures, waxing, acupressure, makeup. Open 8:00 A.M. to 7:30 P.M. By appointment only, and must book 24 hours in advance.

Charlene Trier
(213) 663-8530

Charlene is a traveling masseuse who will come to you if you're anywhere in L.A. She specializes in tension and stress reduction. Brings lotion and table. Flexible hours and appointments can be arranged between 10:00 A.M. and 10:00 P.M. Many East coast travelers call before they fly in to schedule a jet-lag-reducing treatment. $40/hour for massage.

NEW YORK

Hair

Bumble & Bumble
56 West 57th Street, 2nd Floor
New York, New York 10019
(212) 757-3328

A specialty hair cutting salon favored by beauty editors, models and fashion professionals. Hours: Monday, Tuesday, Friday and Saturday, 9:00 A.M.–5:00 P.M. Wednesday and Thursday, 9:00 A.M.–6:30 P.M. Can usually book appointment same day. Scientific hair analysis and permanent waving, coloring, cutting, styling. Manicures and pedicures.

Pierre Michel
6 West 57th Street
New York, New York 10019
(212) 593-1460

Clinic for care of hair as well as fashion of hair. Their philosophy is, "Only healthy hair can be beautiful," and they give special emphasis on getting hair into the best condition. Monday–Saturday appointments. Hours: 9:00 A.M.–6:00 P.M., Wednesday, 9:00 A.M.–5:30 P.M., Saturday, 9:00 A.M.–4:00 P.M. Can usually book same-day appointments. Services, coloring, waving, styling, blowing, streaking, manicure and pedicure. Haircut: $35, Perm: $65+, Shampoo: $4, Blow-dry: $15.

Clive Summers
645 Fifth Avenue, 2nd Floor
New York, New York 10022
(212) 751-7501

An Olympic Tower salon specializing in hair and beauty services. Styling, coloring, waves, perms, waxing, manicures and pedicures. "A Morning for You" includes scalp treatment, facial, shampoo, hair cut, blow dry, manicure, pedicure, make up lesson, color consultation and body wave for $175 ($185 if booked with Clive). Same day appointments are possible, but it is suggested that you call ahead. Open Monday and Saturday, 9:00 A.M.–4:30 P.M. Tuesday, Wednesday and Friday, 9:00 A.M.–6:00 P.M. Thursday, 9:00 A.M.–7:00 P.M.

Skin

Anushka
11 East 67th Street
New York, New York 10021
(212) 249-3615

Individual guidance to nutrition, health and beauty. Specialists in cellulite control with European passive and exercise equipment and deep cellular massage. Personalized nutrition regulation. Special services: head-to-toe body slough, and various facial masks with collagen or elastin treatments to give elasticity and suppleness to skin. You must call for an appointment.

Moi
38 East 63rd Street
New York, New York 10021
(212) 752-4447

Complete skin and nail services. Facials, waxing, eyebrow shaping. Known for sculptured nails, manicures and pedicures. All natural products used for skin care. It is necessary to call for an appointment. Hours: Monday–Friday, 10:00 A.M.–6:00 P.M. (June–August). Tuesday–Saturday, 10:00 A.M.–6:00 P.M. (after August).

Payot Salon
Bloomingdale's (balcony)
1000 Third Avenue
New York, New York 10022
(212) 759-7790

A system of skin care devised 60 years ago by a French doctor. All products are made by Payot in France. Three estheticians at location. Services: facials (including back massage), waxing (lip, bikini, legs, underarm areas). Necessary to make an appointment in advance. Hours: Monday and Thursday, 10:00 A.M.–9:00 P.M., Tuesday, Wednesday and Friday, 10:00 A.M.–6:30 P.M. Saturday, 9:30 A.M.–6:30 P.M.

Christine Valmy
767 Fifth Avenue
New York, New York 10023
(212) 752-0303

Complete skin care program for men and women: deluxe facial, makeup application, manicure and pedicure available. Natural skin care line of products. An on-premise mini-lab will not only test your skin, but it will also test the products you are currently using. If the two are not compatible, they will suggest the right products and follow your progress with them. If necessary, they will reblend products.

Fitness

Cardio-Fitness Center
345 Park Avenue
New York, New York 10022
(212) 838-4570

McGraw-Hill Building at Rockefeller Center
1221 Avenue of the Americas
New York, New York 10020
(212) 840-8240

or

79 Maiden Lane
New York, New York 10038
(212) 943-1510

A monitored, goal-oriented fitness program incorporating strengthening, stretching and cardiovascular exercises. Includes rowing machines, treadmills, Universal equipment, and stationary bicycles. Individual programs are structured based on the results of an exercise stress test, a physical work capacity test, and a skinfold measurement to determine the percentage of body fat. The entire workout—including time for showing and dressing—is about 1 hour. Progress is reviewed and goals are adjusted after every visit. Annual fee lets members use facilities as often as they wish, 6 days a week, although a three-time-a-week schedule is suggested. Lockers, hair dryers, shower facilities and all exercise clothing (except shoes) are provided. Hours: Monday–Friday, 7:00 A.M.–8:30 P.M. Saturday, 9:00 A.M.–3:00 P.M.

Pilates
29 West 56th Street
New York, New York 10019
(212) 974-9511

Regular gym facilities provide the environment for the Pilates method of stretching and strengthening through a system of controlled resistance. Use of springs and mats is geared to improve circulation and breathing habits. Must buy an introductory package of 5 lessons @ $100 per package. After this initial introduction, sessions are $15 each. Workouts run 45 minutes to 1½ hours, depending on your fitness level. Hours: Monday–Friday, 7:30 A.M.–7:30 P.M. Saturday, 9:00 A.M.–2:00 P.M. Sunday, 10:00 A.M.–3:00 P.M.

Sports Training Institute
239 East 49th Street
New York, New York 10017
(212) 752-7111

A specific Nautilus and cardiovascular program will be designed for you by your own individual trainer, based on the results of a complete physical performed by your doctor. The Sports Training Institute will also test your strength, aerobic capacity and fat percentage. The vigorous program includes warm-up, stationary bike and weight machines. Showers, lockers and hairdryers are provided. They suggest a three-time-a-week workout with your trainer. You must book standing appointments and give at least 24 hours' notice to cancel. Hours: Monday–Friday, 7:00 A.M.–8:30 P.M. Saturday, 8:00 A.M.–1:00 P.M.

SAN FRANCISCO

Hair

Gary Price
153 Maiden Lane, 2nd Floor
San Francisco, California 94108
(415) 433-1390

Open Tuesday–Saturday, 9:00 A.M.–4:30 P.M., Thursdays until 7:00 P.M. A contemporary full-service salon located off Union Square. In addition to hair services, you can also get manicures, pedicures, waxing, facial, makeup and a massage. Appointments can be booked with 24-hour notice.

Mr. Lee
834 Jones Street
San Francisco, California 94109
(415) 474-6002

Very old school, but with lots of appeal for a more conservative woman. Full service salon, with a Georgina Scosti skin care area. Call (212) 885-1551 to book a fabulous facial. Tuesday and Thursday, 8:00 A.M.–5:30 P.M. All other days, 4:30 P.M. You can generally book an appointment a few hours ahead of time, unless you want Mr. Lee. Reserve at least a week in advance for him.

Yosh
173 Maiden Lane
San Francisco, California 94108
(415) 989-7704

Specializes in quick service for working women. Good for lunch hours appointments–they don't keep you waiting! You'll need to book 2–3 days in advance for an appointment although they do reserve standing appointment times.

Skin

Fabulous Faces
223 Grant Street
San Francisco, California 94108
(415) 362-4696

Full service (including hair facilities). Two different facials offered, waxing, massages, manicures, pedicures. Own skin care and makeup line of products.

Face Place
339 Kearney Street
San Francisco, California 94108
(415) 781-8153

or

2448 Mission Street
San Francisco, California 94110
(415) 282-7772

Over 800 allergy-tested skin care and makeup products, plus a free makeup lesson to show you the best ways to apply them! The most complete makeup store in town, with prices about 60% less than department stores. Their aim is to create a simple, easy look that's easy to accomplish in a few minutes. Can call or order by mail. Will send out price list on request.

Fitness

Jane Fonda's Workout
170 Maiden Lane
San Francisco, California 94108
(415) 981-4423

Beginning, intermediate and advanced exercise and stretch classes. Also pregnancy and recovery exercises. Each class is 1½ hours, with a special 45-minute lunch hour class. Cost is $6 per class. Hours: 7:00 A.M.–8:30 P.M. You can buy a Workout tape and book and tote them along on business trips to continue your program.

Physis
100 Chestnut Street
San Francisco, California 94111
(415) 781-6400

Intense program geared for executives. Many are sent by their companies as a perk. Medically supervised, owned and run by Dr. Bagshaw. A $425 evaluation fee includes a complete physical, bloodwork, EKG, and stress test. A three-month conditioning program is planned to accommodate your individual level of fitness and either preventive or rehabilitative maintenance needs. Conditioning Program @ $750, consists of aerobics and weight work three times a week. You can also drop in on aerobics classes for $4–$5 each.

Women on the Run
(800) 927-3490

Running training for women, from beginners to marathoners. Classes are held outdoors and include stretching exercises, speed work and pacing, weight lifting, injury prevention techniques and nutrition advice.

WASHINGTON, D.C.

Hair

Antoine
1616 Wisconsin Avenue N.W.
Washington, D.C. 20007
(202) 965-1646

Open Tuesday–Friday, 9:30 A.M.–5:30 P.M., Thursday, until 6:30 P.M. Saturday, 8:30 A.M.–5:00 P.M. Specializing in fast service, classic styling. "No one waits at a lunch hour appointment." Call same week for appointment.

Bogarts
1063 Wisconsin Avenue N.W.
Washington, D.C. 20007
(202) 333-6550

Open Monday–Saturday, 9:30 A.M.–6:00 P.M. Thursday, until 7:00 P.M. A full-service salon, featuring waxing (face and body), manicures, pedicures, facials and skin care along with hair services. You can book a standing appointment. Businesswomen love the no-waiting treatment. Bogarts offers a unique skin care and makeup service. An esthetician mixes products (both care and cosmetic lines) to suit individual skin needs.

Sunshine
5110 Ridgefield Road
Chevy Chase, Maryland 20016
(202) 656-7080

Open 9:00–4:30. Tuesday until 7:30. Hair, manicure, pedicure and facial services offered. Experts in color. If you want Guiseppe, book at least 3 weeks in advance. Otherwise, you can make an appointment 2 to 3 days ahead of time.

Skin

Elizabeth Arden
1147 Connecticut Avenue
Washington, D.C. 20036
(202) 638-6212
or

5225 Wisconsin Avenue N.W.
Washington, D.C. 20015
(202) 362-9895

Complete salon services: facials, waxing, massage, steam cabinets, hair styling, makeup application, manicure and pedicure. Exercise classes (private or with 3–4 people) at the Connecticut Avenue location only.

Elodie France International
51 Wisconsin Avenue N.W.
Washington, D.C. 20016
(202) 686-9310

Open Tuesday–Friday, 9:00 A.M.–9:00 P.M. Complete skin care, featuring any kind of a facial, European waxing, cellulite treatment, manicure and pedicure. Spot reducing programs, contouring and shaping. Passive exercise via Slender-tone equipment.

Robin Weir & Co.
2134 P Street N.W.
Washington, D.C. 20037
(202) 861-0444

Specializes in the Repechage therapy: a series of masks, including a seaweed and mineral one that thoroughly cleanses and recharges the skin. They also do peeling, waxing, conventional facials. Full hair salon. Manicurists. Open 8:00 A.M.–6:00 P.M. You can book lunch hour appointments.

Fitness

K-Bridge Marriot Hotel Health Club
1401 Lee Highway
Arlington, Virginia 22209
(703) 524-6400

Open 10:00 A.M.–10:00 P.M. Exercise room, Universal equipment, stationary bicycles, free weights, indoor-outdoor pool, two locker rooms with sauna, jacuzzi. Individual weight lifting programs, slimnastics. Annual membership: $300 single, $450 couple. Monthly memberships: $40 single, $60 couple. The health club is free for hotel guests.

Saga Club
1000 Potomac Street
Washington, D.C. 20007
(202) 298-8455

A private club (both personal and corporate memberships available), with a 50-ft. pool, sun deck, steam room, whirlpool sauna, weight room. Exercise classes (regular and aquatic), massage, pedicure, manicure, makeup application and facials offered. Co-ed, with separate locker facilities for men and women. All bathing suits, towels, jogging shorts, tee-shirts, and robes are provided.

Somebody's
1070 Thomas Jefferson N.W.
Washington, D.C. 20007
(202) 338-3822

Co-ed classes weekdays from 6:30 A.M.–8:00 P.M. Saturday and Sunday, 7:45 A.M.–2:00 P.M. Classes limited to six people. You must reserve a space. Beginning, intermediate and advanced levels. Hour classes are very vigorous. You will begin with a warm up, then a cardiovascular set, followed by isometrics and isotonics (toning, concentration on form, breathing, spinal alignment), and finish with yoga. Facials, cellulite treatments, Swedish body massages are also available. Changing rooms and shower. Your first class is complimentary. Single classes are $12. A series of four classes: $42, eight classes: $61. Several series are offered, but they must be used within a 30-day period.

Washington Squash and Racquet Club
1 Layfayette Center
1120 20th St. N.W.
Washington, D.C. 20036
(202) 659-9570

Open Monday–Friday, 7:00 A.M.–11:00 P.M. Weekends 9:00 A.M.–9:00 P.M. This facility has a reciprocal membership arrangement with other squash clubs around the country. In addition to the courts there is an exercise room. Annual membership: $75, Family membership: $110. Court: $5–$10 for 1/2 hour.

11

The Woman At The Top: Keeping Your Image Intact

"I've definitely become more feminine, more individual, less concerned about the 'corporate image,' more concerned about my own image."

There's a certain freedom that comes with professional rank, a latitude that affects both performance and appearance. But it's not a blank check to do anything terribly unexpected. To the contrary, executives often reach the top because their moves can be counted upon, their actions confidently anticipated. "We decided to give you a crack at this position because we know you can handle it," is one of the most oft-repeated promotion speeches. Women—and men— who make it to the top have been watched all the way up. In addition to their on-the-job effectiveness, their managerial style, their poise and their very image must all be considered consistently reliable. And you think all of that's going to change once they get the title on the door? It's not very likely.

No matter what stage of career progression you're in, you develop—daily— your own personal ways of relating to superiors, peers and subordinates. Through trial and error, you evolve your individual methods of doing things, saying things, and getting the job done. The more unique it is, the more immediately identifiable as your own it is, the more you'll stand out. Think about the pecking order at your place for a moment. Chances are, those at the top of it have their own unmistakeable ways of doing things and saying things. The sooner you earmark your own style, the more reliable you'll seem. A woman, especially, without a distinct managerial style is often perceived as mercurial, while a man may simply be thought of as not focused enough. Either way, the end result is the same. Neither one of them will get the promotion.

At the same time you are perfecting the way you deal with others, those around you are forming their reaction patterns to you. Each one of us develops a personal, computer-like code for interrelating. Once we establish our set of impressions of someone, we don't have to think about the way we must respond to them in any given situation. The tone of voice we use, the level of camaraderie we select, the sense of reassurance or urgency we convey all become automatic in the interchange. And we like it that way. Because that leaves our minds free to deal with the determining factors—the real issues of the conversation.

That's why establishing a consistent impression is so critical throughout every stage of your career. Part of the input your co-workers "program" into their consciousness about you is based on your performance, part is based on your managerial style, and part is based on your appearance. If one thing goes out of whack along the way, it interferes with everything else.

So what happens when you get closer to your goal? Are you going to throw away your carefully organized style? If it has worked for you, and if people have responded well to you up to this point, chances are you will not. Of course, you may upgrade the quality level of your clothing. Four hundred dollar designer skirts may replace the no-name woolens you've been wearing. Silk may replace silk blends. Softer knit suits may replace more structured ones. Or you may be able to afford an entire wardrobe of businesslike dresses, even though they offer less variety than fewer coordinating skirts/jackets/shirts. But few executive women turn into closet chameleons once the promotion comes. (You won't see the new senior vice president striding down the hall in leather pants and a sweatshirt sweater.) Although the price tag on clothes may change, the professional tone of clothes should not. If you've created an efficient, successful image on your way up, it simply makes sense to stick with it.

The difference—and there is a slight one—between the way women at the top and the up-and-comers dress has to do more with the bottom line than the fashion line. More money simply means you can buy more. But if your style isn't going to change all that radically, it's nothing short of boring to simply buy more of the same. Where you should invest your new-found clothing dollar is on very special, isolated items that can give what you've got extra snap. Look for look-finishers that you couldn't afford before. Try the new accessories of the season, as long as they're in sync with your overall presentation. (A fantastic, antique onyx-and-rhinestone brooch could be, a woven Guatemalan cinch belt would not.) Experiment with newer scarf shapes. Your old-reliable rectangles might go with everything you own, but you can add a little more drama once you can afford more than basics. Try triangles of lace or lightweight lengths of wool, just short enough to wrap around once into a soft jabot. Trade in a few suit jackets for soft cardigan sweaters. If you belt them and finish them just as you would a jacket, the authority remains, but the overall effect is softer. You'll be able to personalize your wardrobe more now—within the parameters of the image you've established. With both better quality and more variety going for you, you will set yourself off, subtly, as a woman at the top. But don't overdo it. Trooping in swathed in fur and dripping in designer labels two weeks after your promotion is only going to alienate everybody. "Ever since she got that promotion, her mind's been more in *Vogue* than on her job," the cattiest co-workers will insist. Once people begin to concentrate more on what you're wearing than on what you're saying, you'll know you've gone too far. Wait a while. The change in your position is going to be enough to get used to. Nobody wants to have to get used to a whole new you in the bargain.

No matter what the accepted standard of dress is in the workplace, women—or men, for that matter—at the top don't deviate very far from it. But that's not to say that standards of what is, and what is not, appropriate won't change. And women will be responsible for that change. With well above 60% of all women aged 18–45 working, and nearly 70% of all women aged 20–24 in the work force, wearing a "uniform" that is not personally pleasing will not be tolerated. As the influx of women numerically approaches the percentages of men in the marketplace (by 1990, 65% of all women are expected to be employed, in comparison to the 79% figure for men today), male dress code expectations will carry less and less clout. When women see more peers and more role models at the executive level, whole new modes of dressing may be devised. Suit looks may finally be discarded as much too imitative. Dresses may become the order of the day. Or we all may choose to walk around in weather-insulated jumpsuits. Whatever the professional style tomorrow's executive women choose to claim as their own, it will succeed. Because women are succeeding.